Think
Read
React
Plan
Write
Rewrite Third Edition

Think
Read
React
Plan
Write
Rewrite Third Edition

W. Royce Adams

Santa Barbara City College

Holt, Rinehart and Winston
New York Chicago San Francisco Philadelphia
Montreal Toronto London Sydney
Tokyo Mexico City Rio de Janeiro Madrid

Library of Congress Cataloging in Publication Data

Adams, W. Royce.
  Think, read, react, plan, write, rewrite.

  Includes index.
    1. English language—Rhetoric.   2. College readers.
I. Title.   II. Title: TRRPWR.
[PE1408.A318   1982]   808′.042   81–6479
ISBN 0–03–059116–3   AACR2

CBS COLLEGE PUBLISHING
Holt, Rinehart and Winston
The Dryden Press
Saunders College Publishing

Preface to the Third Edition

Many changes have been made in this third edition of *TRRPWR*. Although the format of each unit continues to be THINK, READ, REACT, PLAN, WRITE, and REWRITE, modifications occur within these components. The THINK section continues to raise questions about a particular topic in order to gain student attention and thought for the essay in the READ section. Seven of the thirteen essays in READ have been changed. REACT requires student responses both about the essay content and style as well as subjective reactions to the ideas in the essay.

The PLAN sections have been much enlarged. A list of possible topics for student essays is now enhanced with short moral dilemmas containing no pat answers, quotations and short passages from other works that provoke thought, and recommendations and practices in journal keeping and freewriting as a means to thinking through a plan for an essay. In effect, more information for planning an essay is given as well as more aid in selecting possible essay topics.

WRITE is still the rhetorical backbone of the book, where concepts on topic sentences, paragraph control, introductory and concluding paragraphs, transitional elements, refined sentence control, punctuation, grammar, and other points listed in the Table of Contents are explained. In many units, the WRITE sections contain graphics to explain the paragraph and essay form. Sentence-combining exercises have been added to six of the units as well as additional exercises in topic sentences. In addition, whole essays are now called upon from the first unit, although instructors could still modify the assignment to one or two paragraphs if so desired.

REWRITE has been greatly enlarged. Rather than beginning rewriting at the sixth unit, as in previous editions, the rewrite step begins in Unit 1. In addition, a new feature has been added, that of providing sample student first drafts with instructor comments and then a revised student draft with instructor reactions. In each unit, the concept being taught in the WRITE portion is reenforced through the student sample writings used in REWRITE. Then the student is provided a checklist to follow during the revision stage.

Some instructors seem to worry that the presentation of student problem areas such as sentence fragments, run-ons, comma splices, and the like don't appear early enough in the book. It can't be stated strongly enough that it is NOT necessary to work straight through from one unit to the next. It is quite possible to skip around, using whatever unit the instructor feels is more important to cover at a given time. True, the philosophy behind *TRRPWR* is to emphasize thinking, planning, and organizing ideas for an essay before getting involved in the technicalities of grammar and punctuation, as important as they are. But many poor writers, the ones for whom this book is written, have developed inhibitions against writing because they write with the fear of making mistakes and being called on them. But the aware instructor can use, for instance, the THINK, READ, and REACT sections of one unit and then move to the PLAN, WRITE, and REWRITE sections of another unit without difficulty. Or instructors can work straight through the text, referring students with special problems to other units containing information dealing with the problem in question. The book does not, as some may feel at first glance, lock users into a tight structure. But it is there for those who want it.

The Appendixes contain definitions of selected words from each essay and exercises in the use of these words. Work in affixes is also provided. Basic spelling rules and drills are also found here. In addition, a list of verb parts as well as some grammar drills for supplemental use are included.

Suggestions for using this book, along with suggested answers to drills, appear in the *Instructor's Manual* that accompanies the text. The Manual may be obtained through a local Holt representative or by writing to the English Editor, College Department, Holt, Rinehart and Winston, 383 Madison Avenue, New York, NY 10017.

I wish to thank the following reviewers for their helpful comments: Richard S. Beal; Chrysanthy M. Grieco, Seton Hall University; Drewey Wayne Gunn, Texas A & I University; Deborah Long, West Georgia College; Richard Opdahl, Long Beach City College; Alice Sodowsky, University of Northern Iowa; Stephen Sossamon, Westfield State College; Charlotte Tannheimer, Endicott Junior College; Nettye R. Thompson, Tuskegee Institute; Roger. V. Zimmerman, Lewis and Clark Community College. Much appreciation goes to the following people at Holt, Rinehart and Winston for their help in putting this third edition together: Susan Katz, Anne Boynton-Trigg, Lester A. Sheinis.

W. R. A.
Santa Barbara, California

Contents

UNIT 5

Think . . .   100
about college sports

Read . . .   102
about intercollegiate sports
"Away with Big-Time Athletics" by
Roger M. Williams

React . . .   106
to the essay

Plan . . .   108
an essay
Topics for an essay on sports

Write . . .   114
(A) an outline for an essay
(B) the introductory paragraph
(C) supporting paragraphs
(D) the concluding paragraph
Practices in writing concluding
paragraphs

Rewrite . . .   118
your first draft

UNIT 6

Think . . .   123
about stereotyped sex roles

Read . . .   125
about sexist language
"Is Language Sexist? One Small Step
for Genkind" by Casey Miller and Kate
Swift

React . . .   131
to the essay

Plan . . .   133
an essay
Topics for an essay

Write . . .   136
(A) an outline for your essay
(B) a first draft
(C) transitional devices
Transitional words and expressions
Transition between sentences
Transition within paragraphs
Transition between paragraphs
Practices in transitional usage

Rewrite . . .   143
the first draft

Think
Read
React
Plan
Write
Rewrite Third Edition

To the Student

© 1973 United Feature Syndicate, Inc.

Have you ever felt about essays the way Peppermint Patty does? If you have to write reports, essays, or essay exams for many classes, that million-to-one chance to fake your way through isn't much help. The easiest thing to do is to learn how to write essays so you won't have to worry about faking it.

Although you may never have to write an essay once you are finished with your academic career, learning to write has at least three advantages. One advantage is that you will do better work at a less frustrating pace in those courses that require some type of writing from you. A second advantage is that learning to write also teaches you to think in a more organized and logical fashion, even where no writing is involved. A third advantage to learning to write is that it will help your reading comprehension because you will understand better how an author organizes and presents information.

Believe it or not, you can learn to write. This book is organized so that you learn one step at a time. If you look carefully at the Contents (and you should because it's your money that bought it), you will see that each unit is built around sections on THINKING, READING, REACTING, PLANNING, WRITING, and RE-WRITING. Each section requires your involvement by raising questions about, and providing reading information on, various subjects from education to astrology. You haven't lived this long without having had many experiences and emotions about many topics. Each unit tries to stimulate or reawaken experiences and ideas you have on a wide range of subjects. Go take a peek at the Contents, and see for yourself. You probably know something about each topic.

Within each unit only one aspect of writing essays is presented so that your mind won't get boggled with too many concepts at once. Unit 1 provides ideas and practices in organizing thoughts on any given subject so that you can use these thoughts or outlines as a writing guide. From there, each unit presents still one more step in learning to write so that by the time you have worked through this book, you will understand the following aspects of writing essays:

1. How to plan and organize an essay.
2. How to write topic sentences.
3. How to write introductory paragraphs.
4. How to write supporting paragraphs.
5. How to write concluding paragraphs.
6. How to use transitional devices correctly.
7. How to write correct sentences.
8. How to use proper agreement.
9. How to punctuate correctly.
10. How to write with parallelism.
11. How to use the proper word.
12. How to write logically.

Many practices are provided in each unit to help you understand these concepts.

A vital part of learning to write well is the need to develop vocabulary and spelling. If one or both of these areas are not your strong points, you will find helpful the information in the Appendixes. Vocabulary definitions and drills based on the words from the readings in each unit are provided in Appendix 1. Hints and drills in spelling are provided in Appendix 2, and Appendix 3 lists the principal parts of verbs to which you may need to refer from time to time.

It is possible to use the units in this book in a different order from the order used here. However, each unit, though following the same structural plan, is meant to be followed in the sequence presented in the book for best results. Many students have followed the sequence with positive writing results. Take some time now to look over the sequence as shown in the Contents and the Appendixes, and maybe take a quick glance at one or two units before you begin work in the book. If you realize where you are beginning and see where you are going, you will no longer have to worry about "faking it" as Charlie Brown's friend does. You may have an excellent chance to lower the odds on your ability to write a good essay.

SO, as Peppermint Patty would say, HERE WE GO!

UNIT 1

Think. . . .
about writing essays

Read. . . .
about learning to write better
"How to Say Nothing in Five Hundred Words" by Paul Roberts

React. . . .
to the essay

Plan. . . .
an essay
Planning Point One: Selecting a Topic and Thesis
Planning Point Two: Listing Supporting Points
Planning Point Three: Ordering Supporting Points
Practices in Planning an Essay

Write. . . .
(A) a thesis statement and an outline for an essay
(B) an essay

Rewrite. . . .
your first draft

Think...

about writing essays.

To stimulate your thinking and to focus your attention on essay writing, answer the following questions.

1. Do you often read essays, or do you only read them when required to do so?

   _____

   Why? _____

   _____

   _____

2. Explain why you think it is or is not important to learn to write essays.

   _____

   _____

   _____

   _____

3. As most students never write essays once they finish school, why do you suppose learning to write essays is required in college?

   _____

   _____

   _____

   _____

4. Check any of the areas that follow with which you feel you may need help when writing essays in this class:

   _____ a. topics to write about

   _____ b. organizing your ideas

   _____ c. writing good sentences

   _____ d. writing good paragraphs

_____ e. punctuation

_____ f. grammar

_____ g. spelling

_____ h. vocabulary

_____ i. finding a pen and paper

5. Define what you think an essay is:

_____

_____

_____

_____

_____

_____

_____

_____

about learning to write better.

The following essay is written by an English teacher who understands only too well the problems many students have in writing essays. It is an essay you will want to refer to several times during the length of this course. It's a rather long article; and you may want to read part of it, take a break, then read some more. But don't let the length put you off. It's well written and has many helpful suggestions for writing.

As you read, notice how the author begins with the problem all students in English classes have: the problem of getting an essay started and then making it a good one. Then he goes on to offer advice that you should find very useful as you work throughout this book.

How to Say Nothing in Five Hundred Words
Paul Roberts

Nothing About Something

1. It's Friday afternoon, and you have almost survived another week of classes. You are just looking forward dreamily to the weekend when the English instructor says: "For Monday you will turn in a five-hundred word composition on college football."

2. Well, that puts a good big hole in the weekend. You don't have any strong views on college football one way or the other. You get rather excited during the season and go to all the home games and find it rather more fun than not. On the other hand, the class has been reading Robert Hutchins in the anthology and perhaps Shaw's "Eighty-Yard Run," and from the class discussion you have got the idea that the instructor thinks college football is for the birds. You are no fool, you. You can figure out what side to take.

3. After dinner you get out the portable typewriter that you got for high school graduation. You might as well get it over with and enjoy Saturday and Sunday. Five hundred words is about two double-spaced pages with normal margins. You put in a sheet of paper, think up a title, and you're off:

WHY COLLEGE FOOTBALL SHOULD BE ABOLISHED

College football should be abolished because it's bad for the school and also bad for the players. The players are so busy practicing that they don't have any time for their studies.

This, you feel, is a mighty good start. The only trouble is that it's only thirty-two words. You still have four hundred and sixty-eight to go, and you've pretty well exhausted the subject. It comes to you that you do your best thinking in the morning, so you put away the typewriter and go to the movies. But the next morning you have to do your washing and some math problems, and in the afternoon you go to the game. The English instructor turns up too, and you wonder if you've taken the right side after all. Saturday night you have a date, and Sunday morning you have to go to church. (You shouldn't let English assignments interfere with your religion.) What with one thing and another, it's ten o'clock Sunday night before you get out the typewriter again. You make a pot of coffee and start to fill out your views on college football. Put a little meat on the bones.

WHY COLLEGE FOOTBALL SHOULD BE ABOLISHED

In my opinion, it seems to me that college football should be abolished. The reason why I think this to be true is because I feel that football is bad for the colleges in nearly every respect. As Robert Hutchins says in his article in our anthology in which he discusses college football, it would be better if the colleges had race horses and had races with one another, becuase then the horses would not have to attend classes. I firmly agree with Mr. Hutchins on this point, and I am sure that many other students would agree too.

One reason why it seems to me that college football is bad is that it has become too commercial. In the olden times when people played football just for the fun of it, maybe college football was all right, but they do not play football just for the fun of it now as they used to in the old days. Nowadays college football is what you might call a big business. Maybe this is not true at all schools, and I don't think it is especially true here at State, but certainly this is the case at most colleges and universities in America nowadays, as Mr. Hutchins points out in his very interesting article. Actually the coaches and alumni go around to the high schools and offer the high school stars large salaries to come to their colleges and play football for them. There was one case where a high school star was offered a convertible if he would play football for a certain college.

Another reason for abolishing college football is that it is bad for the players. They do not have time to get a college education, because they are so busy playing football. A football player has to practice every afternoon from three to six, and then he is so tired that he can't concentrate on his studies. He just feels like dropping off to sleep after dinner, and then the next day he goes to his classes without having studied and maybe he fails the test.

(Good ripe stuff so far, but you're still a hundred and fifty-one words from home. One more push.)

Also I think college football is bad for the colleges and the universities because not very many students get to participate in it. Out of a college of ten thousand students only seventy-five or a hundred play football, if that many. Football is what you might call a spectator sport. That means that most people go to watch it but do not play it themselves.

(Four hundred and fifteen. Well, you still have the conclusion, and when you re-type it, you can make the margins a little wider.)

These are the reasons why I agree with Mr. Hutchins that college football should be abolished in American colleges and universities.

4. On Monday you turn it in, moderately hopeful, and on Friday it comes back marked "weak in content" and sporting a big "D."

5. This essay is exaggerated a little, not much. The English instructor will recognize it as reasonably typical of what an assignment on college football will bring in. He knows that nearly half of the class will contrive in five hundred words to say that college football is too commercial and bad for the players. Most of the other half will inform him that college football builds character and prepares one for life and brings prestige to the school. As he reads paper after paper all saying the same thing in almost the same words, all bloodless, five hundred words dripping out of nothing, he wonders how he allowed himself to get trapped into teaching English when he might have had a happy and interesting life as an electrician or a confidence man.

6. Well, you may ask, what can you do about it? The subject is one on which you have few convictions and little information. Can you be expected to make a dull subject interesting? As a matter of fact, this is precisely what you are expected to do. This is the writer's essential task. All subjects, except sex, are dull until somebody makes them interesting. The writer's job is to find the argument, the approach, the angle, the wording that will take the reader with him. This is seldom easy, and it is particularly hard in subjects that have been much discussed: College Football, Fraternities, Popular Music, Is Chivalry Dead?, and the like. You will feel that there is nothing you can do with such subjects except repeat the old bromides. But there are some things you can do which will make your papers, if not throbbingly alive, at least less insufferably tedious than they might otherwise be.

Avoid the Obvious Content

7. Say the assignment is college football. Say that you've decided to be against it. Begin by putting down the arguments that come to your mind: it is too commercial, it takes the students' minds off their studies, it is hard on the players, it makes the university a kind of circus instead of an intellectual center, for most schools it is financially ruinous. Can you think of any more arguments just off hand? All right. Now when you write your paper, *make sure that you don't use any of the material on this list.* If these are the points that leap to your mind, they will leap to everyone else's too, and whether you get a "C" or a "D" may depend on whether the instructor reads your paper early when he is fresh and tolerant or late, when the sentence "In my opinion, college football has become too commercial," inexorably repeated, has brought him to the brink of lunacy.

8. Be against college football for some reason or reasons of your own. If they are keen and perceptive ones, that's splendid. But even if they are trivial or foolish or indefensible, you are still ahead so long as they are not everybody else's reasons too. Be against it because the colleges don't spend enough money on it to make it worth while, because it is bad for the characters of the spectators, because the players are forced to attend classes, because the football stars hog all the beautiful women, because it competes with baseball and is therefore un-American and possibly Communist inspired. There are lots of more or less unused reasons for being against college football.

9. Sometimes it is a good idea to sum up and dispose of the trite and conventional points before going on to your own. This has the advantage of indicating to the reader that you are going to be neither trite nor conventional. Something like this:

> We are often told that college football should be abolished because it has become too commercial or because it is bad for the players. These arguments are no doubt very cogent, but they don't really go to the heart of the matter.

Then you go the the heart of the matter.

Take the Less Usual Side

10. One rather simple way of getting interest into your paper is to take the side of the argument that most of the citizens will want to avoid. If the assignment is an essay on dogs, you can, if you choose, explain that dogs are faithful and lovable companions, intelligent, useful as guardians of the house and protectors of children, indispensable in police work—in short, when all is said and done, man's best friends. Or you can suggest that those big brown eyes conceal, more often than not, a vacuity of mind and an inconstancy of purpose; that the dogs you have known most intimately have been mangy, ill-tempered brutes, incapable of instruction; and that only your nobility of mind and fear of arrest prevent you from kicking the flea-ridden animals when you pass them on the street.

11. Naturally, personal convictions will sometimes dictate your approach. If the assigned subject is "Is Methodism Rewarding to the Individual?" and you are a pious Methodist, you have really no choice. But few assigned subjects, if any, will fall in this category. Most of them will lie in broad areas of discussion with much to be said on both sides. They are intellectual exercises, and it is legitimate to argue now one way and now another, as debaters do in similar circumstances. Always take the side that looks to you hardest, least defensible. It will always turn out to be easier to write interestingly on that side.

12. This general advice applies where you have a choice of subjects. If you are to choose among "The Values of Fraternities" and "My Favorite High School Teacher" and "What I think About Beetles," by all means plump for the beetles. By the time the instructor gets to your paper, he will be up to his ears in tedious tales about the French teacher at Bloombury High and assertions about how fraternities build character and prepare one for life. Your views on beetles, whatever they are, are bound to be a refreshing change.

13. Don't worry too much about figuring out what the instructor thinks about the subject so that you can cuddle up with him. Chances are his views are no stronger than yours. If he does have convictions and you oppose them, his problem is to keep from grading you higher than you deserve in order to show he is not biased. This doesn't mean that you should always cantankerously dissent from what the instructor says; that gets tiresome too. And if the subject assigned is "My Pet

Peeve," do not begin, "My pet peeve is the English instructor who assigns papers on 'my pet peeve.' " This was still funny during the War of 1812, but it has sort of lost its edge since then. It is in general good manners to avoid personalities.

Slip Out of Abstraction

14. If you will study the essay on college football [on pages 7–8], you will perceive that one reason for its appalling dullness is that it never gets down to particulars. It is just a series of not very glittering generalities: "football is bad for the colleges," "it has become too commercial," "football is a big business," "it is bad for the players," and so on. Such round phrases thudding against the reader's brain are unlikely to convince him, though they may well render him unconscious.

15. If you want the reader to believe that college football is bad for the players, you have to do more than say so. You have to display the evil. Take your roommate, Alfred Simkins, the second-string center. Picture poor old Alfy coming home from football practice every evening, bruised and aching, agonizingly tired, scarcely able to shovel the mashed potatoes into his mouth. Let us see him staggering up to the room, getting out his econ textbook, peering desperately at it with his good eye, falling asleep and failing the test in the morning. Let us share his unbearable tension as Saturday draws near. Will he fail, be demoted, lose his monthly allowance, be forced to return to the coal mines? And if he succeeds, what will be his reward? Perhaps a slight ripple of applause when the third-string center replaces him, a moment of elation in the locker room if the team wins, or despair if it loses. What will he look back on when he graduates from college? Toil and torn ligaments. And what will be his future? He is not good enough for pro football, and he is too obscure and weak in econ to succeed in stocks and bonds. College football is tearing the heart from Alfy Simkins and, when it finishes with him, will callously toss aside the shattered hulk.

16. This is no doubt a weak enough argument for the abolition of college football, but it is a sight better than saying, in three or four variations, that college football (in your opinion) is bad for the players.

17. Look at the work of any professional writer and notice how constantly he is moving from the generality, the abstract statement, to the concrete example, the facts and figures, the illustration. If he is writing on juvenile delinquency, he does not just tell you that juveniles are (it seems to him) delinquent and that (in his opinion) something should be done about it. He shows you juveniles being delinquent, tearing up movie theatres in Buffalo, stabbing high school principals in Dallas, smoking marijuana in Palo Alto. And more than likely he is moving toward some specific remedy, not just a general wringing of the hands.

18. It is no doubt possible to be *too* concrete, too illustrative or anecdotal, but few inexperienced writers err this way. For most the soundest advice is to be seeking always for the picture, to be always turning general remarks into seeable examples. Don't say, "Sororities teach girls the social graces." Say, "Sorority life teaches a girl how to carry on a conversation while pouring tea, without sloshing the tea into the saucer." Don't say, "I like certain kinds of popular music very much." Say, "Whenever I hear Gerber Spinklittle play 'Mississippi Man' on the trombone, my socks creep up my ankles."

Get Rid of Obvious Padding

19. The student toiling away at his weekly English theme is too often tormented by a figure: five hundred words. How, he asks himself, is he to achieve this staggering total? Obviously by never using one word when he can somehow work in ten.

20. He is therefore seldom content with a plain statement like "Fast driving is dangerous." This has only four words in it. He takes thought, and the sentence becomes:

> In my opinion, fast driving is dangerous.

Better, but he can do better still;

> In my opinion, fast driving would seem to be rather dangerous.

If he is really adept, it may come out:

> In my humble opinion, though I do not claim to be an expert on this complicated subject, fast driving, in most circumstances, would seem to be rather dangerous in many respects, or at least so it would seem to me.

Thus four words have been turned into forty, and not an iota of content has been added.

21. Now this is a way to go about reaching five hundred words, and if you are content with a "D" grade, it is as good a way as any. But if you aim higher, you must work differently. Instead of stuffing your sentences with straw, you must try steadily to get rid of the padding, to make your sentences lean and tough. If you are really working at it, your first draft will greatly exceed the required total, and then you will work it down, thus:

> It is thought in some quarters that fraternities do not contribute as much as might be expected to campus life.
> Some people think that fraternities contribute little to campus life.

> The average doctor who practices in small towns or in the country must toil night and day to heal the sick.
> Most country doctors work long hours.

> When I was a little girl, I suffered from shyness and embarrassment in the presence of others.
> I was a shy little girl.

> It is absolutely necessary for the person employed as a marine fireman to give the matter of steam pressure his undivided attention at all times.
> The fireman has to keep his eye on the steam gauge.

22. You may ask how you can arrive at five hundred words at this rate. Simply. You dig up more real content. Instead of taking a couple of obvious points off the surface of the topic and then circling warily around them for six paragraphs, you work in and explore, figure out the details. You illustrate. You say that fast driving is dangerous, and then you prove it. How long does it take to stop a car at forty and at eighty? How far can you see at night? What happens when a tire blows? What happens in a head-on collision at fifty miles an hour? Pretty soon your paper will be full of broken glass and blood and headless torsos, and reaching five hundred words will not really be a problem.

Call a Fool a Fool

23. Some of the padding in freshman themes is to be blamed not on anxiety about the word minimum but on excessive timidity. The student writes, "In my opinion, the principal of my high school acted in ways that I believe every unbiased person would have to call foolish." This isn't exactly what he means. What he means is, "My high school principal was a fool." If he was a fool, call him a fool. Hedging the thing about with "in-my-opinion's" and "it-seems-to-me's" and "as-I-see-it's" and "at-least-from-my-point-of-view's" gains you nothing. Delete these phrases whenever they creep into your paper.

24. The student's tendency to hedge stems from a modesty that in other circumstances would be commendable. He is, he realizes, young and inexperienced, and he half suspects that he is dopey and fuzzy-minded beyond the average. Probably only too true. But it doesn't help to announce your incompetence six times in every paragraph. Decide what you want to say and say it as vigorously as possible, without apology and in plain words.

25. Linguistic diffidence can take various forms. One is what we call *euphemism.* This is the tendency to call a spade "a certain garden implement" or women's underwear "unmentionables." It is stronger in some eras than others and in some people than others but it always operates more or less in subjects that are touchy or taboo: death, sex, madness, and so on. Thus we shrink from saying "He died last night" but say instead "passed away," "left us," "joined his Maker," "went to his reward." Or we try to take off the tension with a lighter cliché: "kicked the bucket," "cashed in his chips," "handed in his dinner pail." We have found all sorts of ways to avoid saying *mad:* "mentally ill," "touched," "not quite right upstairs," "feeble-minded," "innocent," "simple," "off his trolley," "not in his right mind." Even such a now plain word as *insane* began as a euphemism with the meaning "not healthy."

26. Modern science, particularly psychology, contributes many polysyllables in which we can wrap our thoughts and blunt their force. To many writers there is no such thing as a bad schoolboy. Schoolboys are maladjusted or unoriented or misunderstood or in need of guidance or lacking in continued success toward satisfactory integration of the personality as a social unit, but they are never bad. Psychology no doubt makes us better men or women, more sympathetic and tolerant, but it doesn't make writing any easier. Had Shakespeare been confronted with psychology, "To be or not to be" might have come out, "To continue as a social unit or not to do so. That is the personality problem. Whether 'tis a better sign of integration at the conscious level to display a psychic tolerance toward the maladjustments and repressions induced by one's lack of orientation in one's environment or—" But Hamlet would never have finished the soliloquy.

27. Writing in the modern world, you cannot altogether avoid modern jargon. Nor, in an effort to get away from euphemism, should you salt your paper with four-letter words. But you can do much if you will mount guard against those roundabout phrases, those echoing polysyllables that tend to slip into your writing to rob it of its crispness and force.

Beware of the Pat Expression

28. Other things being equal, avoid phrases like "other things being equal." Those sentences that come to you whole, or in two or three doughy lumps, are sure to be bad sentences. They are no creation of yours but pieces of common thought floating in the community soup.

29. Pat expressions are hard, often impossible, to avoid, because they come too easily to be noticed and seem too necessary to be dispensed with. No writer avoids them altogether, but good writers avoid them more often than poor writers.

30. By "pat expressions" we mean such tags as "to all practical intents and purposes," "the pure and simple truth," "from where I sit," "the time of his life," "to the ends of the earth," "in the twinkling of an eye," "as sure as you're born," "over my dead body," "under cover of darkness," "took the easy way out," "when all is said and done," "told him time and time again," "parted the best of friends," "stand up and be counted," "gave him the best years of her life," "worked her fingers to the bone." Like the other clichés, these expressions were once forceful. Now we should use them only when we can't possibly think of anything else.

31. Some pat expressions stand like a wall between the writer and thought. Such a one is "the American way of life." Many student writers feel that when they have said that something accords with the American way of life or does not they have exhausted the subject. Actually, they have stopped at the highest level of abstraction. The American way of life is the complicated set of bonds between a hundred and eighty million ways. All of us know this when we think about it, but the tag phrase too often keeps us from thinking about it.

32. So with many another phrase dear to the politician: "this great land of ours," "the man in the street," "our national heritage." These may prove our patriotism or give a clue to our political beliefs, but otherwise they add nothing to the paper except words.

Colorful Words

33. The writer builds with words, and no builder uses a raw material more slippery and elusive and treacherous. A writer's work is a constant struggle to get the right word in the right place, to find that particular word that will convey his meaning exactly, that will persuade the reader or soothe him or startle or amuse him. He never succeeds altogether—sometimes he feels that he scarcely succeeds at all—but such successes as he has are what make the thing worth doing.

34. There is no book of rules for this game. One progresses through everlasting experiment on the basis of ever-widening experience. There are few useful generalizations that one can make about words as words but there are perhaps a few.

35. Some words are what we call "colorful." By this we mean that they are calculated to produce a picture or induce an emotion. They are dressy instead of plain, specific instead of general, loud instead of soft. Thus, in place of "Her heart beat," we may write "Her heart *pounded, throbbed, fluttered, danced.*" Instead of "He sat in his chair," we may say, "he *lounged, sprawled, coiled.*" Instead of "It was hot," we may say, "It was *blistering, sultry, muggy, suffocating, steamy, wilting.*"

36. However, it should not be supposed that the fancy word is always better. Often it is as well to write "Her heart beat" or "It was hot" if that is all it did or all it was. Ages differ in how they like their prose. The nineteenth century liked it rich and smoky. The twentieth century has usually preferred it lean and cool. The twentieth century writer, like all writers, is forever seeking the exact word, but he is wary of sounding feverish. He tends to pitch it low, to understate it, to throw it away. He knows that if he gets too colorful, the audience is likely to giggle.

37. See how this strikes you: "As the rich, golden glow of the sunset died away along the eternal western hills, Angela's limpid blue eyes looked softly and trustingly into Montague's flashing brown ones, and her heart pounded like a drum in time with the joyous song surging in her soul." Some people like that sort of thing, but most modern readers would say "Good grief," and turn on the television.

Colored Words

38. Some words we would call not so much colorful as colored—that is, loaded with associations, good or bad. All words—except perhaps structure words—have associations of some sort. We have said that the meaning of a word is the sum of the contexts in which it occurs. When we hear a word, we hear with it an echo of all the situations in which we have heard it before.

39. In some words, these echoes are obvious and discussible. The word *mother*, for example, has, for most people, agreeable associations. When you hear *mother* you probably think of home, safety, love, food, and various other pleasant things. If one writes, "She was like a mother to me," he gets an effect which he would not get in "She was like an aunt to me." The advertiser makes use of the associations of *mother* by working it in when he talks about his product. The politician works it in when he talks about himself.

40. So also with such words as *home, liberty, fireside, contentment, patriot, tenderness, sacrifice, childlike, manly, bluff, limpid.* All of these words are loaded with favorable associations that would be rather hard to indicate in a straightforward definition. There is more than a literal difference between "They sat around the fireside" and "They sat around the stove." They might have been equally warm and happy around the stove, but *fireside* suggests leisure, grace, quiet tradition, congenial company, and *stove* does not.

41. Conversely, some words have bad associations. *Mother* suggests pleasant things, but *mother-in-law* does not. Many mothers-in-law are heroically lovable and some mothers drink gin all day and beat their children insensible, but these facts of life are beside the point. The thing is that *mother* sounds good and *mother-in-law* does not.

42. Or consider the word *intellectual*. This would seem to be a complimentary term, but in point of fact it is not, for it has picked up associations of impracticality and ineffectuality and general dopiness. So also with such words as *liberal, reactionary, Communist, socialist, capitalist, radical, schoolteacher, truck driver, undertaker, operator, salesman, huckster, speculator.* These convey meanings on the literal level, but beyond that—sometimes, in some places—they convey contempt on the part of the speaker.

43. The question of whether to use loaded words or not depends on what is being written. The scientist, the scholar, try to avoid them; for the poet, the advertising writer, the public speaker, they are standard equipment. But every writer should take care that they do not substitute for thought. If you write, "Anyone who thinks that is nothing but a Socialist (or Communist or capitalist)" you have said nothing except that you don't like people who think that, and such remarks are effective only with the most naïve readers. It is always a bad mistake to think your readers more naïve than they really are.

Colorless Words

44. But probably most student writers come to grief not with words that are colorful or those that are colored but with those that have no color at all. A pet example is *nice*, a word we would find it hard to dispense with in casual conversation but which is no longer capable of adding much to a description. Colorless words are those of such general meaning that in a particular sentence they mean nothing. Slang adjectives, like *cool* ("That's real cool") tend to explode all over the language. They are applied to everything, lose their original force, and quickly die.

45. Beware also of nouns of very general meaning, like *circumstances, cases, instances, aspects, factors, relationships, attitudes, eventualities,* etc. In most circumstances you will find that those cases of writing which contain too many instances of words like these will in this and other aspects have factors leading to unsatisfactory relationships with the reader resulting in unfavorable attitudes on his part and perhaps other eventualities, like a grade of "D." Notice also what "etc." means. It means "I'd like to make this list longer, but I can't think of any more examples."

React....

to the essay.

Write in your answers to the following questions in the spaces provided.

1. What is the *subject* of the essay?

_____

_____

2. Every well-written essay or article contains a *thesis* or a main idea about the subject that the author wants the reader to accept or think about. A thesis is not the same as the subject but rather what the author says or feels about his or her subject. The *subject* of the essay you just read is how to write an essay. What is the *thesis* or main point the author is making?

_____

_____

_____

_____

3. Reread paragraph 6. What is the main idea of the paragraph?

_____

_____

_____

4. Authors usually reveal an *attitude* or *tone* about their subject. It may be humorous, serious, pleasant, sarcastic, nasty, biased, or any number of things to get the reader to react to their thesis. What do you think is this author's attitude about his subject?

_____

Why? _____

_____

_____

5. To what group of people (reader audience) do you feel the author is writing?

_____ Why? _____

_____

_____

6. The author has ten parts to his essay, each divided by a heading. In the spaces below, write in each heading and a brief summary of the author's point in that part of the essay.

1st Heading: _____

   Summary: _____

2d Heading: _____

   Summary: _____

3d Heading: _____

   Summary: _____

4th Heading: _____

   Summary: _____

5th Heading _____

   Summary: _____

6th Heading: _____

   Summary: _____

7th Heading: _____

   Summary: _____

8th Heading: _____

   Summary: _____

9th Heading: _____

   Summary _____

10th Heading: _____

Summary: _____

7. The meaning an author wishes to give may be lost if the reader does not understand the author's use of certain words or phrases. Check the following words you don't know or could not use correctly. The number behind the word represents the paragraph number where the word appears in the essay.

_____ a. tedious (6 and 12)

_____ b. trivial (8)

_____ c. trite (9)

_____ d. vacuity (10)

_____ e. abstract (17)

_____ f. hedge (23 and 24)

_____ g. linguistics (25)

_____ h. euphemism (25 and 27)

_____ i. jargon (27)

_____ j. induce (35)

Reread the words as they are used in the paragraphs shown. Then go to the Vocabulary Section in the Appendix on page 313.

an essay.

Writing essays is required in many school courses. Success in these courses often depends on a student's ability to write. Unfortunately, when many students are assigned an essay, they too frequently begin by writing away on the subject until a page or two is full. Or some students sit with a pen and paper in front of them, waiting for some divine inspiration to help them fill the page. To avoid either of these approaches, which are usually drastic measures, try using the following organizational approach before writing your required essay. More will be said about each of the following points later. For now, just read them carefully.

1. Select a topic that is neither too broad nor too narrow, and write a thesis statement that reflects what you want to say about your topic.
2. Write down a list of all the points you can that will support what you want to say about the topic. If you can't think of any, switch to a different topic related to the general assignment.
3. Analyze your list of points by putting together those that are similar. Renumber your list so that the points are in the order in which you will use them in your essay.

Now let's look more closely at each of these planning points.

Planning Point One: Selecting a Topic and Thesis

First select a topic that is neither too broad nor too narrow, and write a thesis statement. Let's assume that in one of your classes your teacher assigns a short essay asking that you write about some aspect of education. Where do you begin if you are not "knocked out" by the subject?

If you stop to think, you probably have many thoughts or ideas you could use in an essay on education. You've spent a good deal of time being exposed to both formal and informal education during your lifetime. You might decide to write about teachers, textbooks, schools, grading systems, school dropouts, the need (or lack of need) for a degree, the history of public education, and so on. The problem should not be: "I don't know what to write about." Rather, the problem is to select a topic about education that you feel will lend itself to a short essay and that you know something about.

Where do you get ideas for essays? Virtually everywhere. You haven't lived as long as you have without personal experiences and exposure to ideas with which you've agreed and disagreed. Finding an essay topic you can handle simply requires some moments of reflection, reacting to ideas in an essay, a book, a movie, or a TV program or newscast. You have experiences and thoughts that you merely need to pursue. Planning and writing an essay is really a "thinking" project. It forces you to think about you in connection with the world around you and to develop your thought processes.

When stuck for an essay topic, skim through the newspaper or a magazine to see what's happening in the world. Let's say, for instance, that you are still looking for a topic on education. You see this item in the paper:

---

3 in 10 Adults Rated Illiterate in World
According to experts at the U.N. Educational, Scientific and Cultural Organization, the number of adult illiterates is currently estimated at 814 million—or three adults in 10—and the problem is increasing because of soaring population growth.

Nearly three-quarters of the world's illiterates live in Asia, approximately 20% in Africa and 5% in Latin America.

Think a moment. What are the lives of those illiterates like? Do you know any illiterates? Would their lives be more meaningful if they could read and write? Do all people really need to know how to read and write? Does being illiterate mean being unhappy or stupid or something of which to be ashamed? Does it really matter in some cultures? Is our desire to have everybody literate based on our society's need others to be like us? Are we so great? What would your life be like if you couldn't read this? An essay on education can easily be developed by pursuing these questions and thoughts.

Or let's say you live in San Francisco, where you go to the public library to check out a copy of *Mary Poppins* for your sister. You can't find it, so you inquire from the librarian why not. The librarian informs you that the book has been removed from the San Francisco libraries because, she says, "*Mary Poppins* treats minorities in ways that are degrading. It is written from the old English view of the white man's burden . . . that is naturally offensive to minorities and others as well." (At the time of this book's writing, 1981, *Mary Poppins* is banned from the San Francisco Public Library for those reasons given.) Is the library submitting to censorship? Do others have a right to supress what you or others may want to read? Should someone or group be in charge of selecting what can and cannot be placed in a public or school library? Are there people who know what is good for you to read and what isn't? Should schools censor books or information from students? Is censorship in education ever appropriate?

The point here is that topics for essays are everywhere. It is simply a matter of training yourself to begin to look at what you know and don't know, what you feel and don't feel. But in all cases, don't ever try to write about something you haven't thought about and planned in an organized way.

Once you have some idea what the general subject of your essay will be, it's necessary to make certain the topic is neither too broad nor too narrow. For instance, you could not use the subject "Grades" for a short essay. The subject of grades is too broad. It needs to be narrowed down to something such as "How Some Instructors Use Grades Against Students" or "The Advantages of the Credit Grading System over the Letter Grading System." In both cases, the topic is more appropriate for a short essay.

Nor could you use the topic "Teachers" for a short essay. It's also too broad. It needs to be narrowed down to something like "My English Teacher" or "Why I Fell in Love with My Sixth-Grade Teacher" or "The Best History Instructor I Ever Had" or "The Qualities Necessary for a Good Teacher." Any of these topics could be used for a short essay assignment.

Selecting a topic means going from the abstract or broad topic to one that you can specifically deal with in an essay of 300–500 words. Start with the broad subject, and narrow it down like this.

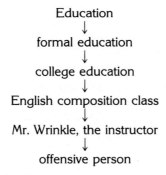

Education
↓
formal education
↓
college education
↓
English composition class
↓
Mr. Wrinkle, the instructor
↓
offensive person

A possible thesis now is "My English instructor, Mr. Wrinkle, is an offensive person." The next step would be to see if you can support that thesis with good examples or proof.

In the space that follows, write down four topics (on any subject you want) that could be used in a short essay of five or six paragraphs. Remember that the topics must not be too broad or too narrow. Here are some suggestions, but feel free to use your own:

    a. My favorite pastime.
    b. What makes a friend.
    c. Is college important?
    d. An invention we are better off without.
    e. Women in the military.
    f. What makes a good parent?
    g. Which sport is best suited for TV?
    h. Criteria in selecting a new car.
    i. What makes a good teacher?
    j. The disadvantages of grades.
    k. What I'd do with a million dollars tax free.
    l. Look in the newspaper for some ideas.

1. _____

2. _____

3. _____

4. _____

Once you have decided on a topic, you need to consider what your *thesis* will be. Remember, your thesis is what you want to prove or say about your subject. For instance, it may be that you decide to write about "How Some Instructors Use Grades Against Students." Your thesis or point of the essay might be "Some teachers at our school take advantage of their power by using grades to punish students." In other words, the point of your essay will be to prove or show the reader the unfairness of those instructors who take advantage of the grading system and use it against students.

Here is another example. Let's say you wanted to write about the topic "The Qualities Necessary for a Good Teacher." Your thesis statement might read something like this: "The most important qualities a good teacher should have are a thorough understanding of the subject he or she teaches, a concern for the students, and a variety of teaching methods." Notice the difference between a topic and a thesis statement. The topic is what will be written about; the thesis is what will be said or the point being made about the topic.

Here are some examples of a few possible theses (that's plural for thesis) for the subject of grading systems:

Example A: Grades should no longer be used in schools.
Example B: Grades are a necessity in completing school work and represent payment for work accomplished.
Example C: Several changes in grading policies as now used need to be made.

Notice that the topic—grading systems—stays the same in all examples, but the opinion or feeling about the topic is different in each example. Yet each example could serve as a thesis for an essay if enough supporting material could be provided.

In the space that follows, write a possible thesis statement for each item you listed earlier as a possible topic for an essay. Make certain your thesis statement is a complete sentence as in the examples previously given.

Thesis Statement 1: _____

_____

_____

Thesis Statement 2: _____

_____

_____

Thesis Statement 3: _____

_____

_____

Thesis Statement 4: _____

_____

_____

Now look closely at each of your thesis statements. Are any of them too broad or too narrow for a short essay? Here are some examples to serve as guides before you check yours.

Example A: All tests and grades should be abolished in schools.

(Although this could be an interesting essay, the term "All tests and grades . . ." is a big generalization. Perhaps "Entrance tests should be abolished" or "Grades in nonmajor courses should be abolished" would be easier and narrower in scope. Unless you are writing a very long essay, Example A is too broad for a short essay.)

Example B: My English teacher "bugs" me.

(The task here would be to come up with several reasons why your English teacher gets to you and be able to give incidents and examples to show how the teacher "bugs" you. It could be a good topic to develop into an essay.)

Example C: Textbooks are boring.

(This subject would be difficult to handle because you probably aren't familiar with enough textbooks—and there are thousands of titles—to prove your point. It's too broad. Narrow it to "My history textbook is boring" or "Every psychology book I've ever read is boring.")

Example D: Education is a necessity in today's world.

(This one is too broad. Education—or what kind of education—needs defining. Also, the word *necessity* is too vague. Besides, how true is the statement? Is education necessary? If so, what kind—high school? college? on the job education? The topic needs narrowing.)

Example E: The dean of men is fat.

(This one is too narrow. What can be said after you say he's fat? You could give examples of weight, size of clothes, compare him with other fat people, but it all sounds repetitious. Something else about the dean of men should be found to write an essay.)

Following is a list of some statements. Place a check mark by the ones you feel are good thesis statements, being neither too narrow nor too broad for a short essay.

_____ 1. Grades are (or are not) a necessity.

_____ 2. The most important human qualities are not gradable.

_____ 3. An *F* grade doesn't mean you are a failure.

_____ 4. There are advantages to the credit–no credit system over the letter grade system.

_____ 5. The history of universities in America.

_____ 6. Plains Indians rode horses in the 1800s.

The first four statements above could probably be used as theses for short essays, although the first one could be narrower and explain why grades are a necessity. Number 5 is not a thesis statement; it's a very broad topic. Number 6 is too narrow; it needs to be changed to something such as, "The horse had several influences on the life-style of the Plains Indians in the 1800s."

Now select one of the four thesis statements you wrote earlier on page 22, and, in the space that follows, write down the thesis you have decided to use for an essay of four or five paragraphs in length. Change the wording if you need to do so.

Essay Thesis: _____

_____

_____

_____

_____

Planning Point Two: Listing Supporting Points

Second, write down a list of all the points you think will support what you want to say about your topic. Suppose, for instance, that you have decided on "My English teacher 'bugs' me." You might list the following supporting points.

Thesis: My English teacher "bugs" me.
Support: 1. always scratching his chin
       2. doesn't believe in giving A's
       3. the course makes me miss lunch.
       4. talks as if we know more than we do
       5. uses too many big words
       6. often comes to class late
       7. gives too many writing assignments
       8. walks around the room too much
       9. never looks at students
     10. I didn't take enough English in high school

Notice that all but two of these reasons deal with why the teacher "bugs" or bothers "me." The key word in the thesis statement is "bug." Thus, all points but numbers 3 and 10 listed show why this is so.

In the spaces that follow, write down the thesis you've selected to write about, and list any points you can use in your essay to support your views. If you can't list at least six points, go back to page 21 and select another topic. Remember, your list should be related to the key words in your thesis statement.

Thesis Statement: _____

_____

_____

Support:

1. _____
2. _____
3. _____
4. _____
5. _____
6. _____
7. _____
8. _____
9. _____
10. _____

Planning Point Three: Ordering Supporting Points

Third, analyze your list of points by putting those that are similar together. Rearrange your list so that the points are in the order in which you will use them in your essay or in categories that are easy to handle. In the case of the topic "My English Teacher Bugs Me," the rearranged list might look like this with items 3 and 10 not used:

Original Order
1. always scratching his chin
2. doesn't believe in giving A's
3. course makes me miss lunch
4. talks as if we know more than we do
5. uses too many big words

① Personal mannerisms

② Attitude toward students

Rearranged Order
1. always scratching chin
8. walks around room too much
9. never looks at students
5. uses too many big words
4. talks as if we know more than we do
6. comes to class late

6. often comes to class too late
7. gives too many essay writing assignments
8. walks around the room too much
9. never looks at students
10. I didn't take enough English in high school

③ Difficult teacher { 7. gives too many easy writing assignments
2. never gives *A*'s

You can see from the reordered list that the points now appear in three general categories: personal mannerisms, attitudes toward students, and difficult teacher. Each of these areas can now be developed into three separate paragraphs. By the time the essay is complete, it will probably be a five-paragraph essay based on the following outline:

Essay Outline

Paragraph 1   I. Introduction, mentioning three main areas
    A. personal mannerisms
    B. attitudes toward students
    C. difficult teacher

Paragraph 2   II. Personal mannerisms
    A. always scratches chin
    B. walks around room too much
    C. never looks at students

Paragraph 3   III. Attitude toward students
    A. uses too many big words
    B. talks as if we know more than we do
    C. comes to class late

Paragraph 4   IV. Difficult teacher
    A. gives too many essays
    B. never gives *A*'s

Paragraph 5   V. Conclusion or summary

You can see from the above outline that an essay could easily be developed from it. Naturally, more rearrangement could be done, placing IV as II, or III as II, and so on. But the basic idea of planning before you write is to give some thought and order to what you say for the sake of your reader.

Practices in Planning an Essay

The following practices will help you develop your organization and outlining abilities. You may not need to do all of them.

Practice 1. Rearrange by color (red, yellow, blue-black) the following ten items of fruit into a more orderly or logical fashion for each in writing an essay.

Unordered Support	Ordered Support
1. strawberries	_____
2. bananas	_____
3. peaches	_____
4. pomegranates	_____
5. red apples	_____
6. grapefruit	_____
7. blueberries	_____
8. tomatoes	_____
9. blackberries	_____
10. lemons	_____

Practice 2. Place the ordered support in Practice 1 into an outline that could be used for writing an essay. The first part has been done for you.

Paragraph 1   I. Introduction, mentioning three main types of fruit

      A. _____ *red fruit* _____

      B. _____ *yellow fruit* _____

      C. _____ *blue-black fruit* _____

Paragraph 2   II. _____

      A. _____

      B. _____

      C. _____

      D. _____

Paragraph 3   III. _____

      A. _____

      B. _____

      C. _____

      D. _____

(continued on next page)   Plan   **27**

Paragraph 4   IV. _____

          A. _____

          B. _____

Paragraph 5   V. Conclusion, summarizing three main types of fruit

          A. _____

          B. _____

          C. _____

Practice 3.   Rearrange the following list of tools into a more logical or orderly fashion.

Unordered Support   **Ordered Support**

1. claw hammer   _____ ⎫
2. pliers   _____ ⎬ A. _____
3. jigsaw   _____ ⎭
4. ball peen hammer _____ ⎫
5. vise grips   _____ ⎬ B. _____
6. handsaw   _____ ⎭
7. sledgehammer   _____ ⎫ C. _____
8. bench vise   _____ ⎭

Practice 4.   Place the ordered support in Practice 3 into an outline that could be used for writing an essay.

Paragraph 1   I. Introduction, mentioning three main types of tools

          A. _____

          B. _____

          C. _____

Paragraph 2   II. _____

          A. _____

          B. _____

C. _____

Paragraph 3   III. _____

        A. _____

        B. _____

        C. _____

Paragraph 4   IV. _____

        A. _____

        B. _____

Paragraph 5   V. Conclusion, summarizing three types of tools

        A. _____

        B. _____

        C. _____

Practice 5. Rearrange the following fish into two categories: freshwater and saltwater fish.

Unordered Support   **Reordered Support**

1. trout   _____

2. shark   _____

3. goldfish   _____

4. saltwater fish   _____

5. sea bass   _____

6. perch   _____

7. freshwater fish   _____

8. stingray   _____

9. bluegill   _____

10. catfish   _____

11. swordfish   _____

12. tuna   _____

Practice 6. Place the reordered list of fish from Practice 5 into an outline that could be used for writing an essay on types of fish. Use the space that follows.

Practice 7. Rearrange the following list into an orderly arrangement. Two items in the list *do not* belong.

Unordered Support	**Rearranged Support**
1. ice skating	_____
2. water sports	_____
3. skin diving	_____
4. snow skiing	_____
5. sports	_____
6. swimming	_____
7. jogging	_____
8. waterskiing	_____
9. winter sports	_____
10. snow sledding	_____
11. table tennis	_____
12. sailing	_____

Practice 8. Place the rearranged list from Practice 7 into an outline that could be used for writing an essay. Do this on a separate sheet and turn it in to your instructor.

(A) a thesis statement and an outline.

In the following spaces, write the thesis statement you decided to use on page 25, and rearrange your list of support so that your ideas are more organized. You should have at least six points to rearrange.

Thesis Statement: _____

_____

_____

Reordered Support:

_____

_____

_____

_____

_____

_____

_____

_____

_____

Outline of your essay: (You should have at least four or five possible paragraphs. The outline should be similar to those in Practices 2, 4, and 6.)

Write...

(B) an essay based on your outline.

Using your thesis statement and outline, write an essay. An essay, at least the kind you'll be expected to write, has three basic parts: the introductory paragraph, the supporting paragraphs, and the concluding paragraph. Usually, college essays run between 400 and 500 words in length. If you have an outline with five major parts, I to V, generally, the *form* of your essay will look like this:

Introductory paragraph based on your outline's Roman numeral I

A. The beginning of each paragraph is indented five spaces.
B. The first paragraph should create reader interest in your topic.
C. The thesis or controlling idea of your essay usually appears in the first paragraph.

Supporting paragraph: Roman numeral II of outline

A. Always indent.
B. A topic sentence, usually at the beginning, controls what will be said in the supporting sentences.
C. The length or number of sentences depends on how much needs to be said to develop topic sentence.
D. Use all the support under II of your outline.

Supporting paragraph: Roman numeral III of outline

A. Always indent.
B. Another topic sentence that supports the thesis.
C. Use all the support listed under III of your outline.

Supporting paragraph: Roman numeral IV of outline

A. Always indent.
B. Another topic sentence that supports the thesis.
C. Use all the supporting points under IV of your outline.

Concluding paragraph: Roman numeral V of outline

A. Always indent.
B. Draw together all that has been said either to summarize or make a concluding point.
C. Final statement should be strong.

Follow your outline as much as possible. However, if new ideas occur to you as you write and if those ideas fit your thesis, feel free to change from your outline. The outline is only a working model to follow so that you don't end up with an unorganized essay. When finished, go to the next step: Rewrite.

Rewrite...
your first draft.

Before you turn in your essay to your instructor, follow the advice that Paul Roberts gives in his essay that you read at the beginning of this unit. Check each one of these points, and rewrite any part of your essay that needs it.

_____ 1. Did you say "nothing about something," or did you write what you know and feel?

_____ 2. Did you "avoid the obvious content," or did you write what everyone else would write?

_____ 3. Did you take the less usual side if that's what you really think?

_____ 4. Did you write using abstractions and generalities, or did you use concrete points to prove or support your thesis?

_____ 5. Did you "get rid of obvious padding," or did you use many words that say little?

_____ 6. Did you "call a fool a fool," or did you hedge on what you really wanted to say?

_____ 7. Did you check your essay for "pat expressions" and change them to fresh expressions?

_____ 8. Did you use "colorful words" to give your essay the right tone and meaning?

_____ 9. Did you get rid of any "colored words" you may have used?

_____ 10. Did you avoid using "colorless words"?

It may be that you will need more practice in recognizing many of the pointers Roberts gives in his essay. That will come with time and more writing, which is what this book is all about.

Turn in your revised essay to your instructor.

UNIT

Think....
about education

Read....
about education
"Schools as Thermostats: Putting Culture's
Beam in Balance" by Neil Postman

React....
to the essay

Plan....
an essay
Topics for an essay on education
The journal

Write....
(A) **an outline for an essay**
(B) **an introductory paragraph**
Method 1: ask a question
Method 2: use an anecdote
Method 3: use a quotation
Method 4: brief overview
Method 5: stress importance of topic
Method 6: use a combination of methods
Practices in writing introductory paragraphs
(C) **an essay**

Rewrite....
your first draft

Think...

about education by answering the following questions.

1. How do you define education; that is, what do you think education is?

_____

_____

_____

_____

2. What was the best educational experience you had during the last two years of your schooling?

_____

_____

_____

_____

3. Is education a right or a privilege?

_____ Explain. _____

_____

_____

_____

_____

4. If you could change the educational process, what would you change first?

_____

_____

_____

_____

5. Do you feel you learn more of value to you from attending school or from the media, such as TV, radio, and magazines? _____

   Explain. _____

   _____

   _____

   _____

6. Should schools try to make education relevant; that is, should teachers deal with what is presently of interest, controversial, and entertaining to students?

   _____

   Why? _____

   _____

   _____

   _____

7. What subjects do you think schools should emphasize the most and why?

   _____

   _____

   _____

about education.

The following essay was written by a professor of media ecology at New York University. He is also well-known for two books on education: *Teaching as a Subversive Activity* and *Teaching as a Conserving Activity*. The author is concerned with defining relevance in education and believes that schools should try to keep the education of youth in balance. What that balance is becomes the thesis of his essay. He compares what the media teach youth with what he feels the schools should teach youth in order to give them balance. As you read Neil Postman's essay, remember the answers you gave to the questions in the THINK section. Do you agree with the author? Are you a victim of the media? Has your education so far taught you exposition—what the author calls the systematic presentation and development of ideas?

Schools as Thermostats: Putting Culture's Beam in Balance
Neil Postman

1. During most of the 1960s and early '70s, the word that received the heaviest pounding in discourses on education was "relevance." Every education writer, it seemed, was expected to work it over thoroughly, and I joined in the fun myself in at least two books I wrote.

2. The prevailing opinion in those years was that educational relevance meant that which was of immediate interest, controversial and, if possible, entertaining. It followed from this that any relevant topic would engage the student's wholehearted attention, and by that sole virtue was deserving of inclusion in the school curriculum. The opposite was also held to be true. That which did not have an immediate and engrossing interest to a student was mere pedantry and a waste of valuable time.

3. By this definition of relevance, the best thing the schools could do would be to close their doors and turn the education of our youth over to the electronic media: television, film, records and radio. For there can be no doubt that the media have our students' wholehearted attention, and that the "curriculum" of the media—"Star Wars," Fonzie, The Who and the like—has a direct and urgent bearing on our students' lives.

4. As a matter of fact, something very close to this has already happened. The average American child, from age 6 to 18, spends about 16,000 hours in front

Reprinted by permission of Neil Postman.

of a television set. The only activity that occupies more of an American youth's time is sleeping. And if we add to TV viewing time the amount of time spent listening to records and radio and watching movies, we get a figure in excess of 20,000 hours of "relevance."

5. Given the fact that the media are already the dominating force in the education of our youth, it is reasonable to ask if there is not some other definition of relevance that might be used by the schools during the 12,000 hours our students are required to be there.

6. I believe there is, and it may be simply stated; What has the most relevance to students is that which their culture *least* provides them. This is what Cicero meant when he said that the purpose of education is to free a student from the tyranny of the present. It is also what André Gide meant in saying the best education is that which goes counter to one's culture.

7. I call this the thermostatic view of schools. It may also be called the ecological view, which is to say that schools should try to keep the education of our youth in balance. When the culture stresses yin, the schools should stress yang. In this way, there is a continuous dialogue sustained between competing points of view; the teachings of the culture and the teachings of the school. Through this dialogue, students are protected against being overwhelmed by the biases of their own times—for to leave students entirely to the influences of the dominating biases of their culture is to guarantee them a one-dimensional education and a half-developed personality. What is relevant, therefore, is what the culture is insisting is irrelevant.

8. In our present circumstances, we may look directly at the electronic media to discover what are the dominant teachings of the culture. The media teach many things, of course, but I should like to mention four of their biases which are in special need of opposition by the schools.

9. The media are, first of all, attention-centered. Their main goal is to capture and hold the attention of their audiences. The content of media is of relatively little importance. It is changeable and disposable. Its only function is as bait.

10. Second, the media are vastly entertaining. Nothing will appear on TV or the movie screen outside of school unless it has "entertaining value." This means it must not be demanding or disturbing, for if it is, the audience will turn away

11. Third, the media, especially television, are image-centered. TV consists of fast-moving, continuously changing visual images which compress time to an extraordinary degree. The average length of a shot on "The Love Boat," for example, is about three seconds. On commercials, the average length of a shot is two seconds. (In the first 20 years of their lives, American children will see approximately 500,000 TV commercials.) Thus TV, as well as movies, work against the development of language.

12. Ironically, the two electronic media best suited to the transmission of human speech—the radio and phonograph—have been given over almost entirely to the transmission of music, a non-linguistic form of communication. Such language as is heard on records is little else but comedy routines, or song lyrics at the level of Neanderthal chanting. On radio, language is largely a commercial message, mostly a parody of human speech—disjointed, semihysterical, almost completely devoid of ideational content.

13. And finally, most of what children see on TV and in the movies takes the form of stories. The media ("Sesame Street" is no exception here) have turned all cultural teaching into a narrative mode. Exposition—the systematic presentation and development of ideas—is practically unknown among our children.

14. The teachings of the media, then, stress instant, not deferred, gratification; entertainment, not serious content; images, not words and stories, not ideas. According to the thermostatic view, our schools must now make a concerted effort to counterbalance such teachings. This would imply that the schools stress, for example, subjects that require students to understand and express themselves in words; that require them to pay attention even when they are not being entertained; that require them to evaluate and criticize ideas; that demand concentration and a confrontation with complexity. If you are under the impression that most of our schools already do this, you might find it sobering to know that more than half the high schools in the United States do not offer a single course in physics.

15. But I do not intend here to criticize what educators have been doing, and certainly do not want to associate myself with a simplistic "back to the basics" movement. The point I am making is that we can no longer ignore the extent to which the teachings of the media are controlling the direction of the intellectual character of our youth. In the future, the schools must promote, as never before, the skills, values and behaviors that the media either disregard or undermine.

16. To be specific, I believe the schools must emphasize more than ever such subjects as history, science and semantics. Even philosophy and comparative religion would be extremely valuable, especially for high school students. Subjects such as these require students to confront serious content, complexity and continuity. They are also uniquely able to provide perspectives on the present.

17. The processes of reading, writing, speaking and listening should, of course, be given the highest priority. And it would be desirable if, at long last, our schools took seriously the teaching of critical thinking. But beyond the subjects we teach, the school may act as a thermostatic agent through its style and ambience. I believe it is important, for example, that school be sharply differentiated from other cultural institutions such as movie theaters, rock concert sites and playgrounds.

18. It is particularly important that schools be seen as places of serious and dignified academic purpose. This implies that schools would attempt to preserve civilized modes of discourse and relatively formal patterns of behavior; that schools insist on a measure of respect for traditional social symbols, and that the schools undertake the task of teaching our youth how civilized intellects disagree with one another and generally what the habits are of well-mannered people.

19. In this way, we will be providing our youth with an alternative idea of relevance—an idea they may use to judge for themselves, in a changing future, what knowledge and values will serve most surely to conserve and enrich their own lives and the life of their culture.

React...

to the essay by answering the following questions. Reread the essay, if need be, in order to answer the questions.

1. What is the author's *subject;* that is, what is he writing about? (Don't merely answer, "Education.")

_____

_____

2. What is the author's *thesis* or main idea about his subject?

_____

_____

_____

3. In what paragraph or paragraphs does the thesis seem best stated?

_____

4. Do you agree with his thesis? _____

   Why? _____

_____

_____

5. What does the author mean by "the thermostatic views of schools" in paragraph 7? _____

_____

_____

_____

6. Postman mentions that the media teach many things, but discusses four of their biases that the schools need to oppose. What are the four?

_____

_____

_____

_____

7. What subjects does the author feel the schools should emphasize?

_____

_____

_____

_____

8. Of what relevance is the content of this essay to you?

_____

_____

_____

_____

9. Place a check mark in front of the following words from the essay that you don't know or could not use correctly. The number behind the word refers to the paragraph number where the word appears in the essay. You will be tested on these words later.

_____ a. relevance (1, 2, 3, 4, 6)

_____ b. pedantry (2)

_____ c. counter to (6)

_____ d. ecological (7)

_____ e. yin and yang (7)

_____ f. dominant (8)

_____ g. devoid (12)

_____ h. semantics (16)

_____ i. ambience (17)

_____ j. alternative (19)

Reread any word you checked by turning to the paragraph number by the word. Then turn to the Vocabulary Section in the Appendix on page 314, where you will receive help in learning the words.

Plan...

an essay on some aspect of education.

In the last unit it was emphasized that planning an essay before attempting to write one will save time and produce a better-organized essay. Three planning points were presented: one, select a topic that is neither too board nor narrow, and develop a thesis—your views or feelings about the topic; two, make a list of as many supporting points as possible to support your thesis; and three, order or reorganize those points into an outline or some form to follow when you actually begin to put words on paper. Doing so will help you "say *something* in 500 words"!

But it isn't always easy to come up with an idea for an essay. Let's say your instructor wants you to write a paper of about 500 words on education. Education is a broad topic, so you'd have to narrow it down. Here are some possible ideas related to education, but narrowed down to manageable topics:

1. Reasons students drop out of school.
2. Causes of student cheating.
3. Is education a right or a privilege?
4. Is a college degree worth the hassle?
5. Should schools teach sex education?
6. The advantages/disadvantages of a junior college.
7. Should professors be required to "publish or perish"?
8. How to select a fraternity or sorority.
9. Should all courses in school be relevant?
10. The most important things schools should teach.
11. The best/worst class I ever had.
12. The food service in my college's cafeteria.

Where did these dozen ideas come from? Just a few moments of sitting and thinking with a pen in hand. That's the real key to a good essay—thinking an idea through. Actually, that's why essay writing is taught. It forces mental discipline, "the systematic presentation and development of ideas," as Neil Postman says in his essay. That's why this textbook deals first with thinking, planning, and organizing essays and later deals with the basics of grammar and punctuation. Those are only tools to good writing used to polish the ideas an essay builds on.

Some students have trouble coming up with good topics for an essay. The "trouble" is usually lack of practice more than anything else. Sometimes it's a fear that "I have nothing important to say." Others don't write because they worry about their spelling, grammar, and punctuation. They get so caught up in their fear of mistakes that they don't really produce any good ideas.

One of the best ways to combat these types of problems is to keep a journal or notebook in which you do some thinking on paper. Don't let anyone read it unless you want to do so, but every day try to write something in it. A journal is not a diary; it's merely a record of some of your thoughts about yourself, others, places, ideas, fantasies, whatever comes to mind. You don't worry about spelling, grammar, or punctuation. You just deal with ideas. Sometimes the ideas that come out are clear, sometimes confused. Sometimes what you write is happy, sometimes sad. Some things you'll write are private and others you'll want to share. But for the undisciplined writer, it's the best way to realize you really do have things to think about—and write about. By writing daily in your journal, you'll soon have a resource of ideas to use in future essays.

You could also use your journal to help you plan an essay. Let's say that you think you might want to write an essay on the reasons students drop out of college. Here's an example of a possible journal entry:

> Think I'll write about student dropouts. Why do students drop out of school? Boredom—I've experienced that. A good job may come along. Fear of failure maybe? Pregnancy. Sickness. Are there other reasons? What are they? Can't think—ah, yeah, disappointment in what the classes teach. I remember how I looked forward to my first psychology (sp?) class, but the teacher only seemed to deal with rats and mazes and I wanted to know more about how the mind works. Man, that class was awful, maybe I should write about the worst class I ever had. That was it! So far, anyway.

Notice how loose and rambling this entry is. It's nowhere near an essay. But it has helped the author. First, there are at least six reasons given regarding student dropouts. All could be developed into supporting points with more thought on each one. Second, the journal entry shows that maybe the author would have more feeling for an essay on a different topic—"the worst class I've ever had." Now the author has plenty to write about. Keeping a journal, then, is one way to capture your ideas on paper and an excellent place to think through and plan an essay. The next section, "Write," will show you how to get the essay itself started.

Practice 1.   On another sheet of paper, or in a notebook you intend to use as a journal, start writing about education. Don't worry about an organized essay. Just let any and all ideas you have that the word education triggers in your mind. In other words, think on paper. Since our thoughts are usually not organized, don't expect your writing to be. Here are some ideas to get you thinking: formal education, informal education, street education, church education, sex education, driver education, elementary, secondary, college . . . start writing your ideas.

Practice 2.   In the space below, trying to use what you just wrote, write down a topic on education that you feel is neither too narrow or too broad for an essay of about 500 words. If you wish, you can use one of the twelve topics listed earlier. However, it's better to have one of your own.

Topic:

Practice 3. Now write a tentative thesis statement that expresses what you want to say about your topic. You may need to alter or change your thesis somewhat after you think through your topic. This is just a working thesis.

Tentative Thesis Statement:

_____

_____

_____

_____

Below, list all the ideas you can think of to support your thesis. If you don't have at least six points, try another topic or thesis.

_____

_____

_____

_____

_____

_____

_____

_____

_____

(A) an outline for an essay.

Now rearrange your list of ideas into an outline or some order you can follow to write your essay. Use the outlining procedure described in Unit 1. Do this on a separate piece of paper.

Write...

(B) an introductory or opening paragraph for your essay. But first read the following information about introductory paragraphs.

A paragraph, as you probably know, is a group of sentences arranged in such a way that *one idea* is developed or discussed. In some ways a paragraph is a mini-essay. More will be said about paragraphs in Unit 3. For now, be concerned only with introductory paragraphs.

An introductory or opening paragraph to an essay is an important one. It should do three things: one, give a statement about the subject or topic; two, state or suggest a thesis or point of view about your subject; and three, convince your readers it is worth their time to read the rest of the essay by drawing their interest. Whenever you write an introductory paragraph, keep these goals in mind.

There is no one way to begin an opening paragraph to an essay. In fact, you should attempt to be as original as you can provided you accomplish the three things mentioned. Authors use several methods for opening essays. Here are some of them. Each one will be discussed more fully later.

Method 1. Ask the reader a question that will interest or irritate him or her.

Method 2. Give a short anecdote or brief incident that interests the reader in the subject.

Method 3. Use a quotation that is related to your topic and that either agrees or disagrees with the essay thesis.

Method 4. Briefly state the supporting detail that will be developed in the essay.

Method 5. Appeal to the reader regarding the importance of the topic.

Method 6. Combine two or more of the above methods into one or two paragraphs.

These methods are used frequently in various ways, but they are not the only means. Once you learn how to handle these devices you will probably find your own methods, depending upon the topic of the essay being written. Just keep in mind that the purpose of an introductory paragraph is to give a statement about the topic, to give or hint at your thesis or viewpoint about the subject, and to convince your readers it is worth their time to read the essay by drawing their interest. Notice how these different methods work.

1. *Ask the reader a question that will interest or irritate him or her.* The question can be one that does not have an easy answer or one that you intend to answer in the essay for the reader. If the subject is controversial, the question may even irritate the reader into reading the essay to see what you think. Here is an example of how an author uses a question in an introductory essay.

> There is much being said about natural foods these days. Often, proponents of natural foods criticize the majority of foods being sold in the supermarkets because they contain preservatives. Yet, what would happen if food processors quit using preservatives in bakery goods, frozen vegetables, breakfast cereals, and canned goods? Would the housewife be prepared to deal with storing foods without preservatives?

Notice in the example how the topic natural foods is brought up and then the fact that preserved food packaging is often criticized, and next questions that the author will answer in the essay are raised. Probably, the author's thesis would be in favor of using preservatives.

2. *Give a short anecdote or brief incident that interests the reader in the subject.* Often, a reader is attracted to an essay because of the incident an author relates. The reader wants to see what the story has to do with the subject. Here is an example:

> The other day I got trapped into going grocery shopping with my wife at the supermarket. I hate to waste time pushing a cart up and down the aisles and standing around in front of items while my wife compares prices and weight. Bored, I just happened to pick up an item she had placed in the shopping cart and read the ingredients: artificial flavoring, artificial color, fumaric acid, sodium ascorbate, propylene glyco, monosodium glutamate, and sodium benzoate. "My God," I cried out, "you're trying to poison me!"

In this opening paragraph, the author has set the stage for discussing the topic of preservatives used in food packaging. Judging from the tone, we can assume that the author's thesis might be a humorous attack against the use of food preservatives.

3. *Use a quotation that is related to your topic and that either agrees or disagrees with the essay's thesis.* If you use a quotation, make certain it is not one that is used so often that it becomes ineffective rather than effective. Here is an example of how a quotation might be used in an opening paragraph.

> I used to hear my grandmother say, "The way to a man's heart is his stomach." I never really thought about it until last night. I gave my husband some bread I baked because he'd been complaining about the preservatives

in the store-bought bread. Well, about an hour after he ate my fresh-baked bread he started suffering from heartburn!

In this opening paragraph, the author has introduced us to the topic of home cooking or baking. It is a good beginning for a humorous essay on comparing grandma's day in the kitchen with a day in today's kitchen or for a paper on trying to bake fresh bread or for an attempt to make fun of the quotation used by giving a meaning to it that was not intended.

4. *Briefly state the supporting detail that will be developed in the essay.* Such a device gets right to the point of the essay and gives a brief, overall view of what will be said. Here is an example:

> There are at least five areas of gross negligence in our food raising. One is the feedlot used on our beef cattle. Another is our overuse of injection of chickens with antibiotics harmful to them and us. Third is the growing pollution of fresh and salt water that produces toxic substances in fish. Still another area of negligence is the question of preservatives added to milk and milk products. Last is the harmful chemical stimulants and fertilizers used on growing crops.

Notice that five areas of neglect are mentioned. The rest of the essay will take each of these points and discuss them in more detail. This is usually the best method to use for essay exams because it gets right to the point.

5. *Appeal to the reader regarding the importance of the topic.* If your subject is of concern and importance to everyone, such as the need to ration meat because of shortages, the pollution of your local water reservoirs, or the need to pass or repeal a law that concerns most everyone, then you should open your essay stating the importance of your topic. For example:

> With all the wealth, power, health standards, luxuries of life, and abundance of food in the United States, it might surprise most people to learn that Americans rank only fourth in the world as the best fed and only sixth in the longevity of life. There are many reasons for this low record, but the main one has to do with America's eating habits.

In this opening paragraph, the importance of the topic is developed by an attempt to startle or jar the reader into becoming aware of the contrast in America's high standard of living and low rank in nutrition and life expectancy.

6. *Combine two or more of the above methods into one or two paragraphs.* This device simply pulls together more than one method.

> What are natural foods?
> For many years nutritionists have been lecturing about the deficiencies in our national diet, but the audience has been very small, and little information ever filtered through to the large middle segment of our population. However, in the last two or three years, more and more people have become aware of the need for change in their nutritional patterns.

This opening paragraph, actually two, uses both the question technique and the appeal of the importance of the topic.

Opening paragraphs are very important to the success of your essay. Remember that they should:

1. Give a statement about the subject or topic.
2. Contain the thesis or viewpoint toward the subject.
3. Convince readers it is worth their time to read the rest of the essay by drawing their interest.

Always check your opening paragraphs for these three points.

 ## Practices in Writing Introductory Paragraphs

Practice 1. List the three elements a good introductory paragraph should contain.

1. _____

2. _____

3. _____

Practice 2. List the six methods that can be used to write an introductory paragraph.

1. _____

_____

2. _____

_____

3. _____

_____

4. _____

_____

5. _____

_____

6. _____

_____

Practice 3. Read the following introductory paragraphs and, in the spaces provided after each, write in which of the six methods for writing opening paragraphs is used; what the topic of the essay is; and, if possible, what the thesis of the essay probably will be. You may not be able to tell the exact topic or thesis in all cases, but guess when you are in doubt.

A. People have used marijuana both socially and medicinally for several thousands of years, and yet today there is little scientific knowledge of its dangers or merits. In spite of our lack of knowledge, an estimated twelve million Americans have used the drug in recent years. Now we are in a near crisis caused by ignorance and the blanket of misinformation that governmental agencies have used to cover their ineptitudes. It is very important for us all to be aware of the following facts.

Paragraph method used: _____

Topic of essay: _____

Probable thesis: _____

_____

B. From the day man first sipped the liquid collecting around honey or fruit left too long in a warm place, alcohol has played an important role in his life. Early in history, wine became—and still is—an integral part of religious ceremonies. The Bible acknowledged the "wine that maketh glad the heart of man" (Psalms 104:15), and Pasteur called it "the most healthful and hygienic of beverages." In the hectic modern world, hundreds of millions of people drink liquor, beer, or wine for enjoyment, solace, and tranquility. Yet today, as it has throughout history, alcohol is also troubling mankind. For in almost every society, there are those who cannot enjoy alcohol without becoming its slave. ("Alcoholism: New Victims, New Treatment," *Time,* April 22, 1974)

Paragraph method used: _____

Topic of essay: _____

Probable thesis: _____

_____

C. The Battle of the Sexes throughout America has suddenly raged to crisis point. No, we're not talking about women's liberation again. We're talking about battles, real bloody battles—the kind where husband and wife beat, batter, bruise, and, worse, kill each other. Suddenly sociologists, psychiatrists, and law-enforcement officials are becoming aware of the fact that the country is in the midst of the worst family crime-wave in history—we call it the "battered spouse syndrome."

Paragraph method used: _____

Topic of essay: _____

Probable thesis: _____

D. Where is the women's equal rights movement? Do women, who represent over 50 percent of our population, have any more liberty or equality with men than they had before the women's lib movement? Has anything been really gained by the push for equal rights for women?

Paragraph method used: _____

Topic of essay: _____

Probable thesis: _____

E. There are at least six different methods a writer can use to develop an introductory paragraph for an essay: one, ask a question; two, use an anecdote or story; three, use a quotation; four, give a brief overview of your subject; five, stress the importance of the topic; or six, use a combination of these methods. Let's examine each method more closely.

Paragraph method used: _____

Topic of essay: _____

Probable thesis: _____

F. Suppose there were no critics to tell us how to react to a picture, a play, or a new composition of music. Suppose we wandered innocent . . . into an art exhibition of unsigned paintings. By what standards, by what values would we decide whether they were good or bad, talented or untalented, successes or failures? How can we ever know that what we think is right? (Marya Mannes, "How Do You Know It's Good?" from *But Will It Sell?*, 1964)

Paragraph method used: _____

Topic of essay: _____

Probable thesis: _____

G. One day a student, Marylou Simmons, dropped by my office. She had not completed a single assignment and had missed perhaps 50 percent of her classes. Her writing, what little I saw of it, was illogical, grammatically incorrect and sloppy. "Can I help you, Marylou?" I said cheerily, ever the understanding and forgiving teacher. Her lip began to tremble; her eyes grew teary. It seemed she had been having trouble with her boyfriend. "I'm sorry, but what can I do?" I asked. Suddenly all business, Marylou said, "Since I've been so unhappy, I thought you might want to just give me a D or an Incomplete on the course." She smiled encouragingly, even confidently. That's when the weariness set in, the moment at which I turned into a flaming conservative in matters educational. Whatever Marylou's troubles, I suddenly saw that I was not the cause, nor was I about to be the solution. (Suzanne Britt Jordan, "I Wants to Go to the Prose," *Newsweek,* November 14, 1977.)

Paragraph method used: _____

Topic of essay: _____

Probable thesis: _____

_____

Practice 4. Following is a list of *common mistakes* students make when writing opening paragraphs. Read them carefully.

1. Does not get to the point quickly enough. Usually, this happens because the writer doesn't really know what his or her own point or thesis is.
2. Uses quotations that have been used so often they are stale or clichés that lack any real punch.
3. Uses unoriginal and tiresome phrases such as "In my essay I would like to tell you about . . ." or "This paper will attempt to discuss. . . ."
4. Apologizes for writing about the subject by stating that "I really don't know a lot about . . . but I think that. . . ."
5. Relies on the title of the essay to say what should be said in the opening. For instance, some students in writing about a movie will use the movie title as the title of their essay and then begin by saying, "This movie is one everybody needs to see."

Using the numbers from the preceding list of common mistakes, place the appropriate number in the blank space for each of the following paragraphs or partial paragraphs.

_____ A. Anyone who bases his daily actions on the position and movement of the stars must not be very bright. I'm no expert on the subject, but I read a book on astrology, and I think it's a fraud.

_____ B. In my essay, I would like to tell you about my nutrition class. It is a very interesting class . . .

_____ D. Jerry is a good friend. He is charming, intelligent, and nice-looking and never seems to get angry. His favorite food is cheese. Tall girls always seem to be attracted to him even though he's short. I met him when we were in the army.

_____ E. There's an old saying, "Where there's smoke, there's fire." This certainly proved true the other night when I saw smoke coming out from under the door of the apartment next to mine . . .

_____ F. The point of my essay will be to discuss the following points in more detail . . .

Practice 5.   On a separate sheet of paper write what could be an opening paragraph for an essay on *one* of the following topics, and use the method indicated with the topic.

1. Topic: your favorite food
   Method: ask a question
2. Topic: men with long hair
   Method: use an anecdote or brief story
3. Topic: your favorite music
   Method: use a quotation
4. Topic: your pet peeves
   Method: state the supporting detail
5. Topic: a law that should be changed
   Method: stress importance of the topic
6. Topic: your favorite person
   Method: combination of two or more methods

Practice 6.   Refer back to your list of supporting details for an essay on page 45. Use it to write an introductory paragraph for an essay on the topic you selected. *You do not need to write the whole essay,* only the opening paragraph. When you have finished writing it, do the following:

1. Check it for any of the common errors mentioned in Practice 4.
2. Identify which method of six mentioned in this Unit you used.
3. State what audience or type of person your essay would appeal to.
4. Turn it in to your instructor.

Write...

(c) an essay based on your outline.

When your instructor returns the opening paragraph you wrote, use it and your outline to write an essay. When finished, go to the next section, REWRITE.

Rewrite...

your first draft.

If you've been following the steps in the WRITE section, you now have an essay written. But it's not finished. The next step—rewrite—is the hardest part for many writers because it often means just that—rewriting. Sometimes only sentences need to be rewritten for clarity's sake. Sometimes whole paragraphs need to be rewritten. Other times new paragraphs need to be added and others completely taken out of the essay. Basically, you are ready to rewrite when you have developed all the ideas your outline contains. Once you have a first draft of an essay that develops your thesis, you are ready to refine your essay, making certain your reader can clearly follow what you've said. Sometimes a good revision is the difference between a *D* and a *B* grade, or a *C* and an *A*.

As stated earlier in this unit, the introductory paragraph of an essay is extremely important in gaining the reader's attention. Sometimes the introductory paragraph may actually be the last one you write because once you've completed your first draft, you may need to go back and change it to fit the main points your essay finally develops. Note the difference below between a student's first draft and revised introductory paragraph.

Student's First Draft	Instructor's Comments
There are many reasons why students drop out of school. Sometimes good job offers come up. Sometimes people get sick and fall too far behind. Others get bored and find school isn't relevant. I'm sure there are many others.	*You have a thesis but it's not very well stated. You say "many reasons" but only give three. Either use only those three or think of more reasons. Also, what students? High school? college? adult ed? Be more specific. And last, your paragraph is flat and needs to draw more interest.*

Below is the student's revised paragraph.

Student's Revised Draft

When a student drops out of college, many instructor's feel that the student is not really interested in the subject or in developing his or her academic potential. However, lack of interest, while one reason for dropping out, is not the only reason. Some students find it financially necessary to leave school and go to work. Others miss too much school because of illness and feel it would be too difficult to catch up on all the work. But many students leave because they find college disappointing.

Instructor's Comments

A much stronger introduction. You give some obvious reasons for college student dropouts—less vague now—and your thesis is narrowed down to discussing reasons some students find college disappointing. Your thesis is now your last sentence.

Realize that rewriting is a must. It is very seldom a writer can say in the first draft everything necessary or say things as well as they might be said.

Now here are some reminders of things you've been told to keep in mind when you write an essay. Check your essay for each one and rewrite whatever is needed.

_____ 1. Have you revised your opening paragraph based on any comments your instructor may have given you?

_____ 2. Does your opening paragraph give a statement about the subject or topic of your essay?

_____ 3. Does your opening paragraph contain a thesis or a hint of a viewpoint toward your topic?

_____ 4. Does your opening paragraph use a method that draws your reader's interest in reading your essay?

_____ 5. Did you write about something you know and feel?

_____ 6. Did you avoid the obvious and take a fresh approach to your topic?

_____ 7. Did you get rid of obvious padding?

_____ 8. Did you check your essay for "pat expressions" and clichés?

_____ 9. Do you use concrete points and avoid generalities and abstractions?

_____ 10. Do you use colorful words and avoid colorless and colored words?

Once you've revised your essay to the best of your ability, give it to a classmate to read. Listen to any comments or suggestions your classmate may have for rewriting your essay. Consider them before you turn in your paper. Revising a paper is often the most difficult part of writing. You must be willing to change the order of ideas, to rewrite entire paragraphs if need be, to eliminate parts, and to get the advice of readers who will tell you what they like and dislike. That's what rewriting is all about.

UNIT 3

Think...
about marriage and the family

Read...
about marriage and the family
"One Mother's Blast at Motherhood" by Shirley L. Radl

React...
to the essay

Plan...
an essay
Topics for an essay on marriage

Write...
(A) an outline for an essay
(B) topic sentences
Control of topic sentences
Practices in writing topic sentences
(C) paragraphs
Paragraphs that illustrate or use examples
Paragraphs that use specific details or facts
Paragraphs that define
Practices in writing paragraphs
(D) an essay

Rewrite...
your first draft

Think...

about marriage and the family by answering the following questions.

1. Do you think marriage is necessary in our society? _____

   Why? _____

   _____

   _____

   _____

2. Why do you think most people get married? _____

   _____

   _____

3. Do you believe people should live together before they get married?

   _____ Why? _____

   _____

4. Do you think that a married couple should stay married for the sake of their

   growing children even when they no longer wish to remain married? _____

   Why? _____

   _____

5. When do you think young people should stop living with their parents?

   _____

   _____

6. Do you think marriage is "old-fashioned" and will eventually become out-

moded? _____

Why? _____

_____

_____

7. What do you think families will be like in the future? _____

_____

_____

8. Is it selfish or socially wrong for married couples not to want children? _____

Why? _____

_____

_____

9. What qualities make good parents? _____

_____

_____

_____

an essay about marriage and the family.

Shirley L. Radl has been active in groups working to curb the population explosion. She was Executive Director of Zero Population Growth and of the National Organization for Non-Parents. She is the author of *Mother's Day Is Over*.

One Mother's Blast at Motherhood
Shirley L. Radl

1. The eight years before we had children were glorious. I had an enjoyable career, an idyllic home life. But friends pitied us, undoubtedly worried we would continue living hedonistic, meaningless but terribly comfortable lives unless we became parents.

2. When I was pregnant the first time, we celebrated our eighth wedding anniversary. My husband gave me an exquisite pearl bracelet. Six years later I was picking up the pearls in my vacuum cleaner. My son had destroyed it. It is a sad symbol of how two children affected a once-beautiful relationship.

3. It's hard to admit that my beautiful, wanted and planned children could arouse rage in me and could disturb my once-ideal marriage. I'd fallen for the Big Lie, that fulfillment automatically comes with motherhood. But now I'm confident there's enough love in our family to withstand a certain amount of truth.

4. A mother, according to TV and most women's magazines, is a happy person suited, without training, to one of the most formidable jobs in the world. But a mother is also *me,* and I'm a failure as one. I'm not cut out to be a service machine, laundress, PTA member, nurse. My kids deserve better than they got.

5. It's not enough for every child to be wanted as Planned Parenthood says. He must be wanted, not only at the start, but forever. Bearing children is a gamble with lives of innocents. The greatest failure is to have children and learn too late you're not equipped for that career. We who learned the truth must level with an unsuspecting generation of potential mothers. They must look beyond the myths, seek the truth, judge their capacities accordingly. Plan carefully: the life you save may be your own.

6. You don't have to justify deciding to be childless. It's no one's business if your ovaries don't work, or if they do. If you are pressured to "prove yourself," take it from one who has been there.

7. We don't tell others what jobs to take, whom they should marry, where to

From *Mother's Day Is Over*, Warner Books, 1974. Reprinted by permission of the author.

vacation. It's bad manners to ask how much money they make. Yet others' breeding habits, *if* they are childless, are considered fair game. The couples with children, who are miserable, don't hesitate to urge others to follow their examples.

8. When we started our family, it didn't occur to us we were succumbing to social pressure and the media. Now we see that all this couldn't fail to have conditioned us. We never discussed the matter thoroughly, and it never occurred to us we might not be cut out for parenthood. Why, we put more thought into buying a car than bringing two children into the world.

React...

to the following questions about the essay.

1. What is the author's *thesis* or main idea about motherhood?

_____

_____

_____

2. In what paragraph is the thesis best stated? _____
   Why is that good or bad in the case of this essay?

_____

_____

3. What reasons does the author give for wishing she had no children?

_____

_____

_____

4. Why does Radl feel that she's a failure as a parent?

_____

_____

_____

5. Are her reasons good ones? _____ Why?

_____

_____

_____

6. Would you want to be one of the author's children? _____

   Why? _____

   _____

   _____

7. Do you think most people "put more thought into buying a car than bringing

   two children into the world"? _____ Explain.

   _____

   _____

   _____

8. Describe your immediate reaction to Radl's essay.

   _____

   _____

   _____

9. Place a check in front of the following words you don't know or could not use
   correctly. The number following the word refers to the paragraph in the essay
   where the word is used.

   _____ a. idyllic (1)

   _____ b. hedonistic (1)

   _____ c. exquisite (2)

   _____ d. suited (4)

   _____ e. formidable (4)

   _____ f. level (5)

   _____ g. potential (5)

   _____ h. justify (6)

   _____ i. fair game (7)

   _____ j. succumbing (8)

   Reread the words in the paragraphs indicated. Then go to the Vocabulary
Section on page 315 in the Appendix for more information and practice using
these words.

Plan....

an essay on some aspect of marriage.

Getting an essay started, even in the planning stage, is not always easy. It takes time to think of an idea, to brainstorm for possible supporting points. In Unit 2, the idea of keeping a journal or a notebook to write down some of your feelings and thoughts was presented. It's a chance to put ideas that pop into your head on paper so you can see what they look and "sound" like. Daily journal writing forces you to put thoughts into words without worrying about any problems you may have with writing skills.

In a book called *Writing Without Teachers,* Peter Elbow states that the most effective way he knows for people to improve their writing is to do freewriting exercises at least three times a week. His idea is to just sit down and begin writing for ten to twenty minutes without stopping. You write quickly, not worrying about what you are saying or how well it is written. You don't stop to think; you merely capture your thoughts on paper. In effect, you write as though you were taping your brain as it thinks. If you are stuck for something to say, you just write, "I can't think what to say, I can't think what to say" as many times as necessary until you do think of something (and you will!). His only requirement in this freewriting process is to never stop putting words on paper the entire time you do the exercise.

Here is an example of freewriting:

> Freewriting—what is freewriting anyway? How can it help me? Why am I doing this? I really don't know what to say, say, say, say! Boring! I have to write an essay on marriage, and I'm not even married so what do I know about it. Maybe I could write about my parents' marriage. Why did they *really* break up? I don't know. It was sad, tragic, hurtful, but I'm over it now. I think mom is but I'm not sure about dad. Do I want to get married? Not today anyway. I could write about marriage ceremonies. They're changing or maybe about contract marriages. Did Radl mean what she said in her essay or was she putting us on? . . .

Notice that there is no order in this example, and sometimes no punctuation. But mistakes don't count in freewriting, which is called just that because it frees your mind. It allows you to think openly and honestly without having to fear grammar and spelling mistakes, awkward phrases, or style. It frees you to think. It forces you to produce words on paper and helps to unblock you from any fears or doubts you have about your writing.

When you look over what you've written, there is usually an idea or two for you to use as an essay. Notice in the example that though the writer isn't married, it doesn't mean that person could not write about the subject. The author could write about his parents' marriage up to the divorce, what's been learned from the parents about marriage, changing marriage ceremonies, contract marriages, or even a reaction to the Radl essay. Freewriting has produced ideas from which an essay can be planned. Try it.

Practice 1. In your journal notebook, if you have one, or on another sheet of paper, try freewriting for ten minutes. Remember, don't stop writing even if you have nothing to say. Write exactly what comes to your mind. Try *not* to think about the topic of marriage as you write.

Practice 2. In the space below, write down a topic for an essay on marriage. Chances are that even though you were told in the first practice *not* to think about marriage, some ideas crept in anyway. We hope so; that was the plan. Here are some topics you might use in case your freewriting or the Shirley Radl essay did not give you some of your own.

1. Why the bride is traditionally "given away."
2. Are marriage customs necessary?
3. Why I don't believe in marriage.
4. The advantages of polygamy (marriage to more than one person at a time).
5. Living together before marriage.
6. Civil marriage ceremonies versus church ceremonies.
7. Are honeymoons wise?
8. What I expect in a spouse.
9. Are marriages really "contracts" between two people?
10. Describe a wedding you attended.
11. Explain what it takes for a good marriage.
12. Should schools teach classes on marriage?
13. Write a rebuttal to Radl's essay.
14. The Family Unit in the year 2051.
15. What I expect from marriage.
16. Compare and contrast who in your family brings you the greatest joy and the greatest sadness.
17. Discuss any rituals your family shares.
18. Write an essay in reaction to the following passage from Allan Watts' *The Book: On the Taboo Against Knowing Who You Are:*

> Furthermore, the younger members of our society have for some time been in growing rebellion against paternal authority and the paternal state. For one reason, the home in an industrial society is chiefly a dormitory, and the father does not work there, with the result that wife and children have no part in his vocation. He is just a character who brings in the money, and after working hours he is supposed to forget about his job and have fun. Novels, magazines, television, and popular cartoons therefore portray "Dad" as an incompetent clown. And the image has some truth in it because Dad has fallen for the hoax that work is simply something you do to make money, and with money you can get anything you want.
>
> It is no wonder that an increasing proportion of college students want no part in Dad's world, and will do anything to avoid the rat-race of the salesman, commuter, clerk, and corporate executive. . . .

If none of these topics interest you, here are two dilemmas or problems that have no specific answers, but they might provide some essay ideas as you think about the dilemmas.

Dilemma A

You have a fifteen-year-old sister. One day you catch her alone, crying. Concerned, you ask her what is wrong, and she cries all the more. After much prompting, she says she'll tell you if you promise not to tell your parents. You give your word. She then tells you she is pregnant and asks you for help. She reminds you that you promised not to tell your mother or father. What should you do? Why?

Dilemma B

Peggy was sixteen and pregnant when she dropped from high school and married. She is now eighteen and has two children. Her husband left her and sends no money for support. She works at a McDonald's at night while her mother watches the children. Most of Peggy's friends are unmarried, working at better jobs or going to city college. She wants to quit her job and go to city college to get her high school diploma and perhaps become a computer technician, but her mother says she will not support Peggy or her children if she quits her job. What are Peggy's options? How could she go to school and still have money to live on? What should Peggy do?

Share these dilemmas with one or two other people. As you think about and discuss these problems, think of possible topics that you feel you might use in an essay. If none of this helps, then skim through the newspaper for possible ideas.

Now, in the space below, write in the topic you have decided to use for an essay.

Topic:

_____

_____

_____

_____

Practice 3. Now write a possible thesis statement that expresses what you want to say about your topic. You may need to alter or change your thesis after you think through your topic. This will become your working thesis.

Tentative Thesis Statement:

_____

_____

_____

_____

Below, list all the ideas you can think of to support your thesis. If you don't have at least six points, try another thesis or topic.

_____

_____

_____

_____

_____

_____

_____

_____

_____

Write...

(A) an outline for an essay.

Now rearrange your list of ideas into an outline or some order you can follow. Use the outlining procedures described in Unit 1. Do this on a separate sheet of paper. Turn it in for your instructor to check.

(B) topic sentences.

Every essay consists of units of thought called paragraphs. Each paragraph contains a *topic sentence*. The topic sentence is the sentence in the paragraph that states what the paragraph is about. Just as every essay has a thesis, so every paragraph should have a topic sentence. Usually, though not always, the topic sentence is the first one in the paragraph. Notice the following example.

> (1) Actually, you begin to prepare for marriage *before* you are born. (2) Your parents did more than conceive you genetically, the controlling factor in such physical things as your stature and the color of your eyes. (3) They also are part of your inherited moods and manners, the emotional, psychological and spiritual makeup that molded your personality into what it is.

Notice that sentence 1, the topic sentence, is more general and states what the paragraph is about: preparing for marriage before birth. Sentence 2 discusses conception and specifics you inherited in preparation. Sentence 3 discusses moods and manners inherited. Thus, you have:

Paragraph's Point: Preparations for marriage before birth
Supporting Details: 1. genetically
                  a. eye color
                  b. stature
            2. moods and manners
                  a. emotionally
                  b. psychologically
                  c. spiritually

Notice the resemblance of the paragraph outline above to the outline for an essay. In effect, a paragraph is a mini-essay with the topic sentence serving as a thesis statement.

Here is another sample paragraph:

(1) One of the ways you emancipate yourself from your parents is through close identification with other persons outside your family. (2) This process has been going on for years, in the series of friendships, crushes, and infatuations that all boys and girls have with persons of both sexes of their own age and older. These close emotional ties are a mixed blessing to most teenagers, partly because they come with such intensity, and also because they shift so suddenly and unpredictably. (4) Over the years, you learn to sort out your feelings for others as you develop your own emotional repertoire. (From "How Long Is Long Enough?" by Evelyn Mills Duvall, *Face to Face* (May 1972), Vol. 4, No. 9.)

If you pay close attention to how this paragraph is put together, you can see that the first sentence controls the main idea of the paragraph: freeing yourself from your parents by close relationships with others outside your family. The other sentences give examples of these relationships. Thus, in outline form, the paragraph looks like this:

Paragraph's Point: Freeing yourself from parents through outside family relationships

Supporting Details: 1. Types of relationships
      a. friendships
      b. crushes
      c. infatuations
   2. Close emotional ties
      a. mixed blessing
      b. unpredictable
   3. Learn to sort out feelings for others

The topic sentence, then, both controls and restricts what you can say in a paragraph.

As with a thesis statement, a topic sentence should be neither too broad nor too narrow. It should contain not only the main idea of the paragraph, but also key words or phrases that control what can and can't be said in the paragraph. Here are some examples of good and poor topic sentences with remarks about them:

TS	Remarks
1. Mr. and Mrs. Garcia have been married for twenty-five years.	That's nice, but it's too limiting a statement. There are no points to develop. A poor topic sentence.
2. During their twenty-five years of troubled marriage, the Garcias learned to tolerate each other's irritating habits.	Better. Key words to develop: *troubled, tolerate, irritating habits.* The rest of the paragraph should unite around those points.
3. Susan has a good husband.	Too general. What does "good" really mean? Needs better key words to develop.

4. Susan's husband is thoughtful, loving, and intelligent.	Better; more specific. The paragraph should show with examples how Susan's husband is *thoughtful, loving,* and *intelligent.* Much better than "good husband."
5. With the population explosion, the pressure on women to marry is going to be reduced.	Good. Not too broad or too narrow; key words *pressure . . . to marry . . . reduced.* This requires that the other sentences in the paragraph show how or why.

You are probably beginning to see that good writing requires thinking before all else. That's really all writing is—exposing the way you think so others can understand you. In the case of topic sentences, you must think beforehand what it is you want to discuss in each paragraph. If you have a good outline, you already have your essay organized into paragraphs. Simply take each one of your major headings, and turn it into a topic sentence, using key words that use the information listed under your headings. For instance, remember the exercise you did in Unit 1 where you classified sports into water sports and winter sports? Here's how part of your outline looked:

> II. Water Sports
>   A. Skin diving
>   B. Swimming
>   C. Waterskiing
>   D. Sailing

Here's a possible topic sentence for a paragraph:

Of all the water sports, there are four that give me the most pleasure: skin diving, swimming, waterskiing and sailing.

The rest of the paragraph would discuss the pleasure of each water sport mentioned.

From now on when you write, check each of your paragraphs for topic sentences that are neither too broad nor too narrow and that have key words or phrases you develop within the paragraph.

Practices in Writing Topic Sentences

Practice 1. Read the following paragraph. Then, using the space provided below, make an outline of the paragraph as the preceding examples show.

(1) All the greatest love stories in every language and in every country are lessons to the effect that . . . total passionate love and marriage do not go together. (2) Were Tristan and Isolde married? (3) Were Antony and Cleopatra, Heloise and Abelard, Dante and Beatrice, Lancelot and Guinevere, Cyrano and Roxanne, Thais and Athael? (4) In fact, there's even a story about

what happened to Sleeping Beauty after she married the Prince. (5) He fell asleep. (From "The Case Against Marriage" by Phyllis Starr Wilson, *Glamour Magazine*, November 1965.)

1. Which sentence is the topic sentence?

_____

2. In the space below, make an outline of the paragraph as was done on the previous sample paragraphs.

Paragraph's Point: _____

_____

Supporting Details: _____

_____

_____

_____

_____

_____

_____

Practice 2. Read the following paragraph, and then answer the questions that follow.

(1) In recent years, many people have taken to writing their own marriage ceremonies in a desperate attempt to make the institution more relevant to their own lives. (2) But ceremonies, they are finding, do not reach the heart of the matter. (3) So some couples are now taking the logical next step of drawing up their own contracts. (4) These agreements may delineate any of the financial or personal aspects of the marriage relationship—from who pays the bills to who uses what birth control. . . . (From Susan Edmiston, "How to Write Your Own Marriage Contract," *The First Ms. Reader*, Warner Books, Inc., 1973.)

1. Which sentence is the topic sentence?

_____

2. Make an outline of the paragraph in the space below.

Paragraph's Point: _____

Supporting Details: _____

_____

_____

_____

_____

_____

_____

Practice 3. Write a topic sentence that could be used for a well-developed paragraph for each of the following subjects.

1. *love:* _____

_____

2. *weddings:* _____

_____

3. *companionship:* _____

_____

4. *marriage:* _____

_____

Practice 4. Check each of your topic sentences in the previous practice, and rewrite any that are too general or too limiting. For instance, the following topic sentence is too general:

> *I love Alice.*

A *better* topic sentence would be:

> One of the reasons I love my dog, Alice, is her attitude toward me.

An example of a topic sentence that is *too limiting* is:

> I love my dog's brown hair.

A *better* topic sentence would be:

> I love my dog because of her appearance, her attitude toward me, and her playful spirit.

Check your topic sentences for their control of the topic.

Practice 5. Rewrite any of the following topic sentences so that the main idea and control are obvious. Some may not need revising.

1. Weddings are an important tradition in our society.

_____

_____

2. I love my wife.

_____

_____

3. My parents are the greatest people I know.

_____

_____

4. Love is a many-splintered thing.

_____

_____

5. Some people marry for companionship.

_____

_____

6. Marriage is more than enjoying being close to each other.

_____

_____

7. *When You Marry* is a good book.

_____

Practice 6. Read the following topic sentences, and circle the key words that control what the rest of the paragraph will develop.

1. There were at least four major reasons for the Civil War.
2. The counselor gave them many examples of broken homes.
3. Our wedding was different from most.
4. There were many types of wedding gowns from which to choose.
5. The couple had several problems to work out between them.
6. Her idea of marriage and his were quite different.

7. The food at the wedding reception was unusual and delicious.
8. The couple had to decide which of these three places to go on their honeymoon.
9. Honeymoons are not a good idea despite the tradition behind them.
10. Some people marry for all the wrong reasons.

Practice 7. On a separate sheet, pick *one* of the topic sentences from Practice 6, and write a paragraph that develops the key words in that sentence. Turn it in to your instructor when finished.

(C) paragraphs.

Summary of Introductory Paragraph Methods from Unit 2
Method 1: Ask a question.
Method 2: Use an anecdote.
Method 3: Use a quotation.
Method 4: Give a brief overview of subject.
Method 5: Stress importance of topic.
Method 6: Use a combination of methods.

Unit 2 discusses how to write an introductory paragraph for an essay. The following information discusses some of the methods useful in developing your supporting detail paragraphs. Here are at least three methods you need to learn to use. More will be discussed in Unit 4.

1. Paragraphs that illustrate or use examples to support the point.
2. Paragraphs that use specific details such as facts, figures, dates, statistics, and such.
3. Paragraphs that define the point or give a thorough definition or meaning to what is being said.

These methods, as well as those to be mentioned in Unit 4, are all useful in helping you write better paragraphs.

1. Paragraphs that illustrate or use examples to support the point

Here is an example of a paragraph that uses *illustration* or *examples* to support the topic sentence.

Topic sentence   Individual reading and discussion of standard texts in marriage and the family may be helpful to those young people for whom formal courses are not available. Such Duvall books as *Before You Marry—101 Questions to Ask Yourself, Being Married, Faith In Families, Family Development, Love and the Facts of Life*, or *When You Marry* should be available in your library or through your church office. Your denominational headquarters has pamphlets, films, filmstrips, and other preparation for marriage study guides.

Examples of readings and discussion materials

Here is another example of a paragraph that uses *illustration* or *examples* to support the topic sentence.

Topic sentence   So what are you going to use for a sweetener if you never allow sugar to cross your lips? Half the amount of honey should be

Examples of
sugar substitutes
that answer topic
sentence
{ used in substituting for sugar in recipes. Beyond that, it's all experimental. Try carob molasses, carob syrup, unrefined sugar cane syrup, date sugar. The best experiment of all is to follow the advice of J. I. Rodale: "We receive many letters from readers asking what kind of sugar to use. So far as we are concerned, the answer is none . . . if you would be healthy, omit all sugar and just get accustomed to doing without it."

Check one of the following topic sentences that would best fit the paragraph development method of using illustration and example.

_____ a. Her wedding gown was very traditional.

_____ b. There were many types of wedding gowns from which to choose.

_____ c. The minister used the New Testament during the wedding ceremony.

2. Paragraphs that use specific details

Here are two examples of paragraphs that use *specific details* or facts to support the topic sentence.

Topic sentence

Specific details
{ Her wedding gown was very traditional. It was white velvet with a lace bodice and lace train. Floor length, the dress was form fitting except for two small pleats in the front. It had a high collar and long sleeves made of velvet and lace facing.

Topic sentence

Factual details
used to support
the idea that the
wedding was
expensive
{ The wedding was very expensive. The flowers for the church and the wedding group cost $78.00. The rental on the social hall for the reception was $150. The fee charged by the caterers ran well over $350. Then there was an additional charge for the bar that was set up in another room. That bill, including the wages of the bartender, was nearly $260. These figures, of course, do not even include the cost of the bride's gown, the rental of the tuxedoes, or the minister's fees.

Check one of the following topic sentences that would best fit the paragraph development method of using *specific details.*

_____ a. The counselor gave them many examples of broken homes.

_____ b. The book on marriage contains specific points for learning to cope with your marriage partner.

_____ c. Some people prefer big weddings.

3. Paragraphs that define or give definitions

Here are two examples of paragraphs that use *definition* to support the topic sentence.

Topic sentence
{ The most fundamental kind of love, which underlies all types of love, is *brotherly* love. By this I mean the sense of responsibil-

Definition
> ity, care, respect, knowledge of any other human being, the wish to further his life. This is the kind of love the Bible speaks of when it says: love thy neighbor as thyself. Brotherly love is love for all human beings; it is characterized by its very lack of exclusiveness. . . . (From Eric Fromm, *The Art of Loving,* Harper & Row, 1956.)

Topic sentence
> A type of maturity is needed before a person enters marriage. This type of maturity, however, is not necessarily a fixed state,

An attempt to define maturity by breaking it into parts
> but an ongoing process that may last throughout the person's life. The question of maturity contains a number of subparts: physical maturity (able to reproduce), moral maturity (a code of life that gives guidance and direction to one's life), emotional maturity (the ability to control one's emotions), social maturity (the ability to play a part within the society), and vocational maturity (the ability to support one's family). Without these elements of maturity, it is doubtful that a solid marriage can be built, although there are always exceptions.

Check one of the following topic sentences that would best fit the paragraph development method of using *definition.*

_____ a. Sometimes a marriage counselor can be of help to couples having problems.

_____ b. It takes time to learn to love.

_____ c. Love is not easy to define.

Unit 4 will discuss other methods for developing paragraphs, but for now concentrate on the three methods just described.

Practices in Writing Paragraphs

Practice 1. Circle the key word or words in the topic sentences that follow. Then fill in the blanks, using the topic sentence as your guide. Don't be afraid to use exaggerations or humor. There are no "right" answers.

A. Using *examples:*

Our wedding was different from most. For instance, _____

_____

Also, we _____

_____

Unlike most weddings, then, _____

_____

B. Using *specific details:*

Their marriage has lasted for several reasons. For one, they always _____

_____

For another, they _____

_____

In addition, they never _____

_____

C. Using *definition:*

The term *marriage counselor* means different things to different people.

To others, it means _____

_____

To others, it means _____

_____

Basically, marriage counselors _____

_____

Practice 2. On a separate sheet of paper, write a paragraph for each of the following topic sentences, using the paragraph development method mentioned.

A. There are several preparations necessary before getting married. (specific details)
B. The ideal honeymoon is one that requires little travel and little effort. (definition)
C. The last wedding I attended can be described as traditional. (illustration/examples)

Practice 3. Using your rearranged list of support for the topic you selected on page 66, write an introductory paragraph and the second paragraph to an essay. Then do the following:

1. Check for a clear thesis in your introductory paragraph.
2. Identify the method of paragraph development you used in your introductory paragraph.

3. Check for a clear-cut topic sentence in your supporting paragraph.
4. Identify the method of paragraph development used in your supporting paragraph.
5. Turn in your paragraphs to your instructor.

#

(D) an essay.

When your instructor returns your paragraphs, make any changes necessary, and then write the rest of the essay developing your thesis fully.

When finished, you should have an essay of about five paragraphs or so giving your essay this form:

Introductory paragraph
—contains thesis
Second paragraph
—contains a main idea or point developed to support your thesis
Third paragraph
—contains a second idea or point developed to support your thesis
Fourth paragraph
—contains a third idea or point developed to support your thesis
Concluding paragraph
—contains a conclusion to or a summary of your essay.

You may have more than three supporting paragraphs, but if you have too many or even fewer than three, chances are your topic is too broad or too narrow for a 500-word essay.

When finished, go to the next section: REWRITE.

Rewrite...

your first draft.

Now comes the difficult part—finding a happy medium between disliking what you wrote and falling in love with what you wrote so that you don't want to change anything.

Notice below a student's first draft of a supporting paragraph from an essay with the thesis that honeymoons are not a tradition worth keeping and the instructor's comments.

Student's First Draft	Instructor's Comments
One of the reasons I think honeymoons are not a good idea is that they are expensive. A honeymoon wastes money that newlyweds could use.	*You have a topic sentence that supports your thesis against honeymoons, but it is not developed. Your point here is the honeymoon expense. How about some examples as a method to support your topic sentence? Do you need to use "I"?*

Here is the student's revision with instructor comments.

Student's Revised Draft	Instructor's Comments
One argument against honeymoons is the expense involved. A couple can spend hundreds to thousands of dollars on a week or two at some exotic place, only to come home with no money to set up housekeeping. It would be better for the couple to use that money to spend on their living quarters, to save for a down payment on a house, to prepare for having a child, or even for a vacation in the future. But to spend all that money to travel somewhere when all a newlywed couple wants to do is "make eyes" at each other is a definite waste.	*A much better topic sentence. There was no need for the use of "I think . . ." in your first draft. You give some examples of how honeymoon expenses can otherwise be used. However, your last sentence is too broad a generalization since not all honeymooners merely want to "make eyes." You may want to revise your last sentence.*

It is probable that another rewrite could make this improved paragraph even better. However, some students get impatient with rewriting and often don't go that one step more that would make for a much better essay.

Here are some reminders to follow as you rewrite your essay. Use them as a checklist for revision.

_____ 1. Have you revised your opening paragraph based on any comments your instructor or others may have given you?

_____ 2. Does your opening paragraph contain a good thesis?

_____ 3. Does your opening paragraph use a method that draws your reader's interest?

_____ 4. Did you write about something you know and feel?

_____ 5. Does each paragraph contain a topic sentence that expresses the main point of the paragraph?

_____ 6. Does each sentence in each paragraph stick to the idea expressed by the topic sentence?

_____ 7. Does each paragraph have a method for development, such as use of examples, compare/contrast, use of details, and so forth?

_____ 8. Did you follow the advice Paul Roberts gives in his essay "How to Say Nothing in Five Hundred Words"? (It would be a good idea to review the subheadings in that essay in Unit 1.)

Once you've revised your essay to the best of your ability, give it to a classmate to read. Listen to any comments or suggestions offered to you. Consider them before you turn in your essay to the instructor.

UNIT

Think...
about the illegal drug problem

Read...
an argument for legalizing drugs
"Drugs: Case for Legalizing Marijuana" by Gore Vidal

React...
to the essay

Plan...
an essay
Topics for an essay on drugs

Write...
(A) an outline for an essay
(B) supporting paragraphs
Paragraphs that compare and/or contrast
Paragraphs that analyze
Paragraphs that use a story or anecdote
Paragraphs that use combinations of methods
Practices in paragraph writing
(C) an essay

Rewrite...
your first draft

# Think...

about the illegal drug problem.

1. Check any of the drugs listed below that you feel should be legalized and explain why.

_____ a. marijuana because _____

_____

_____ b. cocaine because _____

_____

_____ c. heroin because _____

_____

_____ d. alcohol because _____

_____

_____ e. "speed" (in any form) because _____

_____

_____ f. opium because _____

_____

_____ g. LSD because _____

_____

_____ h. None should be legalized because _____

_____

2. Alcoholism is said to be the worst drug problem in the United States and perhaps in the world. Why do you suppose the sale of alcohol is legal, but

marijuana is not? _____

_____

_____

3. How would you define a drug addict?

_____

_____

_____

4. Do you think the government has a right to control what drugs are legal

or not? _____

Why? _____

_____

5. We often read that drug use is growing. Why do you think there is such a
big drug problem?

_____

_____

6. Do you think that if most drugs were made legal there would be a rise in

drug use? _____

Why? _____

_____

7. Do you think drug-related crimes would be reduced if the government gave

drugs to registered drug addicts? _____

Why? _____

_____

_____

an argument for legalizing drugs.

The following essay was written by the novelist, playwright, and critic Gore Vidal. He has written several novels, among them *The City and the Pillar, Myra Breckenridge, Burr,* and *1876.* His essay is a rather sad and pessimistic argument for legalizing marijuana use as well as other drugs. Regardless of your own views, explore his arguments carefully.

Drugs: Case for Legalizing Marijuana
Gore Vidal

1. It is possible to stop most drug addiction in the United States within a very short time. Simply make all drugs available and sell them at cost. Label each drug with a precise description of what effect—good or bad—the drug will have on whoever takes it. This will require heroic honesty. Don't say that marijuana is addictive or dangerous when it is neither, as millions of people know—unlike "speed," which kills most unpleasantly, or heroin, which is addictive and difficult to kick.

2. For the record, I have tried—once—almost every drug and liked none, disproving the popular Fu Manchu theory that a single whiff of opium will enslave the mind. Nevertheless many drugs are bad for certain people to take and they should be told about them in a sensible way.

3. Along with exhortation and warning, it might be good for our citizens to recall (or learn for the first time) that the United States was the creation of men who believed that each man has the right to do what he wants with his own life as long as he does not interfere with his neighbor's pursuit of happiness (that his neighbor's idea of happiness is persecuting others does confuse matters a bit).

4. This is a startling notion to the current generations of Americans who reflect on our system of public education which has made the Bill of Rights, literally, unacceptable to a majority of high school graduates (see the annual Purdue[1] reports) who now form the silent majority—a phrase which that underestimated wit Richard Nixon took from Homer who used it to describe the dead.

[1]A Survey that showed the majority of high school graduates were opposed to the freedoms provided in the first ten amendment to the Constitution. They did not realize they were being asked about the Bill of Rights.

5. Now one can hear the warning rumble begin; if everyone is allowed to take drugs everyone will and the GNP[2] will decrease, the Commies will stop us from making everyone free, and we shall end up a race of zombies, passively murmuring "groovie" to one another. Alarming thought. Yet it seems most unlikely that any reasonably sane person will become a drug addict if he knows in advance what addiction is going to be like.

6. Is everyone reasonably sane? No. Some people will always become drug addicts just as some people will always become alcoholics, and it is just too bad. Every man, however, has the power (and should have the right) to kill himself if he chooses. But since most men don't, they won't be mainliners either. Nevertheless, forbidding people things they like or think they might enjoy only makes them want those things all the more. This psychological insight is, for some mysterious reason, perennially denied our governors.

7. It is a lucky thing for the American moralist that our country has always existed in a kind of time-vacuum: we have no public memory of anything that happened before last Tuesday. No one in Washington today recalls what happened during the years alcohol was forbidden to the people by a Congress that thought it had a divine mission to stamp out Demon Rum and so launched the greatest crime wave in our country's history, caused thousands of deaths from bad alcohol, and created a general (and persisting) contempt for the laws of the United States.

8. The same thing is happening today. But the government has learned nothing from past attempts at prohibition, not to mention repression.

9. Last year when the supply of Mexican marijuana was slightly curtailed by the Feds, the pushers got the kids hooked on heroin and deaths increased dramatically, particularly in New York. Whose fault? Evil men like the Mafiosi? Permissive Dr. Spock? Wild-eyed Dr. Leary? No.

10. The Government of the United States was responsible for those deaths. The bureaucratic machine has a vested interest in playing cops and robbers. Both the Bureau of Narcotics and the Mafia want strong laws against the sale and use of drugs because if drugs were sold at cost there would be no money in it for anyone.

11. If there was no money in it for the Mafia, there would be no friendly playground pushers, and addicts would not commit crimes to pay for the next fix. Finally, if there was no money in it, the Bureau of Narcotics would wither away, something they're not about to do without a struggle.

12. Will anything sensible be done? Of course not. The American people are as devoted to the idea of sin and its punishment as they are to making money— and fighting drugs is nearly as big a business as pushing them. Since the combination of sin and money is irresistible (particularly to the professional politician), the situation will only grow worse.

---

[2]Gross National Product, a measure of economic growth.

React...

to the essay by answering the following questions.

1. What is the *thesis* or main point of the essay?

_____

2. State in your own words the argument the author gives in paragraph 3.

_____

_____

3. Do you agree or disagree with the author's point in paragraph 3?

_____ Why? _____

_____

4. In paragraph 4, Vidal is being sarcastic and makes fun of the "silent majority." How does he do so?

_____

_____

_____

5. Do you agree or disagree with Vidal's argument in paragraph 6?

_____ Why? _____

_____

_____

6. In paragraphs 7–11, Vidal takes some strong swings at the government of the United States. With what points do you agree and disagree?

_____

_____

_____

_____

7. Do you agree with the author's conclusion in his last paragraph?

_____ Why? _____

_____

8. Check the following words you don't know or could not use correctly. The number following the word refers to the paragraph in the essay where the word is used.

_____ a. precise (1)

_____ b. exhortation (2)

_____ c. persecuting (3)

_____ d. literally (4)

_____ e. passively (5)

_____ f. mainliners (6)

_____ g. perennially (6)

_____ h. contempt (7)

_____ i. permissive (9)

_____ j. vested interest (10)

Turn to the Vocabulary Section in the Appendix for some practice with these words.

Name _____ **Section** _____ **Date** _____

Plan...

an essay.

It is to be hoped that the THINK questions, the Gore Vidal essay, and the REACT questions have given you some ideas for a possible essay on the topic of drugs. Keep those in mind. Meanwhile, here's a moral dilemma or problem that should further stimulate some ideas.

Miss Amory, thirty-five years old, had been teaching American history at the high school for twelve years. She was very well respected by students, parents, and faculty. Many of her former students who went on to college often returned to thank her for her part in their success in college. Many parents had recommended Miss Amory to other parents who wanted their children in a "good" class. Students loved her because she knew her subject well, disciplined the class through mutual respect, helped students who had trouble learning, and took a personal interest in students' problems, often acting as a counselor when they sought help. Last year she was awarded the honor of Teacher of the Year.

Last week it was discovered that Miss Amory frequently smoked marijuana and had been smoking it for several years. The Board of Education met and demanded her immediate resignation and suspended her from teaching.

What do you think?

1. Should Miss Amory resign or attempt to keep her job? Why?
2. Would you want your children taught by a teacher who used drugs? Why?
3. If you were on the Board of Education, how would you argue—for or against Miss Amory? Why?
4. If Miss Amory managed to keep her job, how do you think she would be treated by students, parents and other faculty?
5. If you were Miss Amory would you want to remain teaching at the high school? Why?
6. Do you think people's negative reactions to Miss Amory would be the same if she had been accused of being an alcoholic? Why?
7. Should teachers and other public figures be allowed to do what they want in public, such as smoking "pot"? Are there any restrictions that should be made? Why?

Here is another dilemma in case you didn't like the last one. (We don't want you to say you can't think of anything to write about.)

Jake is a sailor in the Coast Guard stationed on the *Point Francis* off the Florida coast. His boat has been ordered to board and inspect any suspicious looking ships that might be carrying illegal drugs to Florida. One night a lobster boat is sighted. A few minutes later the lobster boat cuts its lights and suddenly changes course. The captain of the *Point Francis* orders a chase.

Nearing the lobster boat, the captain, over a megaphone, orders the fishing vessel to stop. It doesn't. The captain then orders Jake to fire their .50 caliber machine gun over the lobster boat. Jake does, but the boat still does not stop. Then the captain orders Jake to fire into the fishing boat's cabin. Realizing he could kill someone, Jake hesitates.

What do you think?

1. Should Jake shoot as ordered? Why?
2. What will happen to Jake if he doesn't follow orders? Is that a reason to disobey?
3. Is the captain doing what he should? Why?
4. Is it worth killing to stop illegal drug traffic? Why?
5. What would you do if you were the captain? Jake? the men on the fishing boat?

Practice 1. In your journal notebook or on another sheet of paper, spend about 10 to 15 minutes freewriting. Remember, freewriting means allowing your mind to be free. Don't think about English skills; just think thoughts. You may want to think through one of the questions above.

Practice 2. Now plan an essay on some aspect of drugs. Let us hope you have some ideas based on the exercises you've done so far. If not, here are some topics to consider. Feel free to change them in any way you want.

1. The definition of a drug addict.
2. Reasons for drug addiction.
3. The case for/against legalizing marijuana (or other drugs).
4. Which is less harmful: alcohol or marijuana?
5. Why teenagers are drinking more alcohol.
6. Tell how you feel and what you actually do about pot and alcohol.
7. The need for drug laws.
8. Should schools teach drug education?
9. How people get hooked on drugs.
10. Why alcohol is socially acceptable.
11. The use of marijuana in medicine.
12. The effects of _____ (cocaine/heroin/opium, LSD, and so on).
13. A rebuttal to Gore Vidal's arguments.
14. Pick a topic of your own.

In the space below, write the topic or subject you've picked to write about. Make certain it's not too broad or too narrow.

Topic:

_____

_____

_____

Practice 3. Now write a possible thesis statement that expresses what you want to say about your topic. You can change it later if you need to do so. For now, this is your working thesis.

Tentative Thesis Statement:

_____

_____

_____

_____

Below, list all the ideas you can think of to support your thesis. If you don't have at least six major points, try another thesis or topic.

_____

_____

_____

_____

_____

_____

_____

_____

_____

_____

(A) an outline for your essay.

Rearrange your list of ideas into an outline or some order you can follow. Do this on a separate sheet and turn it in for your instructor to check.

(B) supporting paragraphs (continued from Unit 3).

Summary of Paragraph Types Discussed in Unit 3
1. Topic sentences supported by examples or illustrations.
2. Topic sentences supported by specific details.
3. Topic sentences supported by definitions of terms.

Unit 3 discusses the topic sentence and three methods of paragraph development often used by writers: (1) illustration/example, (2) specific details, and (3) definition. The following information discusses some more useful methods in developing your supporting detail paragraphs. Here are four more you should learn to use:

4. Paragraphs that *compare* and/or *contrast* things, ideas, or facts to help explain the point being made.
5. Paragraphs that *analyze* by breaking a topic into its parts to show the point.
6. Paragraphs that use *a story* or an *anecdote* to make a point.
7. Paragraphs that use a *combination* of other methods described.

4. Paragraphs That Compare and/or Contrast

Let us pick up where we left off in Unit 3. Here is an example of a paragraph that uses the *comparison/contrast* method to support the topic sentence. You may not agree with the author's logic or ideas, but disregard those feelings, and notice how the paragraph is developed.

Topic sentence

Social harm
from alcohol
compared to
lack of social
harm from
marijuana

Physical harm
from alcohol
compared to no
physical harm
from marijuana

Marijuana is not as harmful as our most popular "drug"— alcohol. One has only to read in the daily newspapers of account after account of arrests of drunken drivers, a menace to our highways, the abuse of children by drunken parents, and the millions of Americans involved in Alcoholics Anonymous because of their inability to cope with their jobs and responsibilities. By comparison, users of marijuana generally do no harm to themselves or society. In fact, marijuana usually has a tranquilizing effect and often relaxes the user to the point of immobility or sleep rather than violent danger. In addition, we know the harmful physical effects of alcohol, whereas as yet no research has shown the use of marijuana to be addictive or harmful to the body.

Check one of the following topic sentences that would best lend itself to the paragraph development method of using comparison and/or contrast.

_____ a. Marijuana users are looking for a "crutch."

_____ b. Ninety-five percent of heroin users started their drug habit with the use of marijuana.

_____ c. The laws regarding marijuana should be the same as the laws for traffic violations.

5. Paragraphs That Analyze

Here is an example of a paragraph that *analyzes* by breaking a topic into its several parts. Again, you may disagree with the author's views, but notice how he uses *analysis.*

Topic sentence stating problem and solution	Before a decision can be made regarding the legalization of the use of marijuana, there are many issues that must be investigated and researched thoroughly. We must learn if the
"Parts" or segments of the problem that must be investigated	long-term usage of marijuana has harmful effects. We must learn if the reproductive processes are adversely affected by its use. We must learn if there is a connection between marijuana and the use of hard drugs. We must be certain that if marijuana is legalized, it will not be made available to nonadults as we know alcohol is despite laws against it. All these, and other facets of the problem, must be thoroughly researched and documented if we are to move towards the legalization of marijuana.

Check one of the following topic sentences that would best fit the paragraph development method of using *analysis.*

_____ a. The following steps are being taken to obtain answers to the problem.

_____ b. Our laws governing marijuana are a mixture of bad science and poor understanding of the role of law as a deterrent force.

_____ c. In spite of our lack of knowledge, an estimated twelve million Americans have used marijuana in the past few years.

6. Paragraphs That Use a Story or an Anecdote

Here is an example of a paragraph using a *story* or an *anecdote* to develop a point.

Topic sentence	Parents are very concerned over the growing use of marijuana among teenagers. Just the other day, a mother came to
Story used to back up topic sentence	my office very distraught because she had found three marijuana cigarettes in her teenage son's sock drawer. Alarmed, she came to me as her physician to see if I would tell her son how his use of marijuana would eventually lead to a worse addiction, heroin. I had trouble assuring her that there is nothing inherent in it to cause him to switch to hard drugs.

Check one of the following topic sentences that would best fit the paragraph development method of using a *story* or an *anecdote* to develop the point.

_____ a. Discussions of drug addiction always seem to turn to the question of what happens to the addict.

_____ b. Some persons believe that crimes caused by drug addiction could be reduced if we gave prescribed doses to addicts.

_____ c. The daughter of one of my best friends got hooked on "grass" when she was in high school.

7. Paragraphs That Use Combinations of Methods

Here is an example of a paragraph using a *combination* of methods to develop the topic sentence.

Topic sentence	Evidence seems now to show that marijuana is not a harmful drug. After the most complete study ever made of social and medical evidence concerning marijuana, decriminalization has been recommended by President Nixon's Commission on Marijuana. In addition, the Los Angeles County Grand Jury, the National Institute of Mental Health, and the American
Mixture of details and examples	Medical Association Drug Committee all concur. These conservative authorities all agree that marijuana is not addictive; does not damage the body; does not produce mental illness, crime, or violence; and has no lethal dose. Though no drug—including aspirin, alcohol, and tobacco—is harmless, the vast majority of people who use marijuana do so without harm to themselves.
Use of anecdote	Yet, when presented with this information, a close friend of mine said, "They don't know what they're talking about!"

Actually, just about any topic sentence can be developed through the use of a combination of any of the six methods now described to you. As a writer, you are free to choose what best develops your topic sentence. In fact, you eventually may even develop your paragraphs with a method of your own. At least these methods will help you get started.

 ## Practices in Paragraph Writing

Practice 1. Fill in the blanks in front of the following topic sentences with the letter or letters of the methods that could be used to develop the sentences into paragraphs.

a. illustration/example
b. specific details
c. comparison/contrast
d. definition
e. analysis
f. story or anecdote
g. combination

_____ 1. The effects of marijuana depend on the user's mood, quantity smoked or eaten, and the potency of the plant.

_____ 2. There is a difference between marijuana and hashish.

_____ 3. An interesting account of addiction was brought to my attention yesterday.

_____ 4. According to the National Institute of Mental Health, there are several known factors regarding the effects of marijuana.

_____ 5. The laws in this state regarding the possession or use of marijuana need to be changed.

_____ 6. There are several reasons why the legalization of marijuana should not be considered.

_____ 7. The ignorance and misinformation regarding marijuana have caused the public to react to it negatively.

_____ 8. It is erroneous to categorize marijuana with narcotics.

_____ 9. I do not believe that marijuana should now be legalized.

_____ 10. The known harmful effects of alcohol and tobacco are greater than those of marijuana.

Practice 2. Circle the key word or words in the following topic sentences. Then fill in the blanks, using the topic sentence as your guide. Don't be afraid to use humor. There are no expected answers.

A. Use comparison or contrast to develop the following paragraph:

Personality-wise, my parents are poles apart. My mother is _____

_____

_____

On the other hand, my father is _____

_____

B. Use analysis to develop the following paragraph:

      In order to understand why the football team lost the game last night, we must examine the players' attitudes prior to the game. _____

_____

_____

_____

_____

C. Use a story or anecdote to develop the following paragraph:

      Yesterday was so frustrating to me that I almost resigned from the human race. It all started when _____

_____

_____

_____

_____

D. Use any combination of paragraph types to develop the following paragraph:

      The last two units of this book have presented six different types of methods for developing topic sentences into paragraphs. _____

_____

_____

_____

_____

_____

_____

_____

_____

Practice 3.   Using the outline you wrote earlier, write an introductory paragraph and two supporting paragraphs as a beginning for an essay. Then check for

a. A clear-cut thesis in your introductory paragraph.
b. What introductory paragraph method you used.
c. Clear-cut topic sentences in each of your other two paragraphs.
d. What paragraph methods of development you used.

Turn in this work to your instructor.

(C) an essay.

When your instructor returns your paragraphs, make any changes necessary, and then finish the rest of your essay. Then go to the next section: REWRITE.

your first draft.

To aid you in rewriting your essay, read the following student first draft of a supporting paragraph from an essay with the thesis that drugs should be given to registered addicts.

Student's First Draft	Instructor's Comments
Giving drugs to registered addicts would keep the addict from resorting to stealing or prostitution. That would then reduce crime. Clinics could be set up to aid the addict and eliminate deaths caused by overdoses.	*Though you have a topic sentence, your ideas are not very organized and lack development. Don't you really have two ideas here— one, registering addicts; the other setting up clinics?*

Here is a revision.

Student's Revised Draft	Instructor's Comments
Giving drugs to registered addicts would keep the addict from resorting to stealing or prostitution in order to buy illegal drugs. The procedure would be simple. Any addict would be able to register with a doctor or a drug clinic and admit to being on a certain drug. If the drug user had no money, the drug would be supplied free. This would alleviate the need to steal or commit crimes in order to buy drugs.	*A definite improvement. You now have two more solid paragraphs, each with its own topic sentence.*
Clinics could be set up to aid the addict and eliminate deaths now caused by overdose or bad drugs. The clinics would not force the addict to take a treatment, but the help would be there if desired. The addict could simply walk in, get his shot, and walk out. If more dosage is required, the addict returns. Although the clinic would be supporting the addict's habit, it would be saving the money and lives of the innocent victims of crimes for drug purchases, which is more important.	*This is much better than just the one sentence of your first draft.* *Good point.*

There is a tendency in first drafts not to develop ideas fully. It's very important to give full support to each topic sentence. Try to do this on your revision.

Before you turn in your completed essay, go over your work by using the following checklist.

_____ 1. Have you revised your opening paragraph based on any comments from your instructor?

_____ 2. Does your opening paragraph contain a good thesis?

_____ 3. Does your opening paragraph use a method that draws the reader's interest?

_____ 4. Did you write about something you know or thought through carefully?

_____ 5. Does each paragraph support your thesis?

_____ 6. Does each paragraph contain a topic sentence that expresses the main point of the paragraph?

_____ 7. Does each sentence in each paragraph stick to the idea expressed in the topic sentence?

_____ 8. Does each paragraph have a method for unifying and developing the main idea, such as compare/contrast, use of detail, use of examples, and so on?

_____ 9. Did you follow the advice of Paul Roberts and avoid those common errors he described in his essay? (Don't be afraid to review that essay in Unit 1 again! It's worth it.)

_____ 10. Have you had another classmate or two read your essay for their reactions and comments?

Remember, rewriting essays is not easy. Often writers get "burned out" because they read and reread their essays so much they no longer see their mistakes. Sometimes it's a good idea to put your writing aside for a day and them come back to it fresh. But there is no way around it: revision is difficult but necessary.

UNIT 5

Think...
about college sports

Read...
about intercollegiate sports
"Away with Big-Time Athletics" by Roger M. Williams

React...
to the essay

Plan...
an essay
Topics for an essay on sports

Write...
(A) an outline for an essay
(B) the introductory paragraph
(C) supporting paragraphs
(D) the concluding paragraph
Practices in writing concluding paragraphs

Rewrite...
your first draft

Think...

about college sports by answering the following questions.

1. In which of the following college sports do you or would you like to participate? Rank your top three choices, using the numbers 1, 2, and 3 in the
blanks provided.

_____ football   _____ wrestling

_____ basketball   _____ swimming

_____ baseball   _____ boxing

_____ volleyball   _____ fencing

_____ hockey   _____ other: _____

2. Which of the following sports do you like to watch? Rank your top three
choices as you did in the preceding question.

_____ football   _____ wrestling

_____ basketball   _____ swimming

_____ baseball   _____ boxing

_____ volleyball   _____ fencing

_____ hockey   _____ other: _____

3. What college or university comes to your mind when you first think of foot-

ball? _____

Why?_____

_____

4. How important do you think college spectator sports (football, basketball,

baseball, and so on) are? _____

Why? _____

_____

_____

5. Do you think some colleges place too much emphasis on having a winning

   team? _____

   Why? _____

   _____

6. In the spaces that follow, list some reasons why colleges should and should
   not take spectator sports so seriously.

   Reasons For   *Reasons Against*

   _____   _____

   _____   _____

   _____   _____

   _____   _____

7. Do you think students should receive sports scholarships to college?

   _____ Why? _____

   _____

   _____

8. What would happen to a college or university that did away with intercolle-

   giate sports? _____

   _____

   _____

   _____

   _____

about intercollegiate sports.

The following article's title makes it very clear what the author, Roger Williams, thinks of college sports. As you read, look for the ideas he used to develop his thesis. In other words, why does he want to do away with big-time college athletics? Are his reasons good ones? Williams is a writer for *Sports Illustrated* and *Time* and a former editor for *Saturday Review*.

Away with Big-Time Athletics
Roger M. Williams

1. At their mid-January annual meeting, members of the National Collegiate Athletic Association were locked in anguished discussion over twin threats to big-time college athletic programs: rapidly rising costs and federal regulations forcing the allocation of some funds to women's competition. The members ignored, as they always have, the basic issue concerning intercollegiate athletics. That is the need to overhaul the entire bloated, hypocritical athletic system and return athletics to a sensible place in the educational process.

2. A complete overhaul of the athletic programs, not the fiscal repair now being attempted by the NCAA, is what is necessary. For decades now big-time football, and to a lesser degree basketball, have commanded absurdly high priorities at our colleges and universities. Football stands at the center of the big-time system, both symbolically and financially; the income from football has long supported other, less glamorous sports.

3. Many American universities are known more for the teams they field than for the education they impart. Each year they pour hundreds of thousands of dollars apiece into athletic programs whose success is measured in games won and dollars earned—standards that bear no relation to the business of education and offer nothing to the vast majority of students.

4. The waste of resources is not the only lamentable result of the overemphasis of intercollegiate ahtletics. The skewing of values is at least as damaging. Everyone involved in the big-time system—players, coaches, alumni and other boosters, school officials, trustees, even legislators—is persuaded that a good football team is a mark of the real worth of an educational institution. Some of the most successful coaches elevate that bizarre notion to a sort of philosophy. Woody Hayes of Ohio State has said that the most important part of a young man's college edu-

Reprinted by permission of Roger M. Williams.

cation is the football he plays. Jim Kehoe, athletic director at the University of Maryland, has said of the games played by Maryland: "You do anything to win. I believe completely, totally, and absolutely in winning."

5. Anyone doubtful of the broad psychic satisfaction provided by winning teams need only observe who it is that shouts, "We're number one!" It is seldom the players and only sometimes other students. The hard core of team boosters is composed of middle-aged men—mainly alumni but also legions of lawyers, doctors, and businessmen with no tangible connection to the school.

6. In the South, where football mania rides at a shrill and steady peak, winning seems to offer a special reward: an opportunity to claim the parity with other regions that has been so conspicuously lacking in more important areas of endeavor. In Alabama in the late Sixties, when Coach Bear Bryant was fielding the first of his remarkable series of national championship teams, both Bear and team were the objects of outright public adulation: that is, *white* public adulation. White Alabamians, reacting to the assaults on George Wallace and other bastions of segregation, took a grim, almost vengeful pride in "their" team. During those years, when I covered the South as a reporter, one could hardly meet a white Alabamian who didn't talk football or display, on an office or den wall, a picture of Bryant and the Crimson Tide squad.

7. The disease of bigtime-ism seems to run rampant in provincial places where there is little else to do or cheer for: Tuscaloosa and Knoxville, Columbus and Lincoln, Norman and Fayetteville. But everywhere, always, it feeds on a need to win—not just win a fair share of games but win almost all of them, and surely all of the "big" ones.

8. At the University of Tennessee last fall, coach Bill Battle nearly lost his job because the Volunteers won a mere 7 of their 12 games. Never mind that Battle's Tennessee teams had previously amassed a five-year record of 46 victories, 12 defeats, and 2 ties and had been to a bowl in each of those years. Although Battle was eventually rehired, he received no public support from a university administration which seemed to agree with the fanatics that, outstanding as his record was, it was not good enough.

9. Everyone knows something about the excess of recruiting high-school players and something about the other trappings of the big-time system: the athletic dormitory and training table, where the "jocks" or "animals" are segregated in the interests of conformity and control, the "brain coaches" hired to keep athletes from flunking out of school; the full scholarships ("grants in aid"), worth several thousand dollars apiece, that big-time schools can give to 243 athletes each year. (Conference regulations restrict the size of football traveling squads to about 60, while the NCAA permits 95 players to be on football scholarships. This means that some three dozen football players at each big-time school are getting what's called a full ride without earning it.)

10. What few people realize is that these are only the visible workings of a system that feeds on higher education and diverts it from its true purposes. The solution, therefore, is not to deliver slaps on the wrist to the most zealous recruiters, as the NCAA often does, or to make modest reductions in the permissible number of athletic scholarships, as it did last year. The solution is to banish bigtime athletics from American colleges and universities.

11. Specifically, we should:

(1) Eliminate all scholarships awarded on the basis of athletic ability *and* those given to athletes in financial need. Every school should form its teams from a student body drawn there to pursue academic interests.

(2) Eliminate athletic dormitories and training tables, which keep athletes out of the mainstream of college life and further their image as hired guns. Also eliminate special tutoring, which is a preferential treatment of athletes, and "red shirting," the practice of keeping players in school an additional year in the hope that they'll improve enough to make the varsity.

(3) Cut drastically the size and cost of coaching staffs. Football staffs at Division I schools typically number 12 or 14, so that they are larger than those employed by professional teams. With practice squads numbering 80 or 50, the present staff size creates a "teacher-pupil" ratio that permits far more individualized instruction on the playing field than in the classroom. The salaries paid to assistant coaches should be spent to hire additional faculty members. The salaries of head coaches, who in some states earn more than the governor, should be reduced to a point where no head coach is paid more than a full professor.

(4) Work to eliminate all recruiting of high-school athletes. It has produced horrendous cases of misrepresentation, illegal payments, and trauma for the young man involved.

12. The worst of the abuses is the athletic scholarship, because it is central to all the others. If members of a college team are not principally athletes, there is no need to lure them to the school by offering special treatment and platoons of coaches. They should be students to whom football or basketball is the season's major extracurricular activity.

13. What will happen if these changes are made? The games will go on. In fact, they may well be more like real games than the present clashes between hired, supertrained, and sometimes brutalized gladiators. Will the caliber of play suffer? Of course, but every school will be producing the same lower caliber. Given a certain proficiency, which the best of any random selection of student-athletes always possess, the games will be as competitive and as exciting for spectators as they are today. Is a 70-yard run by a non-scholarship halfback less exciting than the same run by Bear Bryant's best pro prospect? For spectators who crave top athletic performance, it is available from a myriad of professional teams. We need not demand it of students.

14. Certainly, the counter-argument runs, alumni and other influential supporters would not stand for such changes. There would indeed be ill feeling among—and diminished contributions from—old grads who think of their alma mater primarily as a football team. Let them stew in their own pot of distorted values. Those legislators whose goodwill toward a state university depends on winning seasons and free tickets can stew with them. A serious institution is well rid of such "supporters." They may discover the pleasures of a game played enthusiastically by moderately skilled students who are not in effect paid performers.

15. Will athletic-program revenues drop? They undoubtedly will, at least for a while; not many people will pay seven dollars to see games of admittedly lower quality, nor will the TV networks pay fancy fees for the right to televise them. The fans and the networks will eventually return, because these will be the only college games available. And think of the financial savings, as the costs of the typical big-time athletic program drop by hundreds of thousands of dollars a year. If a revenue gap persists, let it be made up out of general funds. The glee club, the intramural athletic program, and innumerable other student activities do not pay for themselves. Why should intercollegiate athletics have to do so?

16. Supporters of big-time programs often say piously that, thanks to those programs, many young men get a college education who otherwise would have no chance for one. That is true. But there are even more young men, of academic rather than athletic promise, who deserve whatever scholarship money is available. If somebody has to pay an athlete's way to college, let it be the professional teams that need the training that college competition provides.

17. The president of a good Southern university once told me privately that he would like to hire outright a football team to represent his school and let the education process proceed. George Hanford of the College Entrance Examination Board, who has made a study of intercollegiate athletics, would keep the present system but legitimize the preparation of players for professional sports. Hanford would have a college teach athletes such skills as selecting a business agent and would permit student-athletes to play now and return later to do the academic work required for a degree.

18. While Hanford's suggested changes would remove the mask of hypocrisy from big-time college athletic programs, they would not solve the fundamental problem: the intrusions the programs make on the legitimate functions and goals of an educational institution. For institutions with a conscience, this problem has been persistently vexing. Vanderbilt University football coach Art Guepe summed it up years ago, when he characterized Vanderbilt's dilemmas as "trying to be Harvard five days a week and Alabama on Saturday."

19. Because of pressure from alumni and others who exalt the role of football, Vanderbilt is still attempting to resolve this dilemma; and it is still failing. Now it is time for all the Vanderbilts and all the Alabamas to try to be Harvard whenever they can and Small-Time State on Saturday.

React....

to the essay by answering the following questions.

1. What is the thesis or main idea about college sports in the essay?

_____

_____

2. In what paragraph does the thesis first appear?_____
3. Reread paragraph 3. Why do you agree or disagree with the author?

_____

_____

4. The author states that everyone involved in the "big-time system—players, coaches, alumni and other boosters . . .—is persuaded that a good football team is a mark of the real worth of an educational institution." Why do you agree or disagree with this statement?

_____

_____

5. Reread paragraph 11. Explain why you agree or disagree with each of the four points the author lists.

   Point (1), scholarships: _____

_____

_____

_____

Point (2), training facilities: _____

_____

_____

Point (3), staff: _____

_____

_____

Point (4), recruiting: _____

_____

_____

6. Check the following words you don't know or could not use correctly. The number following the word refers to the paragraph in the essay where the word is used.

_____ a. intercollegiate (1)

_____ b. hypocritical (1)

_____ c. fiscal (2)

_____ d. lamentable (4)

_____ e. psychic (5)

_____ f. adulation (6)

_____ g. zealous (10)

_____ h. myriad (13)

_____ i. intramural (15)

_____ j. intrusions (18)

Reread the words in the paragraphs indicated. Then go to the Vocabulary Section in the Appendix for more information and practice using these words.

Plan...

an essay on some aspect of sports.

Essays are really "think pieces," short compositions that usually deal with one subject or topic and express the author's feelings, knowledge, and experiences. The "Plan" stage in writing is important in that it is actually the thinking period, the time when you search for a topic, think topics through to see if you know enough to write about them, and think of an organizational framework for your first draft.

Sometimes we need stimulus to get us thinking about possible essay topics. That is why we include a few dilemmas or problems and a list of topics in this section of each unit. But don't feel tied to any of these aids. They are simply meant to help you get some thoughts moving toward possible essay topics.

Below is an editorial that appeared in the *Los Angeles Times*, October 14, 1980, and relates to the essay, "Away With Big-Time Athletics."

A Beast That Needs Taming

The University of Southern California is to be commended for its courage and honesty in facing up to the scandals besetting its athletic programs. A report made public Monday by USC President John Zumberge acknowledged that the balance between academics and athletics at the school had gone askew.

The report admitted that during the last 10 years 330 academically deficient students were admitted to USC strictly on the basis of their athletic prowess. Many of these students never graduated from college, but played for the university until their athletic eligiblity was used up. They were then, for all intents and purposes, cast aside. In the strong words of the report, this practice was "tantamount to exploitation."

It is reprehensible to think this could have gone on so long at a major university which is striving, as USC has been doing for the last several years, to build an academic reputation that would match its reputation on the football field.

USC has already been penalized for some of the infractions: It was banned by the Pacific 10 Athletic Conference from playing in next year's Rose Bowl [1981]. In releasing the report, Zumberge also announced reforms that would prevent such abuses in the future by bringing USC's powerful athletic department back under the control of the admissions procedures that govern other departments of the university. We can only hope Zumberge's actions will have the intended salutory effect, for the temptation to abuse them will unfortunately continue in the future.

The USC report acknowledged this when it warned, in an introduction, that the problems at USC and other major West Coast schools such as UCLA, were indicative of a larger phenomenon—the fact that big-time college athletics have become so profitable they are taking on an existence of their own that threatens to undermine the integrity of higher education. The reforms at USC will mean little if the schools it must compete against continue to abuse the regulations of the National Collegiate Athletic Assn. Far more must be done on the national level. At least the scandals at the West Coast universities have stimulated discussions about proposals like these:

—The elimination of the freshman eligibility rule, so that the incoming student athlete will have at least one year to adjust to the academic rigors of college before facing the additional pressure of intercollegiate competition.

—A national standard of academic achievement that must be maintained if a student athlete is to be allowed to compete for his or her school.

—Harsher penalties for schools that violate NCAA rules. The most severe sanctions now are for a school to be banned from television appearances and post-season competition, both of which involve revenue losses for athletic programs.

Some observers of the college athletic scene have become so discouraged at the recent scandals that they have even taken to making only half-joking proposals that athletic powerhouses like USC and UCLA simply end the charade and create two levels of athletics—one for real students and one for the young semipros striving to break into the professional ranks.

We would not go quite that far. Intercollegiate athletics have become so closely identified with many excellent universities that they could never be abolished. If intercollegiate athletics has become a beast, then it should be tamed, not killed.

The abuses of intercollegiate athletics, despite the many temptations and the great potential for corruption, can be contained. But it will take strong, determined and concerted action by the NCAA and its member schools. Plain talk like that in the USC report will help, too.

Here are some questions to kick around. Does this editorial want the same thing that Williams wants in his essay? Does the editorial supply any means to stop the exploitation of college athletes? Which of the two represents the stronger argument, the essay or the editorial? Has anything new happened in college sports since either the essay or the editorial were written that has changed the problem of exploitation of college athletes?

It may be that you are not interested in the subject the essay and the editorial deal with. Here's another "think piece" for you. Read the following moral dilemma and think about the problem it portrays.

The Championship

According to PA House Bill #225A, local districts cannot receive state funds without providing equal opportunities for girls to participate in athletics. School districts must show that they are spending money to include girls on their athletic teams.

Prior to the track season Coach Dobisc of Larimer High School learned that all high school coaches should make every effort to allow girls to compete on the varsity teams. Coach Dobisc and Mr. Burns, Larimer's athletic director, agreed that they would comply with the new state law.

During the tryouts, Patty Connors did extremely well in the 440 yard dash. Patty worked very hard and her time for the event was excellent, but several of the boys could run the 440 faster. Patty was about equal to Tom Mitchell, but not as good as John Mardi, Harold Laser, and Paul Badger.

Coach Dobisc told Patty that she had made the team and would run in the mile relay. Usually Paul, Harold, John, and Tom ran the important relay race, but the team agreed that Patty and Tom would alternate for each track meet. Tom would run in every other meet for the season. During the season, the team of Paul, Harold, John, and Tom went undefeated, winning five relay races. When Patty ran, the team won two and lost two.

May 15 was the big day. Seven teams would compete for the county championship. Larimer had a chance to win the county championship for the third straight year. As the meet progressed, it appeared that the mile relay could determine the championship. Patty knew that it was her turn to run on the relay team, and she was doing some warm-up exercises in preparation for the race.

The day before the county championship, Paul, Harold, and John had talked about the possibility that the championship might hinge on the last relay. They knew that they could win the mile relay if the all-boy team ran. They decided that if the last relay was crucial to the outcome of the meet, they would ask Patty to voluntarily withdraw. With only two events to go, the boys looked at the score board. Larimer was one point out of first place and followed by a team one point behind them.

Harold, John, and Paul decided to go ahead with their plan. They approached Patty as she was doing her warm-up exercises. Harold asked Patty to fake a pulled muscle and tell the coach that she could not run in the relay. The boys explained to Patty that Larimer High could win another championship if Tom could run with the team. Patty had to agree that the chances for a win would be better with Tom in the relay. She didn't know what to do.

Now answer these questions either in small discussion groups in class or individually.

1. What is the moral dilemma of the situation?

_____

_____

_____

Reprinted with permission from *Moral Reasoning: A Teaching Handbook for Adapting Kohlberg to the Classroom* by Ronald E. Galbraith and Thomas M. Jones. Copyright © 1976 by Greenhaven Press, Inc., 577 Shoreview Park Road, St. Paul, MN 55112.

2. Should Patty agree to withdraw from the race? _____

   Why? _____

   _____

3. Suppose that a group of college scouts are in the stands to watch Patty run. They are considering her for a track scholarship. Should that make a differ-

   ence in the decision Patty makes? _____

   Why? _____

   _____

4. Suppose the coach asks Patty to withdraw voluntarily for the benefit of the

   team. Should that make a difference in the decision Patty makes? _____

   Why? _____

   _____

   _____

5. Is it important to be a champion? _____

   Why? _____

   _____

6. What is Patty's obligation to the team and winning the championship?

   _____

   _____

   _____

7. How important is the state law in this situation? _____

   _____

   _____

8. What is the purpose of athletic programs in schools?_____

_____

_____

_____

9. Should women be allowed to participate in sports on an equal basis with

   men? _____

   Why? _____

   _____

10. Is it ever right to fake an injury?_____

   Why? _____

   _____

Practice 1. In your journal notebook or on a separate sheet, spend about 10–15 minutes freewriting. If you can, write what comes into your mind about Patty's situation and the answers you gave to the questions above. But remember, freewriting means you are free to write what comes in to your head. Don't worry about spelling, grammar, punctuation, or structure. Just think and write.

Practice 2. Now plan an essay on some aspect of sports. Let us hope that you have some ideas based on Patty's dilemma or your freewriting. If not, here are some other ideas to consider for an essay topic. Feel free to change them in any way.

1. Defend big-time athletics against the arguments in the essay "Away with Big-Time Athletics."
2. The strengths and weaknesses of two outstanding sports teams.
3. The benefits of jogging/walking/roller skating.
4. How to perform a particular play or move in some game (golf, tennis, baseball, and so on) such as putting, backhand swing, hitting grounders, and so on.
5. Where and when to take a good bicycle trip.
6. How to hike/ski/roller-skate/water-ski/whatever.
7. The equipment needed to go backpacking.
8. Are Americans too concerned with sports?
9. Why boxing should or should not be abolished.
10. Should the Olympic teams be subsidized by the U.S. government?
11. Professional baseball players: Children at heart.

12. Is football just an extension of the Roman gladiators?
13. Little League: For children or parents?
14. Compare/contrast tennis with squash or any two similar sports.
15. Compare/contrast being at a sports event with watching it on TV.
16. Pick a topic of your own related to sports.

In the space below, write the topic or subject you've picked for an essay. Make certain it's not too broad or too narrow for a five-to-six paragraph essay.

Topic:

_____

_____

_____

Practice 3. Now write a possible thesis statement that expresses what you want to say about your topic. You should feel free to change it later if you need to do so. This is your working thesis.

Tentative Thesis Statement:

_____

_____

_____

_____

Below, list all the ideas you can think of to support your thesis. If you don't have at least six points, try another thesis or topic.

_____

_____

_____

_____

_____

_____

_____

_____

(A) an outline for an essay.

Use your rearranged list of supporting detail to write an outline for an essay. If you need to do so, refer to Unit 1 for the correct form. Have your instructor check the outline when you are finished. Then go to *B* below.

(B) the introductory paragraph to your essay.

Summary of Methods Used for Introductory Paragraphs
1. Ask a question.
2. Use an anecdote.
3. Use a quotation.
4. Give a brief overview.
5. Stress importance of topic.
6. Use a combination of methods.

If you need to do so, refer back to Units 2 and 3 for a quick review of methods for developing an introductory paragraph and topic sentence control. Try to state your *thesis* regarding your topic in the opening paragraph. Do this on a separate sheet of paper. Then go to *C* below.

(C) supporting paragraphs.

Summary of Paragraph Types Discussed in Units 3 and 4
1. Topic sentences supported by examples or illustrations.
2. Topic sentences supported by specific details.
3. Topic sentences supported by definitions of terms.
4. Topic sentences supported with comparisons/contrasts.
5. Topic sentences supported by analysis.
6. Topic sentences supported by a story or anecdote.
7. Topic sentences supported by a combination of methods.

Now review the types of supporting paragraphs listed above. Then use your outline for your essay, and write supporting paragraphs for your essay. As a practice and to make things easy for you, try making your first sentence the topic sentence in each supporting paragraph. You don't *have* to do this (we don't want to crimp your style); but if you do and if you make certain you use key words in the topic sentence as you were shown in Unit 3, you might find it easier to develop each topic sentence into a strong, unified supporting statement of your thesis.

When you have finished, set your essay aside, and learn some methods for concluding your essay as described in *D* below.

(D) the concluding paragraph.

A concluding paragraph can often make or break your essay. It should not only reaffirm what you have been saying in the body of the essay, it should also leave your reader with a strong feeling of agreement or at least stir up some thinking about your viewpoint toward your subject. As with introductory paragraphs, there is no one way to write a concluding paragraph, but here are some examples of methods you could use:

1. Leave the reader with a question he or she must answer.
2. Use a quotation or anecdote that not only says well what you want to say, but also supports your viewpoint in the essay.
3. Summarize your main points for the reader.
4. Show the need for change or concern regarding the topic.
5. Make conclusions about what you have said.

What method you use will depend on what you have been saying in the essay and should seem to be a natural way to conclude your essay. Here are some examples of each method.

1. *Leave the reader with a question he or she must answer.* This method can be used when you feel your reader needs to be jarred into action as the following example attempts to do.

   Our society cannot continue to allow governmental control of medical prices. The free enterprise system has been the backbone of our democratic system. If we allow the government to dictate and control what prices doctors may charge for office visits, for operations, for prescriptions and the like, we are taking one more giant step toward socialism. Is this what you want to happen? Is this the form of government you want your children to be raised in?

2. *Use a quotation or anecdote that not only says well what you want to say, but also supports your viewpoint.* This method can be useful provided the quotation or anecdote summarizes what you have said in the essay. Notice the example below.

Perhaps a saying that my father told me once can clarify my views regarding those who continue to complain about our hospital facilities: "I complained because I had no shoes, until I met a man who had no feet." We should be grateful we have what we do have in comparison with other hospitals and their problems, at least until such time that we can afford to expand.

3. *Summarize your main point for the reader.* By using this method, you leave your readers with the ideas or points you want them to remember. When you use this approach, be careful you do not merely say in the same words what you have already said. Restate your points with different wording.

   In summary, it is necessary we make certain that: one, the American Medical Association makes an intensive investigation of acupuncture; two, that doctors not be allowed to practice acupuncture until the AMA's investigation is concluded; and three, that those doctors who wish to practice acupuncture be required to take training courses in the procedure if the AMA decides it is safe to use on the public at large. Without these steps, we may be putting many patients in jeopardy.

4. *Show the need for change or concern regarding the topic.* In order to get readers to react to your proposal, you may wish to show great concern for the consequences of what might take place if action isn't taken. Notice the writer's concern in this concluding paragraph.

   From the examples used, you can see that surgeons are taking advantage of their positions and patients. It has been estimated that 30 percent to 40 percent of American doctors are "making a killing" in medicine, some by performing "incredible amounts of unnecessary surgery." The median income for doctors is over $40,000 a year, while some private practitioners make more than $100,000. With doctors charging such high prices, many families are financially ruined when in need of medical aid. We must put pressure on our elected representatives to control the rising costs of becoming ill.

5. *Make conclusions about what you said in the essay.* Depending upon what you have said in your essay, it may be appropriate for you to predict or make conclusions about your topic. Here is an example of this method.

   If the "morning-after" pill proves to be truly nontoxic and 100 percent effective as claimed, it will be placed on the market only then. According to the Planned Parenthood Federation, that time will be long in coming. Until then, we don't know if this new pill will be the answer to the population explosion or not. But this we do know and can predict. Our sexual morals, as we have known them in the past, surely will come crashing down around us when and if the pill hits the market. You can count on it!

The preceding methods for developing paragraphs should not be considered the only ways to write. You will soon develop what best fits your essay and style. But they can serve as models for you until that time.

Practices in Writing Concluding Paragraphs

Practice 1. Read the following concluding paragraphs from essays, and fill in the blank line after them with the method the author used.

A.   Thus, the following steps are necessary. We must allocate more money for investigation of the drug's effect on humans. If the drug proves truly harmless, then we must control the cost of production so that customers will not be overcharged in the stores. Finally, we must make certain that sales are made only through a doctor's prescription. Only then will the drug prove truly safe for the public.

_____

B.   The point of all this is simply that retail prices of drugs have become ridiculously high. The average family is unable to "foot the bill" for drugs that can be produced so cheaply, yet retail for such exorbitant prices. The only sensible solution is to persuade the local drugstores to put pressures on their wholesalers to lower their prices. This can be done if we consumers band together as a common force. Please sign our petition.

_____

C.   Gone are the days of the sympathetic, caring doctors and dentists. Just the other day, a young boy went to his dentist with severe pain from an abscessed tooth. Because he didn't have an appointment, he was turned away. Later, I found out the dentist didn't take the boy not because he didn't have an appointment, but because the dentist had a date to go sailing! Modern "professionals" no longer seem to know what the word means.

_____

D.   In spite of what we hear to the contrary, modern doctors deserve the money they earn. If we consider the cost and time of years of schooling they must cope with, the time required as an intern, the cost of equipment they must purchase, and the long hours spent in their office and hospitals, is it not appropriate they be paid well for their time, knowledge, and skill?

_____

E.   Naturally, the warm and devoted television images of doctors, such as the portrayals of old Doc Adams, young Dr. Kildare, and Marcus Welby, are what we want and hope our doctors are. In reality, I suspect the truth is somewhere in between. Who knows? Perhaps these television doctors will influence our real ones for the better.

_____

Practice 2. Reread the concluding paragraph in the essay in this unit, "Away with Big-Time Athletics," and answer the following questions.

1. Which sentence is the topic sentence? _____

2. Which method for writing concluding paragraphs is used? _____

_____

3. What, if any, other method could have been used? _____

_____

Practice 3. Reread your introductory and supporting paragraphs you wrote earlier in this unit. Review the different types of concluding paragraphs. Then write *two* separate concluding paragraphs for your essay using a different method for each. Your instructor may want to see them.

Practice 4. Pick one of the concluding paragraphs you wrote in Practice 3, and add it to what you've already written. You now have a completed essay, and you are ready to go to the next section: REWRITE.

Rewrite....

your first draft.

Before you rewrite your essay, read the following student essay and the instructor's comments.

Student's First Draft

Dracula

In 1931, the movie *Dracula* was made from Bram Stoker's book by the same name. But there were many vampire stories long before Stoker wrote his book.

Vampire stories have been told for centuries all over the world. Even as far back as the ancient Greeks, vampire stories were around.

There are many stories written about vampires that are supposedly

Instructor's Comments

Title too broad. Doesn't reflect your thesis.

Your thesis is clear, but why do you mention the movie? Try drawing your reader's interest into the subject more.

Good topic sentence, but the paragraph is not developed enough. Notice your key words—"for centuries"

Another paragraph with a good topic sentence but little support. Your

true. Calmet, a French monk, wrote about real vampires. He wrote about a man named Arnold Paole, who was supposed to be a vampire.

In the 1840s, another vampire story was written, *Varney the Vampyre*. It was very popular even though it is over 500,000 words long.

Today few people say they believe in vampires.

key phrase is *"many stories."* You give only one. Can you combine sentences 2 and 3 together?

Shouldn't this paragraph be part of your second paragraph?

Very weak concluding paragraph. Not related to thesis.

The writer of the essay obviously understands what the order of an essay is. It does have an introductory paragraph with a thesis, three supporting paragraphs, and a concluding paragraph. But the essay is very weak in developing ideas expressed in the thesis and topic sentence. All the paragraphs are underdeveloped, especially the conclusion, which does not bring us back to the thesis. The student was told all this as an aid for the rewrite. Here's the student's revision of the rough draft.

Student's Revision

Vampires: Real or Just Stories?

The moonlight shines into her open window. A soft breeze gently moves the curtains. Suddenly, a bat-shaped creature appears at the window. Just as suddenly, the bat turns into a tall man in a dark, formal evening suit with a long cape. He smiles at the beautiful woman asleep on the bed, moves toward her as his teeth grow longer and sharper. He bends over the sleeping woman, sinks two fangs into her neck, and drinks her blood. This, for most of us, is the image we have of Count Dracula. He is the vampire made famous by Bela Lugosi in the 1931 movie *Dracula*, which was based on Bram Stoker's book by the same name. However, there were many vampire stories around long before Stoker wrote his book that give us a different picture of vampires.

Vampire stories have been told for centuries all over the world. For example, the ancient Greeks told a

Instructor's Comments

Good title—fits your thesis and supporting ideas.

Much better introductory paragraph. You use a familiar vampire image to draw our interests, then state your thesis clearly at the end of the paragraph.

Thesis is clearer.

Much better. You give three good examples of vampire stories from different time periods, which

legend about a woman named Lamia, who went mad when her children were killed. As revenge, she started killing other children, drinking their blood, and eating their flesh, which soon turned her from a beautiful woman into an ugly creature who became a birdlike creature, killing and drinking blood. In the sixteenth century, when the Spanish conquerors came back from Mexico, they told stories about vampire bats, night fliers, that drank blood from their victims. Also, in the 1840s, *Varney the Vampyre* became very popular; 500,000 words long, it is considered by some to be the longest novel written.

Many of the vampire stories are supposedly true. Calmet, a French monk, wrote about a Hungarian named Arnold Paole, who was bitten by a vampire in Turkey. He soon died, but people in the town where he was buried began to die mysteriously. The townspeople dug up Paole's grave and found his veins were filled with blood, so they drove a stake in his heart, and the body let out a shriek. But the most famous of all vampire stories is Bram Stoker's *Dracula*, which was based on a real man named Vlad Tepov, whose home was in Transylvania. Tepov is reported to have killed over 100,000 people.

Today few people believe in vampires. But, as recently as 1969, an American history professor traveling in Rumania watched the burial of a young girl supposedly bitten by a vampire. The villagers, afraid she would become a vampire, drove a stake through her heart.

For over 2,000 years there have

support your topic sentence. You moved the third paragraph of your first draft to a place it fits better.

A much better developed paragraph. You again use examples to support your topic sentence. You give more specific details of each example so the reader now knows much more than what you gave in your first draft.

Nice use of an anecdote to set us up for your last paragraph. You go from ancient Greece to the present in time.

Much stronger; gives your essay

been tales about vampire-like creatures. But then, they're only stories, right? Still, it might be best to keep a cross handy—just in case!

a nice touch. It also ties in with your title.

Notice how much more developed—not just padded—all the revised paragraphs are. The introductory paragraph uses an anecdote or story to interest us in the essay and also contains a thesis regarding the topic of vampires. Each supporting paragraph has a topic sentence, two of them using the illustration/example method of development and one using another story or anecdote. The concluding paragraph tries to draw a conclusion, but humorously states doubts about the author's conclusion regarding the reality of vampires.

Now take a close look at your first draft. Use the following checklist, and revise your essay as necessary.

_____ 1. Have you revised your opening paragraph so that it draws the reader's interest and has a clear thesis statement?

_____ 2. Does each supporting paragraph in the body of your essay contain a thesis statement that develops your thesis?

_____ 3. Does each supporting paragraph develop your topic sentence; that is, do you say enough to fulfill the key words or phrases in each topic sentence?

_____ 4. Does each paragraph have some kind of method for unifying and developing the main idea?

_____ 5. Does your last paragraph draw a conclusion or summarize your thesis?

_____ 6. Is your last paragraph weak and vague, or does it really conclude your essay topic?

_____ 7. Have you had someone else read your essay for helpful comments and criticism?

Remember, good essays can't be rushed. You may even need to revise your essay a third or fourth time. That's what good writing is all about.

Turn in your essay to your instructor when you've exhausted all you can do to improve it.

UNIT  6

Think...
about stereotyped sex roles

Read...
about sexist language
"Is Language Sexist? One Small Step for Genkind" by Casey Miller and Kate Swift

React...
to the essay

Plan...
an essay
Topics for an Essay

Write...
(A) an outline for your essay
(B) a first draft
(C) transitional devices
Transitional words and expressions
Transition between sentences
Transition within paragraphs
Transition between paragraphs
Practices in transitional usage

Rewrite...
the first draft

Think...

about stereotyped sex roles by answering the following questions.

1. What do you think the role of a typical husband should be? _____

_____

_____

_____

_____

2. What do you think the role of a typical wife should be? _____

_____

_____

_____

_____

3. Why do you think you answered the first two questions as you did? That is, how or where do you think you got your image of a typical husband or wife?

_____

_____

_____

_____

_____

_____

4. List as many specific things as you can that you are or have been exposed to that create or reinforce stereotyped sex roles (magazines, books, parental attitudes, advertisements, and so on).

_____

_____

_____

5. Define the term *sexist*. _____

_____

_____

_____

6. Are you what could be called a sexist? _____

Why? _____

_____

_____

_____

7. Do you ever wish you were the opposite sex from what you are? _____

Why? _____

_____

_____

8. List some words you think are sexist words (chairman, busboy, girlish, and so on).

_____   _____

_____   _____

_____   _____

_____   _____

_____   _____

the following article about sexist language.

The power of language is often ignored by the masses and used to their advantage by those who know how to use it. Language has always been used to discriminate against groups of people. Lately, whether or not language discriminates against women has become a controversial issue. The following essay was first published in *The New York Times Magazine* and has been reprinted frequently. The authors feel that our language is male dominated, so much so that even our word for the human race is male dominated: *man*kind. Notice the numerous examples they give to support their argument and the solution they offer.

As you read about sexist language, notice the way the authors lead into their thesis and some of the paragraph methods used to support their thesis.

Is Language Sexist? One Small Step for Genkind
Casey Miller and Kate Swift

1. A *riddle* is making the rounds that goes like this: A man and his young son were in an automobile accident. The father was killed and the son, who was critically injured, was rushed to a hospital. As attendants wheeled the unconscious boy into the emergency room, the doctor on duty looked down at him and said, "My God, it's my son!" What was the relationship of the doctor to the injured boy?

2. If the answer doesn't jump to your mind, another riddle that has been around a lot longer might help: The blind beggar had a brother. The blind beggar's brother died. The brother who died had no brother. What relation was the blind beggar to the blind beggar's brother?

3. As with all riddles, the answers are obvious once you see them: The doctor was the boy's mother, and the beggar was her brother's sister. Then why doesn't everyone solve them immediately? Mainly because our language, like the culture it reflects, is male-oriented. To say that a woman in medicine is an exception is simply to confirm that statement. Thousands of doctors are women, but in order to be seen in the mind's eye, they must be called women doctors.

4. Except for words that refer to females by definition (mother, actress, con-

"Is Language Sexist? One Small Step for Genkind" by Casey Miller and Kate Swift. From the *New York Times Magazine*, April 16, 1972. Copyright © 1972 by The New York Times Company. Reprinted by permission of Casey Miller and Kate Swift.

gresswoman), and words for occupations traditionally held by females (nurse, secretary, prostitute), the English language defines everyone as male. The hypothetical person ("If a man can walk ten miles in two hours . . . "), the average person ("the man in the street"), and the active person ("the man on the move") are male. The assumption is that unless otherwise identified, people in general—including doctors and beggars—are men. As the beetle-browed and mustachioed man in a Steig cartoon says to his two male drinking companions, "When I speak of mankind, one thing I don't mean is womankind."

5. Semantically speaking, woman is not one with the species of man, but a distinct subspecies. "Man," says the 1971 edition of the *Britannica Junior Encyclopaedia*, "is the highest form of life on earth. His superior intelligence, combined with certain physical characteristics, have enabled man to achieve things that are impossible for other animals." As though quoting the Steig character, still speaking to his friends in McSorely's, the *Junior Encyclopaedia* continues: "Man must invent most of his behavior, because he lacks the instincts of lower animals. . . . Most of the things he learns have been handed down from his ancestors by language and symbols rather than by biological inheritance."

6. Considering that for the last five thousand years society has been patriarchal, that statement explains a lot. It explains why Eve was made from Adam's rib instead of the other way around and who invented all those Adam-rib words like female and woman in the first place. This inheritance through language and other symbols begins in the home (also called a man's castle) where man and wife (not husband and wife, or man and woman) live for a while with their children. It is reinforced by religious training, the educational system, the press, Government, commerce, and the law.

7. Consider some of the examples of language and symbols in American history. When schoolchildren learn from their textbooks that the early colonists gained valuable experience in governing themselves, they are not told that the early colonists who were women were denied the privilege of self-government; when they learn that in the eighteenth century the average man had to manufacture many of the things he and his family needed, they are not told that this "average man" was often a woman who manufactured much of what she and her family needed. Young people learn that intrepid pioneers crossed the country in covered wagons with their wives, children, and cattle; they do not learn that women themselves were intrepid pioneers rather than part of the baggage.

8. Sexist language is any language that expresses such stereotyped attitudes and expectations or assumes the inherent superiority of one sex over the other. When a woman says of her husband, who has drawn up plans for a new bedroom wing and left out closets, "Just like a man," her language is as sexist at the man's who says, after his wife has changed her mind about needing the new wing after all, "Just like a woman."

9. Male and female are not sexist words, but masculine and feminine are as sexist as any words can be, since it is almost impossible to use them without invoking cultural stereotypes. When people construct lists of "masculine" and "feminine" traits they almost always end up making assumptions that have nothing to do with innate differences between the sexes. We have a friend who happens to be going through the process of pinning down this very phenomenon. He is seven years old and his question concerns why his coats and shirts button left over right while his

sister's button the other way. He assumes it must have something to do with the differences between boys and girls, but he can't see how.

10. What our friend has yet to grasp is that the way you button your coat, like most sex-differentiated customs, has nothing to do with real differences but much to do with what society wants you to feel about yourself as a male or female person. Society decrees that it is appropriate for girls to dress differently from boys, to act differently, and to think differently. Boys must be masculine, whatever that means, and girls must be feminine.

11. Unabridged dictionaries are a good source for finding out what society decrees to be appropriate, though less by definition than by their choice of associations and illustrations. Words associated with males—"manly," "virile," and "masculine," for example—are defined through a broad range of positive attributes like strength, courage, directness, and independence, and they are illustrated through such examples of contemporary usage as "a manly determination to face what comes," "a virile literary style," "a masculine love of sports." Corresponding words associated with females are defined with fewer attributes (though weakness is often one of them), and the examples given are generally negative if not clearly pejorative; "feminine wiles," "womanish tears," "a woman-like lack of promptness," "convinced that drawing was a waste of time, if not downright womanly."

12. One dictionary, after defining the word "womanish" as "suitable to or resembling a woman," further defines it as "unsuitable to a man or to a strong character of either sex." Words derived from "sister" and "brother" provide another apt example, for whereas "sissy," applied either to a male or female, conveys the message that sisters are expected to be timid and cowardly, "buddy" makes clear that brothers are friends.

13. The subtle disparagement of females and corresponding approbation of males wrapped up in many English words is painfully illustrated by "tomboy." Here is an instance where a girl who likes sports and the out-of-doors, who is curious about how things work, who is adventurous, and bold instead of passive, is defined in terms of something she is not—a boy. By denying that she can be the person she is and still be a girl, the word surreptitiously undermines her sense of identity: it says she is unnatural. A "tomboy," as defined by one dictionary, is a "girl, especially a young girl who behaves like a spirited boy." But who makes the judgment that she is acting like a spirited boy, not a spirited girl? Can it be a coincidence that in the case of the dictionary just quoted the editor, executive editor, managing editor, general manager, all six members of the Board of Linguists, the usage editor, science editor, all six general editors of definitions, and ninety-four out of the 104 distinguished experts consulted on usage—are men?

14. Possibly because of the negative images associated with womanish and woman-like, and with expressions like "woman driver" and "woman of the street," the word woman dropped out of fashion for a time. The women at the office and the women on the assembly line and the women one first knew in school all became ladies or girls or gals. Now a countermovement, supported by the very term Women's Liberation, is putting back into words like woman and sister and sisterhood the meaning they were losing by default. It is as though, in the nick of time, women had seen that the language itself could destroy them.

15. Some long-standing conventions of the news media add insult to injury. When a woman or girl makes news, her sex is identified at the beginning of a story, if possible in the headline or its equivalent. The assumption, apparently, is that whatever event or action is reported, a woman's involvement is less common and therefore more newsworthy than a man's. If the story is about achievement, the implication is: "Pretty good for a woman." And because people are assumed to be male unless otherwise identified, the media have developed a special and extensive vocabulary to avoid the constant repetition of "woman." The results—"Grandmother Wins Nobel Prize," "Blond Hijacks Airliner," "Housewife to Run for Congress"—convey the kind of information that would be ludicrous in comparable headlines if the subjects were men. Why, if "Unsalaried Husband to Run for Congress" is unacceptable to editors, must women keep explaining that to describe them through external or superficial concerns reflects a sexist view of women as decorative objects, breeding machines, and extensions of men, not real people?

16. Members of the Chicago chapter of the National Organization for Women recently studied the newspapers in their area and drew up a set of guidelines for the press. These included cutting out descriptions of the "clothes, physical features, dating life, and marital status of women where such references would be considered inappropriate if about men"; using language in such a way as to include women in copy that refers to homeowners, scientists, and business people where "newspaper descriptions often convey the idea that all such persons are male"; and displaying the same discretion in printing generalizations about women as would be shown toward racial, religious, and ethnic groups. "Our concern with what we are called may seem trivial to some people," the women said, "but we regard the old usages as symbolic of women's position within this society."

17. Thoughtful writers and editors have begun to repudiate some of the old usages. "Divorcée," "grandmother," and "blonde," along with "vivacious," "pert," "dimpled," and "cute," were dumped by the Washington *Post* in the spring of 1970 by the executive editor, Benjamin Bradlee. In a memo to his staff, Bradlee wrote, "The meaningful equality and dignity of women is properly under scrutiny today . . . because this equality has been less than meaningful and the dignity not always free of stereotype and condescension."

18. What women have been called in the press—or at least the part that operates above ground—is only a fraction of the infinite variety of alternatives to "woman" used in the subcultures of the English-speaking world. Beyond "chicks," "dolls," "dames," "babes," "skirts," and "broads" are the words and phrases in which women are reduced to their sexuality and nothing more. It would be hard to think of another area of language in which the human mind has been so fertile in devising and borrowing abusive terms. In *The Female Eunuch*, Germaine Greer devotes four pages to anatomical terms and words for animals, vegetables, fruits, baked goods, implements, and receptacles, all of which are used to dehumanize the female person. Jean Faust, in an article aptly called "Words That Oppress," suggests that the effort to diminish women through language is rooted in a male fear of sexual inadequacy. "Woman is made to feel guilty for and akin to natural disasters," she writes. "Hurricanes and typhoons are named after her. Any negative or threatening force is given a feminine name. If a man runs into bad luck climbing up the ladder of success (a male-invented game), he refers to the 'bitch goddess' success."

19. The sexual overtones in the ancient and no doubt honorable custom of calling ships "she" have become more explicit and less honorable in an age of air travel: "I'm Karen. Fly me." Attitudes of ridicule, contempt, and disgust toward female sexuality have spawned a rich glossary of insults and epithets not found in dictionaries. And the usage in which four-letter words meaning copulate are interchangeable with cheat, attack, and destroy can scarcely be unrelated to the savagery of rape.

20. Influenced by sexist attitudes, the language of human reproduction lags several centuries behind scientific understanding. The male's contribution to procreation is still described as though it were the entire seed from which a new life grows; the initiative and generative power involved in the process are thought of as masculine, receptivity and nurturance as feminine. "Seminal" remains a synonym for "highly original," and there is no comparable word to describe the female's equivalent contribution.

21. An entire mythology has grown from this biological misunderstanding and its semantic legacy; its embodiment in laws that for centuries made women nonpersons was a key target of the nineteenth-century feminist movement. Today, more than fifty years after women finally won the basic democratic right to vote, the word "liberation" itself, when applied to women, means something less than when used of other groups of people. An advertisement for the NBC news department listed Women's Liberation along with crime in the streets and the Vietnam war as "bad news." Asked for his views on Women's Liberation, a highly placed politician was quoted as saying, "Let me make one thing perfectly clear. I wouldn't want to wake up next to a lady pipe-fitter."

22. When language oppresses, it does so by any means that disparage and belittle. Until well into the twentieth century, one of the ways English was manipulated to disparage women was through the addition of feminine endings to nonsexual words. Thus a woman who aspired to be a poet was excluded from the company of real poets by the label poetess, and a woman who piloted an airplane was denied full status as an aviator by being called an aviatrix. At about the time poetess, aviatrix, and similar Adam-ribbisms were dropping out of use, H. W. Fowler was urging that they be revived. "With the coming expansion of women's vocations," he wrote in the first edition (1926) of *Modern English Usage*, "feminines for vocation-words are a special need of the future." There can be no doubt he subconsciously recognized the downgrading status implied in the -ess designations. His criticism of a woman who wished to be known as an author rather than an authoress was that she had no need "to raise herself to the level of the male author by asserting her right to his name."

23. The demise of most -ess endings came about before the start of the new feminist movement. In the second edition of *Modern English Usage*, published in 1965, Sir Ernest Gowers frankly admitted what his predecessors had been up to. "Feminine designations," he wrote, "seem now to be falling into disuse. Perhaps the explanation of this paradox is that it symbolizes the victory of women in their struggle for equal rights."

24. If Sir Ernest's optimism can be justified, why is there now a movement back toward feminine gender endings in such words as chairwoman, councilwoman, and congresswoman? Betty Hudson of Madison, Connecticut, is campaigning for the adoption of "selectwoman" as the legal title for a female member of that town's executive body. To have to address a woman as "selectman," she maintains, "is not only bad grammar and bad biology, but implies that politics is still, or should be, a man's business."

25. Some women, of course, have yet to learn they are invisible. An eight-year-old who visited the American Museum of Natural History with her Brownie scout troop went through the impressive exhibit on pollution and overpopulation called "Can Man Survive?" Asked, afterward, "Well, can he?" she answered, "I don't know about him, but we're working on it in Brownies."

26. Nowhere are women rendered more invisible by language than in politics. The United States Constitution, in describing the qualification for Representative, Senator, and President, refers to each as "he." No wonder Shirley Chisholm, the second woman since 1888 to make a try for the Presidential nomination of a major party [Margaret Chase Smith entered Presidential primaries in 1964], has found it difficult to be taken seriously.

27. As much as any factor in our language, the ambiguous meaning of "*man*" serves to deny women recognition as people. In a recent magazine article, we discussed the similar effect on women of the generic pronoun "he," which we proposed to replace by a new common-gender pronoun "tey." We were immediately told, by a number of authorities, that we were dabbling in the serious business of linguistics, and the message that reached us from these scholars was loud and clear: It - is - absolutely - impossible - for - anyone - to - introduce- a - new - word - into - the - language - just - because - there - is - a - need - for - it, so - stop - wasting - your-time.

28. When words are suggested like "herstory" for (history), "hissicane" (for hurricane), and "mistresspiece" (for the work of a Virginia Woolf) one suspects a not-too-subtle attempt to make the whole language problem look silly. But unless Alexander Pope, when he wrote "The proper study of mankind is man," meant that women should be relegated to the footnotes (or, as George Orwell might have put it, "All men are equal, but men are more equal than women"), viable new words will surely someday supersede the old.

29. Without apologies to Freud, the great majority of women do not wish in their hearts that they were men. If having grown up with a language that tells them they are at the same time men and not men raises psychic doubts for women, the doubts are not of their sexual identity but of their human identity. Perhaps the present unrest surfacing in the women's movement is part of an evolutionary change in our particular form of life—the one form of all in the animal and plant kingdoms that orders and interprets its reality by symbols. The achievements of the species called man have brought us to the brink of self-destruction. If the species survive into the next century with the expectation of going on, it may only be because we have become part of what Harlow Shapley calls the psychozoic kingdom, where brain overshadows brawn and rationality has replaced superstition.

30. Searching the roots of Western civilization for a word to call this new species of man and woman, someone might come up with "gen," as in genesis and generic. With such a word, "man" could be used exclusively for males as "woman is used for females, for gen would include both sexes. Like the words deer and bison, gen would be both plural and singular. Gen would express the warmth and generalized sexuality of generous, gentle, and genuine: the specific sexuality of genital and genetic. In the new family of gen, girls and boys would grow to genhood, and to speak of genkind would be to include all the people of the earth.

React...

to the essay by answering the following questions.

1. What is the thesis or main idea of the essay? _____

_____

_____

_____

2. How do the authors define sexist language? _____

_____

_____

_____

3. The authors state that *male* and *female* are not sexist words, but that *masculine* and *feminine* are. What are some other words they label as sexist?

_____

_____

_____

4. What do the authors mean when they refer to sexist language as "oppressive"?

_____

_____

_____

5. The author's concluding paragraph draws a conclusion. What is it?

_____

_____

_____

_____

6. Do you agree or disagree with their conclusion? _____

   Why? _____

   _____

   _____

   _____

7. What ideas has reading this essay caused you to think about? _____

   _____

   _____

   _____

8. Check the following words that you do not know or could not use correctly. The number after the word refers to the paragraph in the essay where the word is used.

   _____ a. hypothetical (4)

   _____ b. semantically (5)

   _____ c. patriarchal (6)

   _____ d. inherent (8)

   _____ e. unabridged (11)

   _____ f. pejorative (11)

   _____ g. surreptitiously (13)

   _____ h. ludicrous (15)

   _____ i. discretion (16)

   _____ j. condescension (17)

   Take the time to reread the words as they are used in the paragraphs shown earlier. Then turn to the Vocabulary Section in the Appendix.

Plan...

an essay.

Here are three "think pieces" that may help you get some ideas for essay topics. Read *all* of the dilemmas, and think about them. Your instructor may have class discussions about these dilemmas that may result in more ideas for an essay.

Dilemma A
Sharon is a corporal in the army. She's been working as a clerk in the supply office. Her record has been a good one, and she is up for a promotion to sergeant. When it is discovered that Sharon is the nude centerfold for the recent issue of *Playboy* magazine, her commanding officer brings charges of immoral conduct against her, stating that is is not a good image to project of women in the services. She must face a court-martial. Is the commanding officer right? What should Sharon do and why? What do you think the outcome of the court-martial will be? Why?

Dilemma B
Bob has been busing tables at one of the best restaurants in town for eight months. Two months ago he asked for a waiter's position. His manager told Bob that the next vacancy for a waiter or waitress would be his. Yesterday, Bob noticed a new young woman waiting tables. When he asked his manager why he was not given the new position as promised, he was told that the restaurant needed a woman waitress because there were already too many men working there. Bob was so angry he almost hit the manager. What should Bob do?

Dilemma C
You have a father who tends to talk down to women. He seems to patronize and condescend to women in conversations. His tone is like that of a parent speaking to a child or of the master of the house speaking to a servant, depending upon his mood. At a party you hear him say, "Men are superior to women. We're bigger and stronger physically. We have historically been the breadwinner for the family, playing the tough games of running business and wars." Believing that "father knows best," your father feels that women should be clinging vines, inferior to the one who wears the pants in the family. Though you have not paid attention before, you realize that your mother has supported him in his beliefs. You have been dating someone you love deeply and may want to marry, but you are afraid to introduce your father to that person. What should you do?

Practice 1. In your journal notebook or on a separate page, spend 10–15 minutes freewriting. Before you start, review your answers to the THINK and REACT sections in this unit, as well as your thoughts about the dilemmas you just read. Perhaps in your freewriting some ideas for an essay will creep in.

Practice 2. Now plan an essay on some aspect of sexism. Let us hope that you have some ideas of your own. If not, here are some topics to think about. Feel free to change them to suit *you*.

1. Why (men, women, adolescents) dress as they do.
2. Sexist laws that should be changed.
3. *Playboy* magazine's image of women.
4. *Playgirl* magazine's image of men.
5. Advertisements that stereotype people.
6. Why there will/will never be a woman president of the United States.
7. The difference between male and female and masculinity and femininity.
8. How slang words create sex stereotypes.
9. What pronography reveals about male/female roles.
10. "I want a girl, just like the girl that married dear old dad."
11. How or why women are discriminated against in certain jobs.
12. What women are doing to raise men's consciousness.
13. Why men generally feel superior to women.
14. Why women generally feel superior to men.
15. Why little boys should be allowed to cry.
16. Why women should/should not be drafted.
17. Pick you own topic related to sex roles.

In the space below, write the topic or subject you've picked for an essay. Make certain it's not too broad or too narrow for a five-to-six paragraph essay.

Topic:

_____

_____

Practice 3. Now write a possible thesis for your topic.

Tentative Thesis Statement:

_____

_____

_____

_____

Below, list all the ideas you can think of to support your thesis.

_____

_____

_____

_____

_____

_____

_____

_____

_____

Write...

(A) an outline for your essay.

Do an outline on a sheet of paper, and have your instructor check it for you.

(B) a first draft based on the outline you had your instructor check.

 Quick Review

Summary of Methods Used for Introductory Paragraphs
1. Ask a question.
2. Use an anecdote.
3. Use a quotation.
4. Give a brief overview.
5. Stress importance of topic.
6. Use a combination of methods.

Summary of Paragraph Methods for Supporting Details
1. Examples or illustrations.
2. Specific details.
3. Definition of terms.
4. Comparison or contrast.
5. Analysis.
6. Story or anecdote.
7. Combination of methods.

Summary of Methods Used for Concluding Paragraphs
1. Ask a question.
2. Use an anecdote.
3. Summarize.
4. Show concern.
5. Make conclusions.

If you need to do so, refer back to previous units for a quick review of methods for developing introductory paragraphs, topic sentence control, and concluding paragraphs. Try to state your thesis regarding your topic in your opening paragraph. Do this on a separate piece of paper; then return here.

(C) transitional devices or words and expressions.

Now that you have completed your essay, you should check it for *transitional expressions. Transition* refers to moving from one idea to another. For your essay to read smoothly, you need to use *transitional words or expressions* that enable your reader to move smoothly from one idea to the next, both between sentences and between one paragraph and the other. Doing so will give your reader the feeling of a unified or cohesive essay.

Notice how the following sentence with a transitional expression reads more smoothly than the sentences without any.

1. *with transitional expression*

   I like going to the movies, *but* I can't afford to go very often.

2. *without transitional expression*

   I like going to the movies. I can't afford to go very often.

In the example without the transitional word *but,* the two sentences seem abrupt and unrelated. One sentence deals with liking to go to the movies; the other one deals with not being able to afford to go often. But when the two sentences are used as one with the transitional word *but,* the two ideas are linked together smoothly.

Here is another example:

1. *with transitional expression*

   John said he was going to the game *even though* his mother said he couldn't go.

2. *without transitional expression*

   John said he was going to the game. His mother said he couldn't go.

Again, notice how the transitional expression *even though* gives the two thoughts a smoother connection. You could, of course, change the sentence with the transitional expression coming first, such as: Even though his mother said he couldn't go, John said he was going to the game. The meaning has not changed, but the sentence is more sophisticated and more coherent than making two separate sentences.

List of Useful Transitional Words and Expressions

1. *Words to use to tell your reader more of the same idea is coming:*

   also, additionally, in addition, and, besides, equally important, further, furthermore, moreover, next, finally

2. *Words to use to show sequence of events:*

   first, second, third, *and so forth,* next, then, last, finally, after, afterward, previously

3. *Words to use to show time relationships:*

   first, second, third, *and so forth,* meanwhile, soon, soon after, afterward, later, after a few days, after a while, immediately, yesterday, today, tomorrow

4. *Words to use to show a place or position:*

   adjacent to, above, across, beyond, below, under, on the opposite side, to the left, to the right, in the background, in the foreground, nearby, close at hand

5. *Words to use to compare things:*

   like, likewise, similarly, in the same manner, also

6. *Words to use to contrast things:*

   however, nevertheless, but, yet, on the contrary, although, at the same time, even so, even though, conversely, on the other hand, still

7. *Words to use to draw a conclusion:*

   therefore, thus, consequently, as a result, finally, accordingly, as a consequence, in conclusion, due to, for these reasons

8. *Words to use to emphasize a point:*

   to repeat, in fact, truly, again, indeed, to this end, with this in mind, for this purpose

9. *Words to use to emphasize an example:*

   for example, for instance, a case in point, as an illustration

10. *Words to use in summarizing a point:*

   to sum up, in summary, this, in brief, in short, as I have said, in conclusion, therefore, consequently, as has been noted, in any event, to conclude, as a result

Practices in Using Transitional Expressions Between Sentences

Practice 1. Using the list of transitional words and expressions on the previous page, circle the transitional words and expressions used in the following sentences. In the blanks, write the number from the above list that explains the function of the transitional words.

_____ 1. She didn't believe what he said; furthermore, she even set about proving he lied.

_____ 2. It is really a simple test. First, get your interests ready. . .

_____ 3. It is necessary to have some background regarding the matter. For this reason, I have prepared this report.

_____ 4. He wanted to prove his point. In fact, he spent hours of research to do so.

_____ 5. The police found it in his car. As a result, they arrested him.

_____ 6. His leg was broken and his wrist badly sprained. In spite of this, he managed to crawl back to camp.

_____ 7. The attorney was accused of attempted bribery in the case; however, it was never proved.

_____ 8. Time ran out. Thus, the game ended with no score.

_____ 9. Now is the time to become concerned with the future use of nuclear power. In particular, we must address ourselves to the use of nuclear power as a source of electricity.

_____ 10. Jones's case was dismissed. Similarly, so were the charges against Smith.

Practice 2. Again using the list of transitional words and expressions, select the words or expressions that best fit the following sentences. When more than one expression can be used, insert the others as well.

1. No one wanted to listen to him. _____, they all left.

2. The procedure is simple. _____, place the key here. _____, turn it to the left.

3. She felt sure she would never make it to the end. _____, she kept trying.

4. No one would speak up in his behalf. _____, the teacher blamed it on him.

5. The doctor treated the patient with a new medicine. _____, other doctors have been trying it.

6. It was a year of many disastrous events. ______________________, very little was accomplished.
7. The issues are vital and pressing. ______________________, these points must be considered before any action is taken.
8. ______________________ the evidence was damaging, he managed to get off with a warning.
9. She wanted to do a good job. ______________________, she prepared herself for the task by taking a night course on the subject.
10. We can see the end result by examining the facts. ______________________, this does not mean it will ever happen again.

Transitional Words and Expressions Within Paragraphs

Transitional words and expression are often necessary within paragraphs in order to make clear the arrangement of the ideas being expressed. Notice the use of transitional words in the example below.

Transitional aids

In summary, Commager states that there are at least six common characteristics of the American. First is his carelessness regarding manners, dress, food, social relationships, education, and politics. Second, his generousness or openhandedness in giving to churches, schools, hospitals, and the like. Third, is the American's self-indulgence regarding comfort and luxury. Still another characteristic is his sentimentality toward his children, his alma mater, his history. Fifth is his gregariousness or friendliness. And last is his quest for materialism.

The use of such transitional devices aids the reader in keeping track of the characteristics being summarized. When you check over your written paragraphs, see if there is a need to insert transitional words to clarify what you are presenting to your reader.

Practices in Using Transitional Words and Expressions Within Paragraphs

Practice 3. Circle the transitional words and phrases in the following sample paragraphs.

A. As has been noted, the need for courses in social consciousness is now. It is more important than ever that educational institutions make students aware of their responsibilities as educated citizens. However, such courses must not become courses merely on theory, but application as well.

B. Most people actually know very little about the American Indian. For example, the stereotyped Indian seen in movies and television is one who wears bright feathered bonnets and war paint, rides bareback, and screeches, "Yip, Yip, Yip," as he attacks the circled wagon train. This, then, is most commonly thought of as "the Indian." In contrast to this, the Indian actually has a very diverse history, a social background and language difference.

Practice 4. Write a paragraph on a separate piece of paper, deliberately using the following transitional words or phrases.

a. first
b. second
c. third
d. in addition
e. finally
f. thus or finally

Transitional Words and Expressions Between Paragraphs

Transitions between one paragraph and the next are also necessary for a smooth reading essay. You already know that each paragraph deals with a single topic or idea. When a new paragraph is started, it is important that you ease your reader from the ideas in the preceding paragraphs to the next. Notice how this is done in the example below.

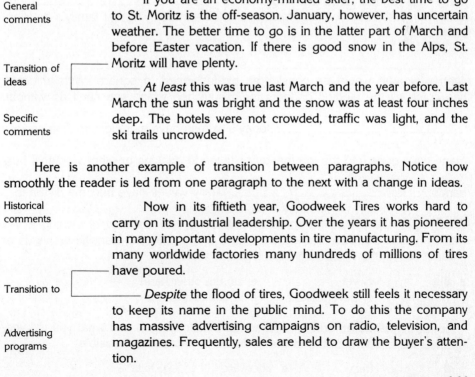

General comments

    If you are an economy-minded skier, the best time to go to St. Moritz is the off-season. January, however, has uncertain weather. The better time to go is in the latter part of March and before Easter vacation. If there is good snow in the Alps, St.

Transition of ideas

Moritz will have plenty.

Specific comments

    At least this was true last March and the year before. Last March the sun was bright and the snow was at least four inches deep. The hotels were not crowded, traffic was light, and the ski trails uncrowded.

Here is another example of transition between paragraphs. Notice how smoothly the reader is led from one paragraph to the next with a change in ideas.

Historical comments

    Now in its fiftieth year, Goodweek Tires works hard to carry on its industrial leadership. Over the years it has pioneered in many important developments in tire manufacturing. From its many worldwide factories many hundreds of millions of tires have poured.

Transition to

    Despite the flood of tires, Goodweek still feels it necessary to keep its name in the public mind. To do this the company has massive advertising campaigns on radio, television, and magazines. Frequently, sales are held to draw the buyer's attention.

Advertising programs

Practices in Using Transitional Words and Expressions Between Paragraphs

Practice 5. In the blanks, supply transitional words or phrases from the list below to make the following two paragraphs read more smoothly.

also	today
for example	in those days
in the past	in fact
last	second
as a consequence	as a result

_____ the housewife was the guardian of the

children. _____ she gave them their early education

and initiated them into principles of religion. _____,

she taught them respect for others. She _____ taught

them to take care of material goods, and _____ she

made them understand the work ethic. _____ the
housewife was busy cooking, making clothes and enjoying her family's development.

_____ such a woman is rare. _____
such a woman would be considered old-fashioned, a square. With affluence
has come all the electric gadgets for her kitchen which she can't do without.

_____, today's women have more leisure time and too

many have gone into the job market or taken to drinking or other women's hus-

bands. _____, family values have become distorted.

Practice 6. Write two paragraphs contrasting the economy of owning a VW with owning a Cadillac. Use at least three of the following transitional words or phrases to link the two paragraphs together smoothly.

a. but	c. yet	e. on the other hand
b. however	d. nevertheless	f. in contrast to this

Practice 7. Write at least two paragraphs describing in part what you did yesterday. Use as many of the following words or phrases as possible.

a. then	c. after	e. afterward	g. later
b. next	d. meanwhile	f. subsequently	h. finally

Rewrite...
your first draft.

In Unit 2 you read an essay by Neil Postman, "Schools as Thermostats." Below, part of his essay is reprinted with all the transitional devices removed alongside Postman's final draft. Notice how much easier it is to follow his ideas when transitional devices are used.

Transitional Devices Removed	**Final Draft with Transitional Devices**
. . . The media teach many things. I should like to mention four of their biases which are in special need of opposition by the schools. The media are attention-centered. Their main goal is to capture and to hold the attention of their audiences. The content of media is of little importance. Its only function is as bait.	. . . The media teach many things, *of course, but* I should like to mention four of their biases which are in special need of opposition by the schools. The media are, *first of all,* attention-centered. Their main goal is to capture and to hold the attention of their audiences. The content of media is of little importance. *In the end,* its only function is as bait.
The media are vastly entertaining. Nothing will appear on TV or the movie screen outside of school unless it has "entertaining value." This means it must not be demanding or disturbing. The audience will turn away.	*Second,* the media are vastly entertaining. Nothing will appear on TV or the movie screen outside of school unless it has "entertaining value." This means it must not be demanding or disturbing; *for if it is,* the audience will turn away.
The media, especially TV, are image-centered. TV consists of fast-moving, continuously changing visual images which compress time. The average length of a shot on "The Love Boat" is about three seconds. On commercials, the average length of a shot is two seconds. TV and movies work against the development of language.	*Third,* the media, especially TV, are image-centered. TV consists of fast-moving, continuously changing visual images which compress time. The average length of a shot on "The Love Boat," *for instance,* is about three seconds. On commercials, the average length of a shot is two seconds. *Thus* TV, *as well as* movies, work against the development of language.
Most of what children see on TV and in movies takes the form of stories	*And finally,* most of what children see on TV and in the movies takes the form of stories. . . .

Though there is nothing "wrong" with the lack of transitional devices in the first column, it is not as easy to follow as the final draft's use of words and phrases, such as *first of all, in the end, second, third, thus,* and the like. As readers, we can keep better track of new ideas, of comparisons and contrasts, and summaries of certain key points. Transitional devices, then, can be used to strengthen and clarify your major points of development.

Use the following checklist as a guide for rewriting your first draft.

_____ 1. Does your opening paragraph create interest in your topic and contain a thesis that is not too broad or too narrow?

_____ 2. Do each of your supporting paragraphs contain a topic sentence?

_____ 3. Do you stick to the development of the topic sentence in each paragraph?

_____ 4. Does your final paragraph make a conclusion or give a summary related to your thesis?

_____ 5. Have you used transitional devices where they are needed for smooth movement from sentence to sentence and paragraph to paragraph?

_____ 6. Have you remembered to follow the advice of Paul Roberts in his essay "How to Say Nothing in 500 Words"?

_____ 7. Have you had one or two others read your essay for helpful comments and criticism?

When you've done the best you can, turn in your essay to your instructor.

UNIT

Think. . .

about social movements in America

Read. . .

about a Chicano's struggle with one social movement
"None of This Is Fair" by Richard Rodriguez

React. . .

to the essay

Plan. . .

an essay
Topics for an essay

Write. . .

(A) an outline for an essay
(B) a first draft for an essay
(C) correct sentences
Sentence fragments
Run-on or fused sentences
Comma splices
Practices in writing correct sentences

Rewrite. . .

your first draft

Think...

about social movements in America by answering the following questions.

1. Social movements generally occur when certain groups who feel they are not being treated equitably band together for change. What social move-

   ments have you witnessed in your lifetime? _____

   _____

   _____

2. During the early 1960s, blacks drew much attention to their problems of un-equal housing, employment, jobs and to other discriminatory practices. Did the protesting and civil rights rallies bring about changes for the better?

   _____ Why do you think so? _____

   _____

   _____

3. What problems still exist for blacks today? _____

   _____

4. In the late 1960s and early 1970s, a movement known as "Women's Liber-ation" gained momentum and attention. How do you feel about "Women's Liberation"?

   _____

   _____

   _____

5. Another social movement in the early 1970s was the push by certain anti-Vietnam War advocates and some veterans to establish amnesty for those persons who left the country or refused to fight in Vietnam. Do you feel amnesty should be granted to those persons who refused to go to war?

_____ Why? _____

_____

_____

6. A social movement called "Gay Liberation" in certain parts of the United States also gained prominence in the news in the early 1970s. Homosexuals banded together in attempts to show the discrimination they felt was taking place against them. What are your feelings toward such a social movement?

_____

_____

_____

7. One social movement that has gained popularity on and off over several hundred years is the awareness of the American Indian's problems. Both historically as well as today, what are some of the problems facing the American Indian? _____

_____

_____

8. Another social movement was the establishment of Affirmative Action to ensure that minority groups were admitted to schools and jobs that before appeared closed to them. Do you feel there should be quotas established to provide opportunities to minorities? _____ Why?

_____

_____

_____

about a Chicano's struggle with one social movement.

The following essay was written by one who has been affected deeply by a social movement's by-product—Affirmative Action. Richard Rodriguez received a B.A. in English from Stanford University and an M.A. in philosophy from Columbia University and studied at the Warburg Institute in London and in the doctoral program at the University of California, Berkeley. He dropped out of the doctoral program for reasons he explains in the following essay. Rodriguez shows us the pressures felt by one who was theoretically being helped by a social movement.

None of This Is Fair
Richard Rodriguez

1. My plan to become a professor of English—my ambition during long years in college at Stanford, then in graduate school at Columbia, and Berkeley—was complicated by feelings of embarrassment and guilt. So many times I would see other Mexican-Americans and know we were alike only in race. And yet, simply because our race was the same, I was, during the last years of my schooling, the beneficiary of their situation. Affirmative Action programs had made it all possible. The disadvantages of others permitted my promotion; the absence of many Mexican-Americans from academic life allowed my designation as a "minority student."

2. For me opportunities had been extravagant. There were fellowships, summer research grants, and teaching assistantships. After only two years in graduate school, I was offered teaching jobs by several colleges. Invitations to Washington conferences arrived and I had the chance to travel abroad as a "Mexican-American representative." The benefits were often, however, too gaudy to please. In three published essays, in conversations with teachers, in letters to politicians and at conferences, I worried the issue of Affirmative Action. Often I proposed contradictory opinions. Though consistent was the admission that—because of an early, excellent education—I was no longer a principal victim of racism or any other social oppression. I said that but still I continued to indicate on applications for financial aid that I was a Hispanic-American. It didn't really occur to me to say anything else, or to leave the question unanswered.

3. Thus I complied with and encouraged the odd bureaucratic logic of Affirmative Action. I let government officials treat the disadvantaged condition of many

Mexican-Americans with my advancement. Each fall my presence was noted by Health, Education, and Welfare department statisticians. As I pursued advanced literary studies and learned the skill of reading Spenser and Wordsworth and Empson, I would hear myself numbered among the culturally disadvantaged. Still, silent, I didn't object.

4. But the irony cut deep. And guilt would not be evaded by averting my glance when I confronted a face like my own in a crowd. By late 1975, nearing the completion of my graduate studies at Berkeley, I was so wary of the benefits of Affirmative Action that I feared my inevitable success as an applicant for a teaching position. The months of fall—traditionally that time of academic job-searching— passed without my applying to a single school. When one of my professors chanced to learn this in late November, he was astonished, then furious. He yelled at me: Did I think that because I was a minority student jobs would just come looking for me? What was I thinking? Did I realize that he and several other faculty members had already written letters on my behalf? Was I going to start acting like some other minority students he had known? They struggled for success and then, when it was almost within reach, grew strangely afraid and let it pass. Was that it? Was I determined to fail?

5. I did not respond to his questions. I didn't want to admit to him, and thus to myself, the reason I delayed.

6. I merely agreed to write to several schools. (In my letter I wrote: "I cannot claim to represent disadvantaged Mexican-Americans. The very fact that I am in a position to apply for this job should make that clear.") After two or three days, there were telegrams and phone calls, invitations to interviews, then airplane trips. A blur of faces and the murmur of their soft questions. And, over someone's shoulder, the sight of campus buildings shadowing pictures I had seen years before when I leafed through Ivy League catalogues with great expectations. At the end of each visit, interviewers would smile and wonder if I had any questions. A few times I quietly wondered what advantage my race had given me over other applicants. But that was an impossible question for them to answer without embarrassing me. Quickly, several persons insisted that my ethnic identity had given me no more than a "foot inside the door"; at most, I had a "slight edge" over other applicants. "We just looked at your dossier with extra care and we like what we saw. There was never any question of having to alter our standards. You can be certain of that."

7. In the early part of January, offers arrived on stiffly elegant stationery. Most schools promised terms appropriate for any new assistant professor. A few made matters worse—and almost more tempting—by offering more: the use of university housing; an unusually large starting salary; a reduced teaching schedule. As the stack of letters mounted, my hesitation increased. I started calling department chairmen to ask for another week, then 10 more days—"more time to reach a decision"—to avoid the decision I would need to make.

8. At school, meantime, some students hadn't received a single job offer. One man, probably the best student in the department, did not even get a request for his dossier. He and I met outside a classroom one day and he asked about my opportunities. He seemed happy for me. Faculty members beamed. They said they had expected it. "After all, not many schools are going to pass up getting a Chicano with a Ph.D. in Renaissance literature," somebody said laughing. Friends wanted to know which of the offers I was going to accept. But I couldn't make up my mind. February came and I was running out of time and excuses. (One chairman guessed my delay was a bargaining ploy and increased his offer with each of my calls.) I had to promise a decision by the 10th; the 12th at the very latest.

9. On the 18th of February, late in the afternoon, I was in the office I shared with several other teaching assistants. Another graduate student was sitting across the room at his desk. When I got up to leave, he looked over to say in an uneventful voice that he had some big news. He had finally decided to accept a position at a faraway university. It was not a job he especially wanted, he admitted. But he had to take it because there hadn't been any other offers. He felt trapped, and depressed, since his job would separate him from his young daughter.

10. I tried to encourage him by remarking that he was lucky at least to have found a job. So many others hadn't been able to get anything. But before I finished speaking I realized that I had said the wrong thing. And I anticipated his next question.

11. "What are your plans?" he wanted to know. "Is it true you've gotten an offer from Yale?"

12. I said that it was. "Only, I still haven't made up my mind."

13. He stared at me as I put on my jacket. And smiling, then unsmiling, he asked if I knew that he too had written to Yale. In his case, however, no one had bothered to acknowledge his letter with even a postcard. What did I think of that?

14. He gave me no time to answer.

15. "Damn!" he said sharply and his chair rasped the floor as he pushed himself back. Suddenly, it was to *me* that he was complaining. "It's just not right, Richard. None of this is fair. You've done some good work, but so have I. I'll bet our records are just about equal. But when we look for jobs this year, it's a different story. You get all of the breaks."

16. To evade his criticism, I wanted to side with him. I was about to admit the injustice of Affirmative Action. But he went on, his voice hard with accusation. "It's all very simple this year. You're a Chicano. And I am a Jew. That's the only real difference between us."

17. His words stung me: there was nothing he was telling me that I didn't know. I had admitted everything already. But to hear someone else say these things, and in such an accusing tone, was suddenly hard to take. In a deceptively calm voice, I responded that he had simplified the whole issue. The phrases came like bubbles to the tip of my tongue: "new blood"; "the importance of cultural diversity"; "the goal of racial integration." These were all the arguments I had proposed several years ago—and had long since abandoned. Of course the offers were unjustifiable. I knew that. All I was saying amounted to a frantic self-defense. I tried to find an end to a sentence. My voice faltered to a stop.

18. "Yeah, sure," he said. "I've heard all that before. Nothing you say really changes the fact that Affirmative Action is unfair. You see that, don't you? There isn't any way for me to compete with you. Once there were quotas to keep my parents out of certain schools; now there are quotas to get you in and the effect on me is the same as it was for them."

19. I listened to every word he spoke. But my mind was really on something else. I knew at that moment that I would reject all of the offers. I stood there

silently surprised by what an easy conclusion it was. Having prepared for so many years to teach, having trained myself to do nothing else, I had hesitated out of practical fear. But now that it was made, the decision came with relief. I immediately knew I had made the right choice.

20. My colleague continued talking and I realized that he was simply right. Affirmative Action programs *are* unfair to white students. But as I listened to him assert his rights, I thought of the seriously disadvantaged. How different they were from white, middle-class students who come armed with the testimony of their grades and aptitude scores and self-confidence to complain about the unequal treatment they now receive. I listen to them. I do not want to be careless about what they say. Their rights are important to protect. But inevitably when I hear them or their lawyers, I think about the most seriously disadvantaged, not simply Mexican-Americans, but all of those who do not ever imagine themselves going to college or becoming doctors: white, black, brown. Always poor. Silent. They are not plaintiffs before the court or against the misdirection of Affirmative Action. They lack the confidence (my confidence!) to assume their right to a good education. They lack the confidence and skills a good primary and secondary education provides and which are prerequisites for informed public life. They remain silent.

21. The debate drones on and surrounds them in stillness. They are distant, faraway figures like boys I have seen peering down from freeway overpasses in some other part of town.

React...

to the essay by answering the following questions.

1. What is the *thesis* or main idea of this essay?

_____

_____

2. Do you agree with the thesis? _____

   Why? _____

   _____

3. What paragraph writing pattern or patterns are used in the following?

   a. paragraph 2: _____

   b. paragraph 3: _____

   c. paragraph 7: _____

   d. paragraph 9: _____
4. What makes Rodriguez's concluding paragraph different from those you've studied so far?

   _____

   _____

5. Why does Rodriguez decide to abandon his career he had been planning for years?

   _____

   _____

   _____

6. What is your opinion of Rodriguez and his decision? _____

_____

_____

7. Check each of the following words or phrases you don't know or could not use correctly.

_____ a. beneficiary (1)

_____ b. gaudy (2)

_____ c. oppression (2)

_____ d. complied (3)

_____ e. evaded (4 and 16)

_____ f. dossier (6 and 8)

_____ g. ploy (8)

_____ h. diversify (17)

_____ i. plaintiffs (20)

_____ j. drones on (21)

Reread the words you checked as they are used in the paragraphs shown. Then turn to the Vocabulary Section in the Appendix for more information and practice with them.

Plan...

an essay.

Here are two dilemmas that may provide you with an idea or two for an essay. Read both, think about them, and perhaps discuss everyone's reactions in class. Compare your ideas with those of others.

Dilemma A
You've been working at the same job for twelve years. Suddenly, because of the economy, you find yourself without a job. You spend weeks looking for a job and finally find one. However, it pays about the same amount you would receive if you went on unemployment. In fact, if you stayed unemployed long enough, you could go on the welfare program, receive food stamps, and be better off than if you worked on a job you didn't really like. What are you going to do and why? Are welfare and unemployment programs worthwhile social programs for your well-being?

Dilemma B
Mitch manages the only grocery store in a rural lettuce growing area. The field hands, primarily migrant Mexican farm workers, go on strike for better wages and working conditions. The farmers, one of whom also owns the grocery store, let Mitch know that if the strike continues and the farm workers ask for credit, he is not to give it to them. Soon, however, farmers approach Mitch for credit for food during the strike. Mitch knows he will lose his job if he does. What should he do? Why?

Practice 1. In your journal notebook or on a separate page, spend 10 to 15 minutes freewriting or tinkering with an idea for an essay. Before you start, review your answers to the THINK and REACT sections in this unit, as well as your thoughts about the dilemmas you just read.

Practice 2. Now plan an essay on some aspect of social values or movements. Let us hope you have some ideas of your own. If not, here are some topics to think about. Feel free to change them to something you can handle.

1. The plight of the migrant farm workers.
2. The problem of illegal aliens.
3. The future of the (black, Indian or Mexican-American) in America.
4. Why racial problems will increase (or decrease) during the next ten years.
5. The Gay Liberation Movement.
6. What's a "minority" group?
7. Why laws won't change prejudice.
8. What "liberation" means.

9. Social problems our children will face.
10. What it is like to be a member of a minority.
11. The pros/cons of Affirmative Action.
12. Who should get scholarships?
13. Why women should/should not be drafted.
14. The problems with welfare programs.
15. Who deserves food stamps?

In the space below, write the topic or subject you've picked for an essay. Make certain it is not too broad or too narrow.

Topic:

_____

_____

Practice 3.   Now write a working thesis for your topic.

Tentative Thesis Statement:

_____

_____

_____

_____

Below, list all the ideas you can think of to support your thesis.

_____

_____

_____

_____

_____

_____

_____

_____

_____

Write...

(A) an outline for your first draft based on your rearranged list of supporting details.

Do an outline on a separate sheet of paper. Then go on to *(B)*.

(B) a first draft.

On still another sheet of paper, write your first draft of your essay based on the outline you did in *(A)*. Feel free to alter or change your rough draft from the outline if you feel the change is for the better. *Your outline is only a guide for writing, not the final word.* When finished, go on to *(C)*.

(C) correct sentences.

Among the common errors found in college freshman compositions are (1) sentence fragments, (2) run-on or fused sentences, and (3) comma splices. Each of these improper sentence formations is now explained.

Sentence Fragments

Sentence fragments are sentences that are not complete. They are just fragments or pieces of sentences. Usually, sentence fragments are incomplete because the subject or the verb of the sentence is missing. Sometimes a sentence fragment is created by the wrong punctuation. Still other times, a fragment is created because of a missing object. Here are some examples.

1. Examples of fragments caused by a missing subject

The subject of a sentence is that part of a sentence *about* which something is said. For instance, in the sentence "The man sat on a chair," *man* is the subject. If the subject were left out it would read, "Sat on a chair" and thus be a fragment.

    a. Everyone enjoyed her cake. Made it yesterday afternoon. (Notice that the second sentence needs the subject "She." Otherwise, we don't know who [subject] made the cake yesterday.)

b. During the half time, the football team was "chewed out" by the coach. Listened uncomfortably. (The second sentence needs the subject "They." Without the subject, we don't know who listened carefully.)

This type of fragment is usually caused by carelessness in writing or by assuming your reader knows whom you are talking about. Remember, every sentence must have a subject unless it is a command where the "you" is implied, such as:

Go to the store for me. ("You" is understood.)
Hurry downstairs! ("You" is understood.)
Drop dead! ("You" is understood.)

Check Your Understanding

Which of the following are sentence fragments? If a subject is missing, supply one.

1. Run to Jerry's house, and borrow some milk.
2. Made his way through the crowd.
3. Shut the door, please.
4. Finished the job and cleaned up after himself.

2. Examples of sentence fragments caused by a missing verb

The verb (often called predicate) of a sentence is the word or words that say something about the subject. In the sentence "The man sat on a chair," *sat* is the verb because it tells what the subject is doing. If the sentence read, "The man on a chair," it would be a fragment.

    a. Around the corner, Jack and his dog. (What did Jack and his dog do? There's no verb to tell us.)
    b. The man who came to the house. (What did the man who came to the house do? There is no verb to tell us.)
    c. A famous author with many books to his credit. (Again, there is no verb to tell us what the author is doing.)

The examples above all fail to tell us what the subject of the sentence is doing. Verbs, besides describing a subject, also tell us what is happening. Notice the connections from fragments to complete sentences.

    a. Around the corner, Jack and his dog *stopped* at a fireplug.
    b. The man who came to the house was *selling* real estate.
    c. A famous author with many books to his credit *gave* a lecture at school.

Check Your Understanding

Which of the following sentences are fragments? Supply any missing subjects or verbs.

1. Near the end of the pier, John and Mary.
2. The dentist with the pretty assistant.
3. Watched the television show very carefully.
4. John, the president of his class.
5. Watch the game on Saturday.

3. Examples of sentence fragments caused by the wrong punctuation

Notice in the following sentences how incorrect punctuation causes sentence fragments.

> Wrong: He ran into a tree. Because he was sleepy.
> Right: He ran into a tree because he was sleepy.
> Or: Because he was sleepy, he ran into a tree.
> Wrong: If I arrive late. I will get more demerits.
> Right: If I arrive late, I will get more demerits.
> Wrong: I will get more demerits. If I arrive late.
> Right: I will get more demerits if I arrive late.
> Wrong: While I was gone. The house was robbed.
> Right: While I was gone, the house was robbed.
> Or: The house was robbed while I was gone.

Check Your Understanding

Which of the following sentences are fragments? Correct any fragment so that it is a complete sentence.

1. I was happy. Because finals were over.
2. An idea that appealed to us.
3. He slipped and fell. Walking across the campus.
4. Close the door, please. Before it gets cold.
5. The teacher with the red hair.

4. Examples of sentence fragment "cliff-hangers"

Many sentence fragments are like "cliff-hanger" stories or movies that don't have clear or understandable endings and leave you "hanging in the air" regarding what happened. These types of sentence fragments are dependent clauses, which means they are dependent on a more complete statement to complete the thought. Notice the following examples.

> a. After the party was over. (What happened after the party?)
> b. Until I arrive home. ("Until I arrive . . ." where? what?)
> c. If John wants to go. ("If" what?)
> d. Because the end of the project is nearing completion. ("Because" what?)
> e. While the teacher talked about verbs. (What happened while the teacher talked?)

Also notice in the preceding sentences that they would be complete and not fragments if the first word were left off. But with "cliff-hanger" words they are all dependent on something more for a complete thought. Avoid beginning sentences with "cliff-hanger" words that can cause fragments unless you complete the whole thought of the sentence.

Here are some cliff-hanger words. If you use them in sentences you write, check to make certain you have written a complete thought.

after	because	although
until	unless	that
if	where	what
since	when	how
while	as	before
rather	inasmuch as	with

Check Your Understanding

Correct any of the following sentence fragments.

1. If you never go to school.

_____

2. Because I thought I saw you there.

_____

3. As we all left together.

_____

4. Unless you think we should drive separate cars.

_____

5. Until the bell rang.

_____

Run-On or Fused Sentences

A run-on or fused sentence is created when a writer fails to use correct punctuation and capitalization between two or more independent sentences. In other words, the sentences "run-on" together, or else they are "fused" together by improper punctuation. Notice the following examples.

Wrong: My mother is coming home tomorrow I'm going to meet her.
Right: My mother is coming home tomorrow. I'm going to meet her.
Wrong: Hemingway wrote *The Old Man and the Sea* he won the Pulitzer Prize for it.

Right: Hemingway wrote *The Old Man and the Sea.* He won the Pulitzer Prize for it.
Wrong: Mike pushed his bike up the hill Carl rode his.
Right: Mike pushed his bike up the hill. Carl rode his.
Or: Mike pushed his bike up the hill; however, Carl rode his. (Note the use of a semicolon and a transitional word.)
Wrong: He enjoys watching them practice he thinks they are good players.
Right: He enjoys watching them practice. He thinks they are good players.
Or: He enjoys watching them practice because he thinks they are good players. (Note the use of the transitional word rather than punctuation.)

The main thing to remember about run-on sentences is that they confuse your reader by not providing the proper pause for thought control. Correct punctuation or transitional devices (as mentioned in Unit 6) will help you avoid writing run-on sentences.

 ## Check Your Understanding

Correct any sentence that is a run-on or fused sentence.

1. I went to the theater I sat in the last row.
2. Her name is Sally she was raised in Missouri.
3. I waited in line a long time it made me very impatient.
4. Because of his voice, he was asked to be the announcer on the program for next week.
5. John came to take Gayle to the movies she had already left, however.

Comma Splices

To splice means "to link" or "join together." Comma splices are created when a writer splices or attempts to link two sentences together with a comma. In other words, two completely different sentences or complete thoughts are connected with a comma rather than with the correct punctuation. Notice the following examples.

Wrong: We packed all our luggage, then we were on our way.
Right: We packed all our luggage. Then we were on our way.
Wrong: Highway 5 is a very busy road, thousands of trucks, cars, and motorcycles use it every day.
Right: Highway 5 is a very busy road. Thousands of trucks, cars, and motorcycles use it every day.
Wrong: Because of the publicity, my friends and I went to see the play, I didn't care for it though.
Right: Because of the publicity, my friends and I went to see the play. I didn't care for it though.

Check Your Understanding

Correct the following comma splices.

1. I spoke to the district attorney, he remembered the case clearly.

_____

2. Two distinct reasons can be presented for your actions, one is the concern for grades, the other is your misconception regarding what learning is.

_____

3. I see no reason to wait any longer, let's go on into the theater.

_____

4. The weather has been unusually warm, this is not generally the case for this time of year.

_____

5. She actually thought she had won, by the time she learned differently it was too late.

_____

_____

Practices in Writing Correct Sentences

Practice 1. Correct any of the following sentences that need correcting and identify what type of error you are correcting. Some need no correcting.

1. She does not have the prettiest teeth in the world. As you can see when she

smiles. (Type of error: _____)

_____

_____

2. While I was heading for school, hitchhiking as usual.

   (Type of error: _____)

   _____

   _____

3. Critically evaluate the books we have read by ranking them in order of your favorite to least liked explain the reasons for your ranking. (Type of error:

   _____)

   _____

   _____

4. He would rather watch television than read, as I'm sure many boys his age

   would. (Type of error: _____)

5. Dr. Causet lectured on many interesting things. For example, black magic,

   devil worship, and other occult ideas. (Type of error: _____)

6. A sentence is usually described as a group of words expressing a complete thought, it contains a subject and a predicate and is an independent unit of

   expression. (Type of error: _____)

   _____

   _____

7. Every morning, my grandmother used to go for a walk in the park in the afternoons she watched her favorite television serials.

   (Type of error: _____)

   _____

   _____

8. As we are all going in the same general direction.

   (Type of error: _____)

   _____

   _____

9. We used to walk through the woods in the fall finding a nice spot in the warm sun, we usually stopped and had lunch.

(Type of error: _____)

_____

10. When the irate customer asked for his money back.

(Type of error: _____)

_____

_____

Practice 2. In each of the following paragraphs there is a *sentence fragment.* Find it, and rewrite it correctly in the space provided.

1.   If you stand to lose a considerable sum. Don't be reluctant to threaten legal action if your complaint is justified but a merchant refuses to refund your money. More and more often, courts are backing the customer who has a legitimate grievance.

_____

2.   The judge ruled he should receive a cash refund, notwithstanding the fact that the warranty period had expired, inasmuch as repairmen had been unable to make the air conditioner work. Dozens of others who bought similar defective air conditioners yanked them out of their cars and took a heavy loss. Rather than engage in legal action.

_____

3.   Few families can afford to waste money if goods or services are not satisfying, especially with inflation a grim reality. Think back on your own purchases in the past year. Did you throw out expensive meat because it was spoiled by the time you got it home from the market? How about the blanket that shrank after a first washing? The $7.00 wash-and-wear shirt whose color faded mysteriously?

_____

4.   We aren't chronic complainers, but if a roast is of poor quality or a child's coat has a defective lining, we speak right up to the butcher or the clothing store manager. We're not bashful about asking for a replacement or a refund. If we believe our request is justified.

_____

Practice 3. Circle all the cliff-hanger words, and then change all of the following fragments into complete sentences.

1. Inasmuch as there is no school tomorrow. _____

_____

2. Before we leave on our cruise. _____

_____

3. Because of the grades I earned in high school. _____

_____

4. Unless the money arrives before Tuesday. _____

_____

5. If I were the president of the United States. _____

_____

6. After you have finished this week's assignment. _____

_____

7. When we all heard that Aunt Sally was coming for a visit. _____

_____

8. Although the students knew of the teacher's feelings. _____

_____

9. As I mentioned to you the last time we met. _____

_____

10. Until the end of the week. _____

_____

Practice 4. Rewrite the following run-on sentences and comma splices by inserting transitional words and/or the correct punctuation. Review the section on transitional words in Unit 6 if necessary.

1. The brakes went out on his bike he managed to stop it.

_____

2. His dentist has never hurt him, he still hates the thought of going.

_____

3. He was happy that finals were over, he wasn't certain of his grades.

_____

4. The instructor was friendly enough his assignments were not easy.

_____

5. Everything seemed to go wrong, the projector blew a bulb and the screen fell off the wall.

_____

_____

Practice 5. Below are sets of sentences. Combine each set of sentences into _one_ sentence by eliminating words you don't need. The first one has been done for you. Don't end up with fragments or run-on sentences.

1. a. The American flag is red.
   b. The American flag is white.
   c. The American flag is blue.

   The American flag is red, white, and blue.
   _____

2. a. Milo's car is a '65 Chevy.
   b. Milo's car is painted maroon.
   c. Milo's car is a convertible.

   _____

   _____

3. a. My history teacher is distinguished.
   b. My history teacher has been invited to speak at the United Nations.
   c. My history teacher was once nominated for the Nobel prize.

   _____

   _____

4. a. José is proud of his Mexican heritage.
   b. He does not like to be called a Chicano.

   _____

   _____

5. a. Our biology textbook is well illustrated.
   b. It has many study guides.
   c. It is fairly easy to understand.

   _____

   _____

6. a. Larry is more handsome than clever.
   b. He should learn to keep his mouth shut.

   _____

   _____

7. a. Sandy is better at English than the rest of us.
   b. Sandy is always impressing our teacher.
   c. She has a better background in languages.

   _____

   _____

8. a. Julie is afraid of the instructor.
   b. She seldom speaks in class.
   c. Julie hates our psychology class.

   _____

   _____

9. a. Shelly wrote a story.
   b. Shelly wrote a poem.
   c. Shelly wrote an essay.
   d. While she was recovering from her accident, Shelly wrote.

   _____

   _____

10. a. Richard Bach is the author of *Jonathan Livingston Seagull*.
    b. He also wrote *Illusions*.
    c. *Illusions* is about the adventures of a reluctant messiah.

   _____

   _____

Rewrite...

your first draft.

Before you begin to revise your essay, take time to review what you've learned so far. If you need to, go back and review the units or drills that deal with the following:

 Quick Review

Summary of Methods Used for Introductory Paragraphs

1. Ask a question.
2. Use an anecdote.
3. Use a quotation.
4. Give a brief overview.
5. Stress importance of topic.
6. Use a combination of methods.

Summary of Paragraph Methods for Supporting Details

1. Examples or illustrations.
2. Specific details.
3. Definition of terms.
4. Comparison or contrast.
5. Analysis.
6. Story or anecdote.
7. Combination of methods.

Summary of Methods Used for Concluding Paragraphs

1. Ask a question.
2. Use an anecdote.
3. Summarize.
4. Show concern.
5. Make conclusions.

Summary of Where to Use Transitional Devices

1. Between sentences.
2. Between paragraphs.
3. List of transitional devices is in Unit 6, page 138.

Return now to the first draft you wrote on a separate sheet of paper at the beginning of this unit. Place a check mark in front of each of the following points as you reexamine your essay.

_____ 1. Does your introductory paragraph contain your thesis or main idea regarding your topic?

_____ 2. Does your introductory paragraph attempt to draw your reader's interest?

_____ 3. Can you identify your topic sentence in each of your paragraphs?

_____ 4. Does your concluding paragraph summarize or clarify your point of view regarding your thesis?

_____ 5. Have you used transitional words or expressions within sentences and paragraphs so that your ideas move smoothly from one to another?

_____ 6. Have you written any sentence fragments, run-ons, or comma splices?

_____ 7. Have you shared your essay with others to get their comments and reactions?

When you are certain you have corrected your essay as needed, rewrite it, and give both your first draft and the final draft to your instructor.

UNIT

Think. . . .
about astrology and horoscopes

Read. . . .
about astrology
"Astrology Revisited: Hit or Myth?" by Mort Weisinger

React. . . .
to the essay

Plan. . . .
an essay
Topics for an essay

Write. . . .
(A) an outline for your essay
(B) a first draft
(C) using correct punctuation
Practices in punctuation

Rewrite. . . .
your first draft

Think...

about astrology and horoscopes by answering the following questions.

1. What is your astrological sign; that is, are you a Leo, a Gemini, a Pisces, or

   what? _____

2. Do you believe that your personality corresponds to your astrological sign?

   _____ Why? _____

   _____

3. Do you read your horoscope on a regular basis? _____

   Why? _____

   _____

4. Have you ever purchased an astrology book or a personal astrological fore-

   cast? _____ Why? _____

   _____

5. Do you feel there is any truth in astrological forecasts? _____

   Why? _____

   _____

6. Have you ever done something because of an astrological prediction? _____

   Why? _____

   _____

7. Why do you feel astrology is so popular with so many people? _____

   _____

   _____

the following essay on astrology, and compare the author's views with your views on the subject.

Astrology Revisited: Hit or Myth?
Mort Weisinger

1. The final splashdown on the Apollo lunar exploration program has terminated one phase of man's search for truth among the planets. Yet while the creepers are beginning to twine around the launch towers of Cape Kennedy, millions of space-age Americans apparently believe that the route to true knowledge of the stars lies in the ancient and arcane art of the astrologer.

2. It seems a most curious possibility that Congress might today find more public support for the funding of an investigation of astrology than for a new manned space venture. That such an expenditure might some day be approved is by no means unlikely. The Governor of California, not exactly your garden-variety flower child, is known to have consulted a noted astrologer, and while there has been no direct word from the White House on the subject as yet, the number of public officials who thank their lucky stars—in advance—is bound to have increased along with the legions of astrology-minded among the electorate. But the casual acceptance of astrology's modern revival is what warrants another, deeper look.

3. One thing is clear: Astrology is the staminal champion of the occult world; it refuses to be permanently debunked, even by the best scientific minds of this or any other age. Nor is it suppressed by the leaps and bounds of technology. In fact, periods of technological upheaval seem to be media in which astrological interest is most likely to flourish. In England at the time of the Industrial Revolution several astrology magazines competed for a mass audience that, if projected to today's population level, would support a newsstand sales bonanza any modern publisher would envy. Technology is the irritant that assails the senses, shakes the faith and generally blooms in the shade of war. The astrologer is time's gypsy traveling through the ages, always camped on the outskirts of town waiting for the time when his services will be in heavy demand.

4. In the U.S. today, he is more likely camped in a chic office suite, a townhouse in a swinging neighborhood or in a suburban shopping mall. Some 10 million Americans are estimated to be actively seeking astrological counsel. Like horse

players flocking to their bookies for the morning line, they patronize perhaps as many as 200,000 astrologers (counting part-timers and amateurs) to buy their previews of fate. Millions more consult the daily horoscopes which are a fixture in 1,200 newspapers. While the youth culture is most often identified as the sensational base of the new astrology, from the Broadway musical *Hair* down to a current chart-climbing ditty titled "Jesus Was a Capricorn," it is the bankers and beldames who spend freely on it. They may not openly flaunt their astrological affinity but they are giving the phenomenon the kind of impetus only cash can provide.

5. Lengthy and detailed horoscopes spewed from a computer, technology's Beelzebub, are regularly gobbled up at $20 a throw. A personal chart cast by a name astrologer, such as New York's Zolar, a former clothing salesman, can cost $200. The showbiz element is the continuing mother lode of astrological faith, and the casebooks are full of performers who choose managers or refuse ever to get into an airplane on the advice of their astrologers. So high is Hollywood on astrology, a standing gag is that bankrupt producers always consult their astrologers for the best time to commit suicide.

6. The accompanying boom in astrology-related merchandise is typically American. You can trace the traverse of your sign on a handsome zodiac clock that Tiffany's sells at $2,000. A "space clock" invented by the University of Minnesota's Dr. Athelstan Spilhaus offers a lot more solid astronomical information at half the price of Tiffany's but was a back number at the scientific mail-order houses until astrology fans saw the potential. Décor items have been blitzed by the zodiac, everything from calendars to carpets and wallpaper.

7. Largely without manufacturers' trappings, astrology is either still going strong or renascent in many other parts of the world. It is a profession in countries where a chicken or a sack of rice is the annual retainer. In Vietnam, the stars have been consulted on the question of whether a man—or even an entire unit—should fight or flee. Some Indian astrologers made a bad call on the end of the world several years ago, but the publicity was probably worth it. At the other end of the Asian standard-of-living spectrum, the Crown Prince of Sikkim put off his marriage to New York socialite Hope Cooke for an entire year on the advice of court astrologers.

8. Can the five million French fans in her radio audience be wrong about Madame Soleil, a middle-aged astrologer who is probably better known in her country than Brigitte Bardot? In Scotland, astrologers lobbied for the mandatory recording of the exact second of an infant's birth, as well as the exact location, claiming this data would enable them to cast horoscopes of maximum accurancy. The statute is now on the books.

9. The horoscopic consultant to the British Royal Family sets the coronation date. Everywhere, foundations are laid, ships are launched and ribbons are cut in sync with the propitious Sun Signs or similar portents from whichever brand of astrology is native to the area—considered worldwide, they are varied and often conflicting.

10. Obviously there is something deep in humankind that gives rise to a need to believe in the existence of a key to fate's closet. That this should have been firmly sky-centered by the dawn of history is completely logical. Undiverted by television, ancient seers from Babylon to Britain peered over the years into a night

sky bereft of smog. Only through patient observation could the slow passage of the planets become an intricate pattern of dips and whorls. One of the features of the still mysterious ruin of Stonehenge, which some scientists believe to have been constructed as a giant astronomical computer, is a perimeter of holes that may correspond to a complicated 56-year cycle of lunar eclipse. This would indicate sustained observation and detailed record-keeping over a period of many generations.

11. The initial plotters of these cycles were the intellectuals of their societies, to whom the relationship of mystique to power was clear. Astrologers have counseled kings—rightly and wrongly—since monarchy was born.

12. The body of astrological "knowledge" which American believers find so deliciously esoteric today is a great amalgam of pseudo-science from civilizations of every time and description. Even by the Middle Ages it was strong enough to survive repeated ecclesiastical denunciations. Most remarkable of all, it survived the astronomer Johannes Kepler's proof, in the 16th century, of a heliocentric solar system—up until which time both astronomers and astrologers had handed down theory and prediction based on the notion that the sun orbited the earth. Kepler could only mutter that astrology was "the foolish daughter of the respectable mother astronomy," when astrologers failed to revise their charts.

13. Later, when improved telescopes revealed the most distant planets— Neptune, Uranus and Pluto—astronomers pointed out that it was impossible for ancient astrologers to have plotted accurate horoscopes, based on the premise of planetary "emanations." Only five planets were known to them. Unaware of the additional emanations from out in the void, astrologers had been shortchanging their customers.

14. The naming of planets after imagined deities, and relating them to human destiny is astrology's most obvious caprice. Suppose the first chap who spotted Mars had named it Eve, because its crimson hue recalled the apple in the Garden of Eden? Wouldn't it follow that a woman born under the ascendary of Eve be curious, sinful, and a temptress?

15. And what if this chap had named the yellow planet Midas, because it shone like gold? Wouldn't those born under it be prone to greed?

16. In the face of such an arbitrary origin, whatever faith, hysteria or other force sustains the planets as governing bodies in the believers' horoscopes is remarkable. But since it persists and recurs, some nonbelievers, including scientists, have begun to suggest that, apart from divination, astrology's one aspect of validity may underlie its very arbitrariness. The planetary jargon—cusps, trines, aspect lines, medium coeli, etc.—might all be a synthetic code that is partially or occasionally synchronous with a real system of cycles that could be stimulated or regulated by an extraterrestrial force. Many cyclic patterns, called bio-rhythms, in both man and lower forms of life, remain unexplained. Cosmic rays, subatomic particles from space, the magnetic and gravitational fields of the solar system and various forms of radiation have all been advanced in speculation. Thus far, no shred of connection of known forces to the signs of the zodiac has been established.

17. To compensate for the lack of any scientific case, today's astrology advocates quote scientists out of context, offer undocumented evidence and befuddle initiates to the cult with the jargon culled from centuries of blissfully ignorant star-

gazing. Despite such efforts to dignify the trade, no school for astrologers exists. I know of no astrologer who holds a degree in astronomy, physics, mathematics, biology or any of the other sciences in which they dabble.

18. Many astrologers invent exotic qualifications. Sybil Leek claims to be a witch. In her recent book, *My Life in Astrology,* she implies she has had official contact with Cape Kennedy regarding astronauts' horoscopes. When I checked that out, NASA officials said the claim was nonsense.

19. Linda Goodman, author of the current astrological best-seller, *Sun Signs,* is a former Miss America candidate who reveals she was an astrologer in a former incarnation. Linda also insists that anybody born on May 25th, 27th, 28th or 29th of 1951 broke his arm or finger before he was five.

20. Scientists cannot accept the marriage of convenience between the occult and the sciences that astrologers attempt to legitimize. Astronomy professor Gibson Reaves of the University of Southern California simply says "there is very little evidence that astrology works." Dr. Harold Spencer-Jones of Britain's Royal Observatory in Greenwich puts it more harshly: "The claims of the astrologers are absolute rubbish. If astronomy is the Queen of Sciences, astrology is the Queen of Humbug."

21. J. B. S. Haldane, the eminent British biochemist, asks three questions of astrologers:

1. Why didn't astrologers predict such large-scale disasters as the Chicago Fire, the Johnstown Flood or the San Francisco Earthquake?

2. Did all the millions of Jews murdered by Hilter have death written into their horoscopes?

3. Of the thousands who die annually of cancer, is there a common denominator in their birth charts?

22. Yet astrologers shrug this off by arguing that the destiny of the individual is "subsumed" in the greater destiny of the state, nation, race, tribe or geographical area. Others race to their literature to show that through the ages they have indeed predicted plagues, wars, famines and other catastrophes. The examples are almost totally apocryphal, but indicative of the tendency of devotees to remember their astrologers' hits and forget their misses.

23. "They tend to ignore the predominant misfirings over the few bull's-eyes, because the latter are so impressive," observes anthropology professor A. Bharati of Syracuse University.

24. The world was not always so charitable. One Egyptian Pharaoh, Thutmost III, had 14 astrologers executed in one year.

25. If the Executive Department were in a beheading mood today, none of the big name astrologers who have ventured from the security of private clients and into prediction of world events would have to worry about shaving or coiffure.

26. Astrology lives on. A new champion, Joseph Goodavage, plays a wild card in his book, *Astrology: The Space Age Science.* He claims to have investigated numerous "time twins"—individuals born the same hour. Reports the author: "In 100 percent of the lives of the people who were born within a few minutes of each other, the same tendency kept reappearing. Major events in the lives of these people paralleled one another as though they were practically synchronized."

27. Startling statistics, indeed. To substantiate them, I turned to geneticist

Amram Scheinfeld, who has lectured at Yale, Cornell, and Columbia. He is the author of a standard college text on heredity and probably knows more about twins than anyone else in the world, having spent several years researching hundreds of case histories for his comprehensive book, *Twins and Supertwins.*

28. Scheinfeld's records tell a different story. "In the cases of twins who are born within three minutes of each other," he assured me, "there are scores of examples where one died on the delivery table while the other survived. In numerous other cases of twins born during the same brief interval, one of the pair remainded single, the other married. I have solid evidence that they differ considerably, often extraordinarily, in their traits, life histories and longevities. Their careers give no validity to astrological principles."

29. From Kepler to Scheinfeld, countless discreditors have assailed astrology, with little enduring effect. "You pay your shrink, I'll pay my stargazer—it's all the same," seems to be a prevalent modern defense.

30. Perhaps. But one is haunted by examples from primitive as well as not-so-primitive societies of the power of suggestion. A man is told he will become sick. He gets sick. The chief is told he will lose the battle. He loses. It is ordained.

31. Successful astrologers are not stupid. Horoscopes are often intentionally vague, they point out, to avoid a client's conversion of them into self-fulfilling prophecies of a specific—drastic—nature. The moral seems to be, never tell an astrologer to stop fooling around and get to the point. If you have a good one, he's probably telling you what you want to hear most of the time anyway.

React...

to the essay.

Answer the following questions.

1. What is the theme or main idea of the essay?

_____

2. According to the author, "[Astrology] refuses to be permanently debunked, even by the best scientific minds of this or any other age." Does this mean the author believes in astrology? _____ Why?___

_____

_____

3. How many Americans are estimated to be actively involved or seeking astrological counsel? _____

What does this signify to you? _____

_____

4. Why do you suppose so many people are concerned with horoscopes? ___

_____

_____

5. Are you willing to spend money on a personal horoscope? _____

Why? _____

_____

6. Have you changed, reaffirmed, or formed an opinion about astrology after reading this essay? _____ Why? _____

_____

_____

7. What is your answer to the question raised in the title of the article? _____

_____

_____

8. Why does the author place quotation marks around the word "knowledge" in

paragraph 12? _____

_____

9. Check the following words from the essay that you do not know or could not use correctly.

_____ a. staminal (3)

_____ b. occult (3)

_____ c. debunked (3)

_____ d. flaunt (4)

_____ e. renascent (7)

_____ f. statute (8)

_____ g. mystique (11)

_____ h. esoteric (12)

_____ i. emanations (13)

_____ j. stargazer (9)

Take the time now to reread the words in the paragraphs indicated. Then go to the Vocabulary Section in the Appendix, and do the exercises with these words.

Plan...

an essay on astrology.

If you do not have an idea for an essay of your own, look over the suggested list of topics to see if there is one you can use.

1. Why I read my daily horoscope.
2. The qualities of a . . . (Gemini, Cancer, Leo, Pisces, or whatever).
3. Why astrologists will continue through the ages.
4. Why people panic when astrologers predict doom.
5. Famous people who believe in astrology.
6. Arguments for believing (or not believing) in astrology.
7. The difference between astrology and astronomy.
8. Computerized astrology: Science comes to witchcraft.
9. Using astrology to select a marriage partner.
10. Are you what your sign says you are?
11. What makes a successful astrologer?
12. Why horoscopes are vague.
13. Which is funnier: the daily comics or horoscopes?
14. The link between astrology and the occult.
15. Why I believe/do not believe in witchcraft.

If none of these topics suit you, think about the following dilemmas and how they might become possible ideas for an essay.

Dilemma A

Sara usually pays no attention to her horoscope, but one day a friend of hers reads Sara's horoscope for the next day. Basically, it tells her not to engage in sports because she might get hurt, to avoid conflict with one she loves, and to expect to hear from an old friend. Sara laughs, paying little attention to the horoscope. But the next day Sara breaks her wrist when she falls playing tennis and has to be taken to the hospital. Her older brother wants her to stay in bed and rest when she gets home from the emergency ward, but Sara yells at him and claims she can take care of herself. They fight. In the mail, she receives a letter from a childhood friend she hasn't seen or heard from in years. Sara tells her boyfriend, Chip, that her horoscope came true and she is now thinking of going to an astrologist to have her chart done. Chip thinks Sara is being silly. They argue. Should Chip try to talk her out of it? What arguments could Chip give Sara? What arguments could Sara give Chip? Who is right?

Dilemma B

A very well-known clairvoyant has predicted the last four major earthquakes within a day of occurrence. He predicts there will be a disastrous earthquake in Washington State near where you and some friends have planned for six weeks to go backpacking. Your friends don't feel concerned about the prediction, but you are now afraid to go. You are the only one with a car big enough to take everyone and all the gear. What should you do? How many alternatives do you have? Should you be afraid to go?

Dilemma C

Here are two horoscopes, both for the same day, year, and astrological sign. They were written by two different astrologers and appeared in two different newspapers.

1. Define terms. Study Scorpio message for hint. Emphasize ability to locate needed material. You are now able to perfect techniques, to discard superfluous concepts. You'll gain "backstage view."
2. Study your money situation and make plans to have more financial security. Strive to be more efficient in your work.

Study each one carefully. What do they really say? What does the first one mean by "Define terms"? Are these helpful guides for the day? Why are they so different if they are meant for the same person? What might this say about astrology?

Practice 1.   In your journal notebook or on a separate page, spend 10 to 15 minutes freewriting or exploring possible essay topics.

Practice 2.   Now plan an essay on some topic. In the space below, write the topic or subject you've picked.

Topic:

_____

_____

Practice 3.   Now write a working thesis for your topic.

Tentative Thesis Statement:

_____

_____

_____

_____

Below, list all the ideas you can think of to support your thesis. Then rearrange or group them into a proper order.

_____

_____

_____

_____

_____

_____

_____

_____

_____

Write...

(A) an outline for your essay.

On a separate sheet of paper, write an outline for your essay, basing it on your rearranged list of support. When finished, turn it in to your instructor for a final check before you actually begin writing your essay. When it has been approved by your instructor, start on (*B*).

(B) a first draft of your essay using the outline you completed.

Do a first draft on a separate sheet of paper. When finished, go on to (*C*).

(C) using correct punctuation.

The need to use correct punctuation has already been shown in Unit 7. Faulty punctuation can cause sentence fragments, comma splices, and run-on sentences. In addition, punctuation can guide your reader to react to what you say in the way you intend him or her to react. Much of the following information may already be familiar to you. Use it for review or to learn what you don't know.

The Period

The period is used for two purposes:

1. after a complete statement, such as:

   Here is the book I want.

2. after abbreviations, such as:

   Ms.   Calif.   U.S. Senate

The Exclamation Mark

The exclamation mark is used for two purposes:

1. after a sentence that carries a strong emotion or excitement, such as:

   We won the game!
   I don't believe it!

2. after a word or expression that carries a strong emotion, such as:

> Oh! That's fantastic!
> Super! Far out!

The Question Mark

The question mark is used after a *direct* question, that is, a question that requires an answer such as:

> May I go with you?
> Did you see it happen?
> *Important:* Do not use a question mark for *indirect* questions, such as:
> I asked if I might go with you.
> I asked if you saw it happen.

 Check Your Understanding

Place the correct punctuation in the following sentences.

a. What did the teacher want
b. I asked what the teacher wanted
c. Oh I bet I'm late for class again
d. I am late for class
e. I just don't believe it

The Comma

The comma is used for six purposes:

1. Commas are used to divide two sentences linked by *but, nor, or, for,* or *and.*

> He won the game, but he hurt himself in the process.
> They went to church in the morning, and later that afternoon they went to the park.

   Note: Without the words *but* or *and* in the preceding examples, the sentences would be comma splices as was discussed in Unit 7.

2. Commas are used to divide descriptive words or a group of words in a series, such as:

> The VW is economical, small, and easy to drive.
> The novel has well-developed characters, an unusual plot, and an entertaining story.
> He talked about his travels in Ireland, particularly Irish pubs, Howth Castle, and the Blarney Stone.

3. Commas are used to separate two or more adjectives (words that describe nouns) used before a noun, such as:

His short, plump brother hurt his knee.
The trophy was a tall, thin, silver cup with his name engraved on it.

Important: To test whether or not two or more adjectives can be used together and separated by a comma, read the sentence inserting only one adjective at a time. For instance:

His *short* brother hurt his knee.
His *plump* brother hurt his knee.
or,
The trophy was a tall cup . . .
The trophy was a thin cup . . .
The trophy was a silver cup . . .
or, read the sentence putting the word *and* where the commas go.
The trophy was a tall *and* thin *and* silver cup . . .

 ## Check Your Understanding

Place the correct punctuation in the following sentences.

a. He saw the doctor last week but he didn't go back as he should have.
b. The history course was interesting informative and unlike any class I've had before
c. The car was painted red had white sidewall tires and cost less than the blue one
d. The long thin velvet dress has been sold

4. Commas are also used to separate words or groups of words in a sentence that could be removed from the sentence without changing its meaning, such as:

My cousin, I believe, will arrive tomorrow.
Dr. Fast, who loves auto racing, will be a judge at tomorrow's race.
John, who is my youngest brother, works for a contractor.
John, my youngest brother, works for a contractor.
His father, however, is smaller than he.

Important: In each of the preceding sentences, the words or phrases surrounded by commas could be taken out of the sentence without destroying the sentence's meaning.

Special Note: When the subordinate clause or words in a sentence are needed to identify the subject, no commas are used. For example, in the following sentence, commas are used to separate the subordinate section because it is not needed to identify the subject.

Mr. Stevens, who loves building model planes, lives down the block.

However, in the following sentence, the subject is not specific and the subordinate clause is needed to clarify the subject.

The man who loves building model planes lives down the block.

5. Commas are also used to set off introductory words or phrases, such as:

For example, we need to establish a new set of rules for the club.
In addition, I want to clarify those statements.
On the other hand, we must be prepared for change.
Although we arrived late, we still found good places to sit.

Important: Commas usually are used after the following words or phrases when they begin a sentence:

for example	however	in the first place
in fact	therefore	after
in addition	nonetheless	although
in general	furthermore	on the other hand

6. Commas are used to set off material using numbers, dates, addresses, and salutary comments such as:

numbers: 3, 452, 611 *or* nine feet, six inches long
dates: December 12, 1930
addresses: 711 Sunset Boulevard, Hollywood, California 90012
salutations and closings: Dear Dad,
                           Yours truly,

 ## Check Your Understanding

Place the correct punctuation in the following sentences.

a. His teacher however has other things to say about him
b. Sally who never misses class was absent today
c. The girl who looks like Shirley MacLaine sat near me
d. In fact we should take care of that now
e. He lives at 6431 Oakdale Avenue San Francisco California 94124
f. The man at the lumber yard cut the board two feet one inch short

The Semicolon

The semicolon is used for two major purposes:

1. The semicolon (;), rather than a period, is used between two sentences that are related in thought and equal in importance.

The car is severely damaged; it may never run again.
John rode his bike; Jane pushed hers.

2. The semicolon is used to separate a series of phrases that contain commas, such as:

The three important speakers were Harry Berry, an actor; Oliver Diddle, the director; and Metro Mayer, the producer.

The Colon

1. The colon is used to direct attention to particular items or statements in a sentence, such as:

   There is only one thing on my mind: food.
   (A dash could be used in place of the colon.)
   The following novels must be read by the end of the month: *Deliverance, Slaughterhouse-Five,* and *The White Dawn.*

2. The colon is also used to distinguish the following odds and ends:

   a. Time: It's exactly 4:15 A.M.
   b. Biblical chapters and verse: John 3:16
   c. Title and subtitle: *New World Beginnings: Indian Cultures in America*
   d. Business salutations: Dear Sir:

The Dash

A dash is generally used in informal writing more than formal writing. It is used in two ways:

1. A dash, like a colon, can be used to direct attention to something in particular, such as:

   There's only one thing left to say—forget it!
   (A colon could be used in place of the dash.)

2. A dash is also used to set off information or comments for dramatic effect:

   The BIA (Bureau of Indian Affairs) refused—as it so often has in the past—to listen to the Indians' requests.
   James Dickey's novel *Deliverance*—his first novel, by the way—was made into a movie.

Quotation Marks

1. Double quotation marks are used to show the exact words that someone has said. This is called a direct quote. Do not use quotation marks with an indirect quotation.

   Direct: George said, "I need to borrow five dollars."
   Indirect: George said that he needs to borrow five dollars.
   Direct: "I thought," she said, "that you weren't going."
   Indirect: I thought she said that she wasn't going.

2. Use double quotation marks to show words being used in a special sense or to indicate slang:

> He looked up the word "doppelganger."
> That's just a "cop out" on your part.
> (In formal writing, avoid the use of slang.)
> He's what I term a real "pro" when it comes to sports.

3. Use double quotation marks to indicate the title of short stories, poems, song titles, magazine articles, and chapter titles in books:

> "A Day in the Life Of" is my favorite song in the Beatles' Sgt. Pepper album.
> "Witches and Warlocks" is an interesting article in this week's Time magazine.

Important: Titles of complete works such as books, magazines, and record albums are underlined, as the preceding examples show. Titles of chapters, essays, or songs within a complete volume take quotation marks.

4. Single quotation marks are used only to show a quotation within another quotation.

> "I thought," the student said, "that the statement 'To err is human, to forgive is divine' was from the Bible."

5. Do not use quotation marks when quoting long passages. Instead, indent what you are quoting five spaces to the right, and single-space if you are typing. Notice the following example:

Your writing
> Today when we think of Puritans and the Puritan ethic, we imagine rather gloomy, over religious, hellfire and damnation people who worked hard all day and prayed over everything. According to Frakes's text, that was not the case:

Quoted material
> There were some not-so-pure Puritans. If everyone had been a good Puritan, the laws and sermons would not have been necessary. Something that tempted the Puritans was the practice of *bundling.* Bundling was the colonial answer to the energy crisis in the bedroom, where couples, often unmarried, would share a bed. . . . Puritans were lovers of the bottle as well as the bed.

Your writing
> Obviously, Puritans had their moments of fun contrary to popular belief.

This is called a block quote and is usually used when you quote over two lines of print.

Parentheses

Parentheses are used to set off comments or information that has no direct point in the sentence's thought and to set off numbers or letters used to list items in a sentence.

According to Bill (and he is no authority), there will be an eclipse of the moon tomorrow night.

This Unit deals with punctuation, such as the use of (1) the colon, (2) the semicolon, (3) the question mark, (4) quotation marks, and (5) parentheses.

 Check Your Understanding

Correctly punctuate the following sentences.

a. Fred said Let's go bowling Friday.
b. *Newsweek's* article Down and Out for the Last Time is interesting reading if you like sports
c. I have only one thing to ask why me
d. What does the word stereotype mean

The Apostrophe

Apostrophes are used for these basic purposes: to form contractions, possessions, and plurals of letters and numbers.

1. Apostrophes are used to form contractions; that is, to show that a letter or letters of a word have been left out.

   they're = they are
   it's = it is
   you're = you are
   we're = we are

2. Apostrophes are used to form singular and plural possessives, such as:

   my mother's car
   the man's hat   } Singular possessive
   the camera's shutter

   the instructors' workroom
   the girls' locker room   } Plural possessive
   the cameras' cases

   Important: If a word ends in *s*, just add the apostrophe: Adams' book.

3. Apostrophes are used to form the plural of letters and numbers, such as:

   7's and 11's
   fifteen *d*'s

   Important: Numbers under 100 should always be written out: seven and eleven.

Check Your Understanding

1. Correctly punctuate the following sentences.
   a. Its time to go now
   b. We havent eaten yet
   c. She wore her sisters shoes today
   d. Are three 10s and two 8s a good poker hand
   e. We have to read at least three of James Jones novels
2. Form contractions for the following words.

   a. let us _____

   b. I will _____

   c. there is _____

   d. we will _____

   e. she had _____

   f. John is _____

   g. are not _____

   h. would not _____

   i. would have _____

   j. who would _____

   k. does not _____

   l. do not _____

 ## Practices in Punctuation

Directions. You may not need to do all of the following practices. Do only those you need to do or the ones assigned by your instructor.

Practice 1. Place commas and periods wherever they belong in the following sentences.

1. A Jeep just might make it but our little VW Bug won't
2. Swamps they warned sometimes bury the road
3. The letter was simply addressed, "Dr. Frankenstein"
4. For my next dangerous trick I would like to attempt to cut this lady in half with no harmful effects to her person
5. Mr. Johnson is a US Senator from California

Practice 2. Use whatever end punctuation (period, exclamation, question mark) is necessary for the following sentences.

1. I just can't believe we won
2. His only response was, "You're kidding"
3. May I ask where you bought that dress
4. I asked where she bought her dress
5. Oh, man It's too impossible to believe

Practice 3. Place commas wherever they belong in the following sentences.

1. He never asked for the book but I knew he wanted it.
2. Here's what I need: four cans of oil two boxes of concrete floor cleaner and a new broom.
3. She is long-legged willowy blond and has a great sense of humor.
4. My father as far as I know wants to go too.
5. Although she didn't say it I think her feelings were hurt.
6. In fact we need to do more of this.
7. Mr. Smythe who is my English professor just published his first novel.
8. Mr. Smythe my English professor just published his first novel *Sweet Sweet Smythe.*
9. My doctor however wants to consult another doctor.
10. It was four feet six inches.
11. He was born December 12 1901 near Mobile Alabama.
12. She has a new address: 722 Nepal Avenue Phoenix Arizona.

Practice 4. Place semicolons, colons, and commas where they belong in the following sentences.

1. The tire is ruined it is irreparable.
2. The three new employees are John Small the young man Richard World the dark-haired one and Sam Jackson the oldest-looking of the three.
3. Here's what I want for Christmas a new Mercedes new sails for my yacht preferably blue ones and a subscription to *Playboy.*
4. There seems to be only one thing to do forget it.
5. At exactly 320 P.M. he says the world will end. He predicts this on the basis of a passage from Revelation 325.

Practice 5. Place quotation marks and commas where they should be appropriately used in the following sentences.

1. We wanted to go but we didn't have time she explained.
2. I thought she said that I already told you.
3. The teacher explained the term alienation effect.
4. A & P is a short story written by John Updike.
5. His sister yelled Close the door.

Practice 6. Follow the directions for each of the following tasks. If you don't understand the direction, review the unit for the section that deals with the underlined word in the directions.

1. Write an example of a *direct* quotation.

_____

2. Write an example of an *indirect* quotation.

_____

3. Write an example of an *exclamatory* sentence.

_____

4. Write a sentence that uses the title of a short story, poem, or song. Use *quotation marks* correctly.

_____

5. Write a sentence, using a *colon* and listing at least three items in a series.

_____

6. Write a sentence, using your street address, city, state, and zip code. Use *commas* correctly.

_____

7. Write a sentence, using *parentheses*.

_____

8. Write two sentences about this book, using a *semicolon* to link them as one.

_____

9. Write a sentence, using *dashes* correctly.

_____

10. Write a sentence, using an introductory clause and the correct punctuation.

_____

_____

11. Write a sentence, using *therefore* correctly.

_____

_____

12. Write a sentence, using the contraction for "they are." (*apostrophe* usage)

_____

_____

13. Write a sentence, showing that Robert possesses some object. (*apostrophe* usage)

_____

_____

_____

14. Write a sentence, using a *quote within a quote.*

_____

_____

15. Write a sentence, using "who is . . ." as part of the sentence. It cannot be a question.

_____

_____

Practice 7. Using the words indicated in italic type, combine the following sets of sentences, eliminating unneeded words. The first one has been done for you. Remember to punctuate correctly.

1. a. The scuba diver nearly drowned.
   b. He didn't check his tank valve before entering the water.
   Use *who:* The scuba diver who didn't check his tank valve before entering the water nearly drowned.
2. a. The tests did not place us very well.
   b. They gave tests at the beginning of the course.

Use *which:* _____

_____

3. a. John Ambrose is our state senator.
   b. He is being charged with taking a bribe.

   Use *who:* _____

_____

4. a. Until recently, Mexicans were stereotyped in a limited way.
   b. Until recently, Mexicans were portrayed as lazy or as bandits.

   Use *that:* _____

_____

5. a. The mother picked up her daughter.
   b. The daughter's leg was broken.

   Use *whose:* _____

_____

6. a. The old woman accidentally set fire to her house.
   b. She lives down the street.

   Use *who:* _____

_____

7. a. Harry's business netted a huge profit last year.
   b. Harry's business may be in for financial trouble this year.

   Use *which:* _____

_____

8. a. James Michener is the author of the best-seller *Centennial.*
   b. He also wrote *Hawaii, The Drifters,* and *The Source.*

   Use *who:* _____

_____

9. a. The money was returned.
   b. The money belonged to the lady down the street.
   c. The thief was caught.

   Use *that* and *when*: _____

_____

10. a. My dad wanted nothing to do with the military.
    b. My dad wanted nothing to do with politics.
    c. His grandfather was a General.

    Use *whose:* _____

    _____

Rewrite...

your first draft.

Before you begin the revision of your essay, carefully read the following paragraphs from a student's first draft and revised draft based on the instructor's comments. The entire essay is not shown, but the student's thesis is that astrology is a farce.

Student's First Draft

To help prove my point that astrology is really lame is my girl friend, Marya. She's a Gemini. Gemini's are supposed to be bright and quick-witted. Open minded and anxious to learn new things as well as easy going. Well, let me tell you Maryas not like that shes not stupid but not quick-witted either. Shes not very open minded or anxious to learn either.

Instructor's Comments

Your topic sentence here supports your thesis, which is good. Try rewriting it and not using "really lame."

Your fourth sentence is a fragment.

Reread the section on apostrophes and contractions.

Your fifth sentence is a run-on.

Instead of repeating the same descriptive words used for Geminis, use different descriptive words for Marya.

Notice the changes, including the corrections of faulty sentence structure and punctuation.

Student's Revised Draft

One of the reasons astrology is not to be relied on is that the characteristics attributed to people born under certain signs is not necessarily true. For instance, my girlfriend Marya is a Gemini. Geminis are supposed to be bright, quick-witted, open minded, anxious to learn new things, and easy going. But that's not my Marya. She's not stupid, but she's not what can be called "quick-witted" either. Unlike Geminis are supposed to be, Marya has a short temper, doesn't seem to be curious, and resists learning anything new.

Instructor's Comments

A much better topic sentence that ties in with both your thesis and what you want to develop here in this paragraph.
Good use of transitional words. You use a combination of examples and compare/contrast. You've eliminated previous errors.

Return now to the first draft you wrote on a separate sheet of paper at the beginning of this unit. Place a check mark in front of each of the following points as you reexamine your essay for those items. Rewrite or make any corrections you feel would strengthen your essay.

_____ 1. Does your introductory paragraph contain your thesis or main idea regarding your topic?

_____ 2. Does your introductory paragraph attempt to draw your reader's interest?

_____ 3. Can you identify your topic sentences in each of your paragraphs?

_____ 4. Does your concluding paragraph summarize or clarify your point of view about your topic?

_____ 5. Have you used transitional words or expressions within sentences or paragraphs?

_____ 6. Have you corrected any sentence fragments, run-ons, or comma splices?

_____ 7. Have you checked for correct punctuation on the basis of what you learned in this unit?

_____ 8. Have you shared your essay with others for their comments and suggestions?

When you are certain you have corrected your essay as needed, rewrite it, and turn in the final draft to your instructor.

$$\text{UNIT } 9$$

Think....
about material values

Read....
about material values
"Things: The Throw-Away Society" by Alvin Toffler

React....
to the essay

Plan....
an essay
Topics for an essay

Write....
(A) an outline for your essay
(B) a first draft of your essay
(C) with sentence variety
Simple sentences
Compound sentences
Complex sentences
Compound-complex sentences
Practices in writing with sentence variety

Rewrite....
your first draft

Think...

about your material values, that is, your attitude about possessions such as clothes, cars, stereos, boats, guns, and other personal property.

1. Do you still have any toys you owned when you were twelve? _____

   Why? _____

   _____

   _____

2. What is your "dream" car—the car you would like to own if you could afford

   it? _____

   How long do you think you would keep the car? _____

   _____

3. If you had to leave your home because of a fire, what three possesions would you want to take with you?

   a. _____ Why? _____

   _____

   b. _____ Why? _____

   _____

   c. _____ Why? _____

4. List some items you use only once or twice and then throw away.

   _____

   _____

5. What is your definition of materialism? _____

_____

_____

_____

6. In what ways are you a materialist? _____

_____

_____

_____

7. In what ways are you *not* a materialist? _____

_____

_____

_____

8. What do you think of such items as Kleenex, nonreturnable bottles, paper napkins, paper towels, throw-away baking pans, and other disposable products?

ucts? _____

_____

_____

_____

Read...

an article by Alvin Toffler, author of *The Culture Consumers* and *Future Shock*, who feels that our culture produces a "throw-away mentality" that is dangerous to our sense of values.

Things: The Throw-Away Society
Alvin Toffler

1. "Barbie," a twelve-inch plastic teen-ager, is the best-known and best-selling doll in history. Since its introduction in 1959, the Barbie doll population of the world has grown to 12,000,000—more than the human population of Los Angeles or London or Paris. Little girls adore Barbie because she is highly realistic and eminently dress-upable. Mattel, Inc., makers of Barbie, also sells a complete wardrobe for her, including clothes for ordinary daytime wear, clothes for formal party wear, clothes for swimming and skiing.

2. Recently Mattel announced a new improved Barbie doll. The new version has a slimmer figure, "real" eyelashes, and a twist-and-turn waist that makes her more humanoid than ever. Moreover, Mattel announced that, for the first time, any young lady wishing to purchase a new Barbie would receive a trade-in allowance for her old one.

3. What Mattel did not announce was that by trading in her old doll for a technologically improved model, the little girl of today, citizen of tomorrow's super-industrial world, would learn a fundamental lesson about the new society: that man's relationships with *things* are increasingly temporary.

4. The ocean of man-made physical objects that surrounds us is set within a larger ocean of natural objects. But increasingly, it is the technologically produced environment that matters for the individual. The texture of plastic or concrete, the iridescent glisten of an automobile under a streetlight, the staggering vision of a cityscape seen from the window of a jet—these are the intimate realities of his existence. Man-made things enter into and color his consciousness. Their number is expanding with explosive force, both absolutely and relative to the natural environment. This will be even more true in super-industrial society than it is today.

5. Anti-materialists tend to deride the importance of "things." Yet things are highly significant, not merely because of their functional utility, but also because of their psychological impact. We develop relationships with things. Things affect our sense of continuity or discontinuity. They play a role in the structure of situations and the foreshortening of our relationships with things accelerates the pace of life.

6. Moreover, our attitudes toward things reflect basic value judgments. Nothing could be more dramatic than the difference between the new breed of little girls who cheerfully turn in their Barbies for the new improved model and those who, like their mothers and grandmothers before them, clutch lingeringly and lovingly to the same doll until it disintegrates from sheer age. In this difference lies the contrast between past and future, between societies based on permanence, and the new, fast-forming society based on transience.

7. That man-thing relationships are growing more and more temporary may be illustrated by examining the culture surrounding the little girl who trades in her doll. This child soon learns that Barbie dolls are by no means the only physical objects that pass into and out of her young life at a rapid clip. Diapers, bibs, paper napkins, Kleenex, towels, non-returnable soda bottles—all are used up quickly in her home and ruthlessly eliminated. Corn muffins come in baking tins that are thrown away after one use. Spinach is encased in plastic sacks that can be dropped into a pan of boiling water for heating, and then thrown away. TV dinners are cooked and often served on throw-away trays. Her home is a large processing machine through which objects flow, entering and leaving, at a faster and faster rate of speed. From birth on, she is inextricably embedded in a throw-away culture.

8. The idea of using a product once or for a brief period and then replacing it, runs counter to the grain of societies or individuals steeped in a heritage of poverty. Not long ago Uriel Rone, a market researcher for the French advertising agency Publicis, told me: "The French housewife is not used to disposable products. She likes to keep things, even old things, rather than throw them away. We represented one company that wanted to introduce a kind of plastic throw-away curtain. We did a marketing study for them and found the resistance too strong." This resistance, however, is dying all over the developed world.

9. Thus a writer, Edward Maze, has pointed out that many Americans visiting Sweden in the early 1950's were astounded by its cleanliness. "We were almost awed by the fact that there were no beer and soft drink bottles by the roadsides, as, much to our shame, there were in America. But by the 1960's, lo and behold, bottles were suddenly blooming along Swedish highways . . . What happened? Sweden had become a buy, use and throw-away society, following the American pattern." In Japan today throw-away tissues are so universal that cloth handkerchiefs are regarded as old fashioned, not to say unsanitary. In England for sixpence one may buy a "Dentamatic throw-away toothbrush" which comes already coated with toothpaste for its one-time use. And even in France, disposable cigarette lighters are commonplace. From cardboard milk containers to the rockets that power space vehicles, products created for short-term or one-time use are becoming more numerous and crucial to our way of life.

10. The recent introduction of paper and quasi-paper clothing carried the trend toward disposability a step further. Fashionable boutiques and working-class clothing stores have sprouted whole departments devoted to gaily colored and imaginatively designed paper apparel. Fashion magazines display breathtaking sumptuous gowns, coats, pajamas, even wedding dresses made of paper. The bride

pictured in one of these wears a long white train of lacelike paper that, the caption writer notes, will make "great kitchen curtains" after the ceremony.

11. Paper clothes are particularly suitable for children. Writes one fashion expert: "Little girls will soon be able to spill ice cream, draw pictures and make cutouts on their clothes while their mothers smile benignly at their creativity." And for adults who want to express their own creativity, there is even a "paint-yourself-dress" complete with brushes. Price: $2.00.

12. Price, of course, is a critical factor behind the paper explosion. Thus a department store features simple A-line dresses made of what it calls "devil-may-care cellulose fiber and nylon." A $1.29 each, it is almost cheaper for the consumer to buy and discard a new one than to send an ordinary dress to the cleaners. Soon it will be. But more than economics is involved, for the extension of the throw-away culture has important psychological consequences.

13. We develop a throw-away mentality to match our throw-away products. This mentality produces, among other things, a set of radically altered values with respect to property. But the spread of disposability through the society also implies decreased durations in man-thing relationships. Instead of being linked with a single object over a relatively long span of time, we are linked for brief periods with the succession of objects that supplant it.

React...

to the essay by answering the following questions.

1. What is the thesis of the essay? _____

_____

_____

2. Do you agree or disagree with the thesis? _____

   Why? _____

   _____

   _____

3. How does Toffler's use of the Barbie doll help him develop his thesis?

   _____

   _____

   _____

4. Reread paragraph 4. What "man-made things enter into and color" your consciousness; that is, what values toward material things have become an ac-

   cepted and natural part of your life? _____

   _____

5. Toffler says "our attitudes toward things reflect basic value judgments" (par-

   agraph 6). What does he mean? _____

   _____

   _____

   _____

6. Do you think Toffler is against the use of disposable products, such as Kleenex, paper towels, cigarette lighters, and toothbrushes? _____

Explain. _____

_____

_____

_____

_____

7. Do you consider yourself a part of the "throw-away" society Toffler discusses? _____ Why? _____

_____

_____

_____

8. Check any of the words below you don't know or could not use correctly.

_____ a. eminently (1)

_____ b. humanoid (2)

_____ c. iridescent (4)

_____ d. continuity (5)

_____ e. transience (6)

_____ f. inextricably (7)

_____ g. sumptuous (10)

_____ h. boutiques (1)

_____ i. radically altered (13)

_____ j. supplant (13)

Take the time now to reread the words in the paragraphs indicated in parentheses
beside the word. Then go to the Vocabulary Section in the Appendix.

Name _____ Section _____ Date _____

Plan...

an essay on some aspect of material values.

This is a very broad topic, and you need to narrow it down to some area that you feel you can develop in an essay. Here are some suggestions, but don't feel you must use any of these.

1. The need to have possessions.
2. A definition of American materialism.
3. Your value system.
4. Why automobile manufacturers change body styles every year.
5. Why I won't trade in my Barbie doll.
6. The effect advertising has on buying unneeded possessions.
7. Write a review of Vance Packard's *Hidden Persuaders*, Jeffrey Schranks's *Deception Detection*, or Alvin Toffler's *Future Shock*.
8. A rebuttal to Toffler's thesis.
9. How what you own reflects your true sense of values.
10. Life without disposable goodies.
11. Define materialism.
12. How advertising supports a materialistic society.
13. The value in disposable products.
14. The benefits of a materialistic society.
15. What our clothes say about our sense of values.

If none of these ideas interests you, try this. Following is a list of fifteen experts and a brief explanation of what their expertise is. Their skills are guaranteed to be 100 percent effective. You are going to be allowed to pick only three of the experts who will then apply their skills to help you obtain what it is you want. Read about all fifteen; then pick the three you want to help you. The experts are:

1. *Dr. Dorian Grey*—A noted plastic surgeon, he can make you look exactly as you want to look by means of a new painless technique. (He also uses hormones to alter body structures and size!) Your ideal physical appearance can be a reality.
2. *Baron VonBarrons*—A college placement and job placement expert. The college or job of your choice, in the location of your choice, will be yours! (He also provides immunity from the draft if you wish.)
3. *Jedediah Methuselah*—Guarantees you long life (to the age of 200) with your aging process slowed down proportionately. For example, at the age of 60 you will look and feel like 20.

4. *Drs. Masters Johnson and Fanny Hill*—Experts in the area of sexual relations, they guarantee that you will be the perfect male or female, will enjoy sex, and will bring pleasure to others.

5. *Dr. Yin Yang*—An organismic expert, he will provide you with perfect health and protection from physical injury throughout your life.

6. *Dr. Knot Not Ginott*—An expert in dealing with parents, he guarantees that you will never have any problems with your parents again. They will accept your values and your behavior. You will be free from control and badgering.

7. *Stu Denpower*—An expert on authority, he will make sure that you are never again bothered by authorities. His services will make you immune from all control which you consider unfair by the school, the police, and the government (the armed forces included!)

8. *"Pop" Larity*—He guarantees that you will have the friends you want now and in the future. You will find it easy to approach those you like and they will find you easily approachable.

9. *Dr. Charlie Smart*—He will develop your common sense and your intelligence to a level in excess of 150 I.Q. It will remain at this level through your entire lifetime.

10. *Rocky Fellah*—Wealth will be yours, with guaranteed schemes for earning millions within weeks.

11. *Dwight D. DeGawl*—This world famed leadership expert will train you quickly. You will be listened to, looked up to, and respected by those around you.

12. *Dr. Otto Carengy*—You will be well-liked by all and will never be lonely. A life filled with love will be yours.

13. *Dr. Claire Voyant*—All of your questions about the future will be answered, continually, through the training of this soothsayer.

14. *Dr. Hinnah Self*—Guarantees that you will have self-knowledge, self-liking, self-respect, and self-confidence. True self-assurance will be yours.

15. *Prof. Val U. Clear*—With his help, you will always know what you want, and you will be completely clear on all the muddy issues of these confused days.

After you've picked the three experts you want to serve you, write an essay that explains *why* you picked the three experts you did. What does your selection say about your values? What seems to be most important to you? Are these good values you have selected for yourself? for others?

Practice 1. In your journal notebook or on a separate page, spend 10 to 15 minutes freewriting or exploring possible essay topics.

Practice 2. Now plan an essay on some topic. In the space below, write the topic or subject you've picked.

Topic:

_____

_____

Practice 3.   Now write a working thesis for your topic.

Tentative Thesis Statement:

_____

_____

_____

_____

Below list all the ideas you can think of to support your thesis. Then rearrange or group them into a proper order.

_____

_____

_____

_____

_____

_____

_____

_____

_____

_____

Write...

(A) an outline for your essay

One a separate piece of paper write an outline for your essay, basing it on your preceding notes. When finished, turn it in to your instructor for a final check before you actually begin writing your essay.

(B) a first draft of your essay, using the outline you completed for your topic.

Do a first draft on a separate sheet of paper. When finished, go on to (C).

 Quick Review

Summary of Methods Used for Introductory Paragraphs
1. Ask a question.
2. Use an anecdote.
3. Use a quotation.
4. Give a brief overview.
5. Stress importance of topic.
6. Use a combination of methods.

Summary of Paragraph Methods for Supporting Details
1. Examples or illustrations.
2. Specific details.
3. Definition of terms.
4. Comparison or contrast.
5. Analysis.
6. Story or anecdote.
7. Combination of methods.

Summary of Methods Used for Concluding Paragraphs
1. Ask a question.
2. Use an anecdote.
3. Summarize.
4. Show concern.
5. Make conclusions.

Avoid the Following
1. Sentence fragments.
2. Run-on sentences.
3. Comma splices.

(c) with sentence variety.

In order for your essay to read at an easier and more understandable level, you should make certain your sentences have variety of construction and related meanings. There are four categories of sentences. Once you understand these four categories, try to apply this information to your own sentences. Do *not* try to memorize the names of the types of sentences; rather, note their structure or form as sentences.

1. *SIMPLE SENTENCES* are sentences with only one subject and one verb. Here are some examples:
   a. The warranty for the TV set is good for one year.
   S   V
   b. The customer demanded the return of his money.
   S   V
   c. The goods were damaged during their shipment.
   S   V

Notice in each of the examples that the SUBJECT is what the sentence is about and the VERB tells what the subject is doing or did, or it may describe the subject. In the last unit, remember that sentence fragments occurred when either the subject or verb was left out.

2. *COMPOUND SENTENCES* are two or more simple sentences connected as one sentence with a conjunction such as *and, but, however,* and so on. Notice the examples that follow:

   a. The warranty for the new TV set is good for one year, and I think we may need it.
   b. The customer demanded the return of his money, but the manager would not give it to her.
   c. The goods were damaged during their shipment; however, the shipping company agreed to replace them.

Notice in each of the examples that if the conjunctions (the circled words) were removed, each sentence would really be two separate sentences, such as:

The warranty for the new TV set is good for one year. I think we may need it.

The conjunction words keep the sentences from being run-on or fused sentences, which were discussed in Unit. 7.

Check Your Understanding
Place an *S* in the blanks in front of the simple sentences below and a *C* in front of the compound sentences.

_____ a. The guarantee does not cover your problem.

_____ b. You are supposed to fill out the warranty card, but I'll do it for you.

_____ c. The turntable does not work correctly.

_____ d. I just discovered the dryer doesn't work; however, the washer works very well.

_____ e. Today he bought a new suit, and tomorrow he wants to buy new shoes to match.

3. *COMPLEX SENTENCES* are sentences with one main clause (simple sentence) and at least one dependent clause (part of a sentence). Here are some examples:

    a. Because you did not fill out the warranty, the company will not replace the bad tubes.

    b. When I bought my car, I expected better service than this.

    c. Prices being the way they are, it is better to repair your old washer than to buy a new one.

Notice that *each* of the beginning elements of the preceding sentences is only a part of a sentence (clauses) and depends on the independent clause or simple sentence. For instance, in example *a*, "Because you did not fill out the warranty" is a fragment and needs the rest of the sentence to make it whole. It is the same for examples *b* and *c*.

4. *COMPOUND-COMPLEX SENTENCES* are sentences with two or more main clauses (compound sentences) and at least one dependent clause (part of a sentence). Notice the examples that follow:

    a. Because you did not fill out the warranty, the company will not replace the bad tubes, and unfortunately I can't do anything about it.

    b. When I bought my car, I expected better service than this; I feel I am being "taken."

    c. Prices being the way they are, it is better to repair your old washer than to buy a new one, but I'll do whatever you say.

In the preceding examples you can see that they are the same examples used for defining complex sentences with the addition of another simple sentence.

Check Your Understanding

In the space in front of each of the following sentences, write in whether it is a simple, compound, complex, or compound-complex sentence.

_____ a. The guarantee does not cover your problem, but I will fix it anyway.

_____ b. When the clock stopped for the sixth time for no apparent reason, I knew it was time to buy a new clock.

_____ c. After trying to fix the TV set myself, I gave up and took it in to be repaired; little did I know my troubles were only beginning.

_____ d. The new smog devices do not seem to be working as well as they should.

_____ e. Because of the warranty, I was able to have the iron replaced at no cost to myself.

Practices in Writing with Sentence Variety

Practice 1.   Following is a list of some conjunctions or connector words that can be used to make simple sentences into compound sentences. Use them or others you know to make compound sentences of the following simple sentences. Remember to use semicolons where necessary.

and	nor	meanwhile	thus	also
but	however	instead	consequently	besides
or	therefore	otherwise	meanwhile	so

1. I forgot to mimeograph the test today. The test will be tomorrow.

_____

2. The game was called because of rain. It will be played later this week.

_____

3. English courses can be fun. Many of them are a drag.

_____

4. She was late turning in her paper. It made a difference on the grade she received.

_____

5. My English teacher is a mean dude. He's really teaching me how to write.

_____

6. I never really knew what a conjunction was. I know one when I see it.

_____

Practice 2.   Turn the following fragments or dependent clauses into complex sentences.

1. Because of you. _____

2. When the teacher started toward me, _____

_____

3. After the test was over, _____

_____

4. Because the course is almost over, _____

_____

5. If I complete this essay, _____

_____

6. As long as the essay covers the topic, _____

_____

Practice 3. Fill in the blanks that follow with dependent clauses so that the simple sentences are then complex sentences.

1. _____, I have to write another essay,

2. _____, I fell into the hole.

3. _____, she let out a scream.

4. _____, it was no longer possible.

5. _____, my name is going to be mud.

6. _____, he wants to try again.

Practice 4. In some of the following compound sentences, a better choice of conjunction might have been used to link the two main clauses together. In the blanks that follow each sentence, write in a conjunction you feel would make the sentence read better or make more sense.

1. The teacher made us write a lot, and she always returned our graded pap-

ers quickly. _____

2. I finally got to see another movie; however, I was disappointed with it.

_____

3. He misplaced his pen, and he finished the essay with pencil.

_____

4. The essay topics were too broad for a short paper; meanwhile, I narrowed one down. _____

5. The essay is short; so I'll accept it anyway. _____

Practice 5. Change each of the following sentences twice. First, change them to compound sentences using conjunctions. Second, change them to complex sentences with a dependent and independent clause. The first one has been done for you as an example.

1. The tide went out last night. Our boat went with it.
   a. *The tide went out last night, and our boat went with it.*
   b. *When the tide went out last night, our boat went with it.*
2. The book my father wanted was in the store, I couldn't resist buying it for him.

   a. _____

   b. _____
3. Cigarette smoking has been linked with cancer. People continue to smoke anyway.

   a. _____

   b. _____
4. The snow fell for fifteen hours. My car was practically buried under it.

   a. _____

   b. _____
5. Essay writing has never seemed to be a necessary skill. I see the reason for it now.

   a. _____

   b. _____
6. John Updike's novels are interesting. His poetry is better.

   a. _____

   b. _____

Practice 6. Some dependent clauses fit better in the middle of a sentence. Finish the clauses in the following sentences, noticing the punctuation.

1. My teacher, who _____ , taught me well.

2. His father, who _____ , let me borrow his car.

3. The elevator, from which _____ , became stuck between the third and fourth floors.

4. The math problem, which _____ , seemed easy to do once the teacher explained it the third time.

5. The Better Business Bureau, which _____ , put pressure on the company to refund my money.

6. The essay I wrote, which _____ , pleased the teacher.

Practice 7. Write a compound-complex sentence for each of the following topics:

1. food: _____

_____

_____

2. parents: _____

_____

_____

3. advertisements: _____

_____

_____

4. television: _____

_____

_____

Practice 8. Combine these simple sentences into one as directed. Use correct punctuation when necessary. The first one has been done for you.

1. a. The old man clutched his chest.
   b. He was wheezing.
   c. He was frightened.
   Omit needless words: *Wheezing and frightened, the old man clutched his chest. Or: The old man clutched his chest, wheezing and frightened.*

2. a. Tom was unable to stop.
   b. He drove too fast.
   c. He hit the truck head on.
   Change *drove* to *driving,* and *hit* to *hitting:*

   _____

   _____

3. a. Tom just sat in his car.
   b. He was stunned by the accident.
   c. He was unable to move.

   Omit needless words: _____

   _____

4. a. The truck driver felt that death was near.
   b. He yelled in pain.
   c. He panicked for fear the truck would burst into flames.
   Change *yelled* and *panicked* to *yelling* and *panicking:*

   _____

   _____

5. a. Finally, Tom came to his senses.
   b. He rushed to the aid of the truck driver.
   c. The truck driver was now out of his head.
   Change *rushed* to *rushing* and use *who:*

   _____

   _____

6. a. Tom acted none too soon.
   b. He yanked on the truck door.
   c. He pulled the driver out.
   Change *yanked* and *pulled* to *yanking* and *pulling:*

   _____

   _____

7. a. The truck exploded.
   b. It lit up the dark night.
   c. It sent shock waves that stunned Tom.
   Change *lit* and *sent* to *lighting* and *sending:*

_____

_____

8. a. Tom carried the truck driver to safety.
   b. He did not know where he got the strength.
   c. The truck driver had passed out.
   Change *know* to *knowing* and use *who:*

_____

_____

Practice 9. On a separate page, write a paragraph using the combined sentences you wrote in Practice 8.

Rewrite...

your first draft.

Before you begin rewriting your essay, read carefully the following paragraphs taken from a student essay whose thesis is that advertising creates a false sense of needs in us. Note the difference between the first draft and the revision.

Student's First Draft

Advertising subconsciously teaches us. It teaches us that failures can be avoided if we use the right products. Are you having trouble getting a girl friend? Maybe its your breath. Try Listermint. Maybe your smile. Try Ultrabrite. Maybe you have body odor. Try Ban. Such ads create a problem. It teaches us that there are instant solutions to almost every problem.

Instructor's Comments

Combine your first two sentences.

its or it's?

Frag *here. See it?*
More examples or explanations needed to fit your last two sentences. Combine last two sentences?

Here is the student's revised paragraph.

Student's Revised Draft

Advertising subconsciously teaches us that failures can be avoided if we use the right products. Are you having trouble getting a girl friend or boy friend? Maybe it's your breath. Try Listermint. Maybe it's your smile. Try Ultrabrite. Maybe you have body odor. Try Ban. Do you look pale and unhealthy? Try Suddentan. And if none of these works and you get a headache from it all, pop a couple of Excedrin or Alka-Seltzer for fast-fast-fast relief. Such ads eventually create problems because they falsely teach us to believe there are instant solutions to almost every problem.

Instructor's Comments

Much tighter topic sentence.

Good punctuation.

You found the frag. *Good.*

Better. You've elaborated on examples.

Better conclusion.

Return now to the first draft you wrote on a separate sheet of paper at the beginning of this unit. Place a check mark in front of each of the following points as you reexamine your essay. Rewrite or make any corrections you feel would strengthen your essay.

_____ 1. Does your introductory paragraph contain your thesis or main idea regarding your topic?

_____ 2. Does your introductory paragraph attempt to draw your reader's interest?

_____ 3. Can you identify your topic sentences in each of your paragraphs?

_____ 4. Does your concluding paragraph summarize or clarify your point of view about your topic?

_____ 5. Have you used transitional words or expressions within sentences and paragraphs so that your ideas move smoothly from one to another?

_____ 6. Have you written any sentence fragments, run-ons, or comma splices?

_____ 7. Have you written good sentences, using the patterns discussed in this unit and sentence-combining techniques?

_____ 8. Have you shared your essay with others for their comments and suggestions?

When you are certain you have corrected your essay as needed, rewrite it and give both your first draft and the final draft to your instructor.

UNIT 10

Think...
about human behavior

Read...
about rationalizing our behavior
"The Thin Grey Line" by Marya Mannes

React...
to the essay

Plan...
an essay
Topics for an essay.

Write...
(A) an outline for an essay
(B) a first draft
(C) sentences with proper agreement
Subject-verb agreement
Subject-pronoun agreement
Practices in agreement

Rewrite...
your first draft

Think...

about human behavior by answering the following questions.

1. a. What do you think about a man who reports someone he knows to the Internal Revenue Service because he heard him mention he "screwed the government royally" on his last income tax return?

   _____

   b. What do you think of the man who cheated the government?

   _____

   c. What do you think of the man when you later learn he donated all the money he saved cheating on his taxes plus more to your church?

   _____

2. What do you think of a college student who sells marijuana to high school students to pay his tuition?

   _____

3. What would you do if you saw two men beating up a woman and no one else and no telephone were near? (Pretend you're a male, if you aren't.)

   _____

   _____

4. What do you think of students who cheat on tests and homework?

   _____

   _____

5. What do you think of a white couple who decide not to have babies of their

   own and adopt two black children? _____

   _____

6. What do you think of a college registrar who admits good athletes to the college, knowing their academic transcripts are phoney?

   _____

7. Is there ever a good reason for telling a lie? _____

Why? _____

_____

_____

_____

the following essay on behavior.

The author of the next essay, Marya Mannes, is a prolific author who has written many essays as well as novels, plays, and poetry. Occasionally she can be seen on TV and heard on radio talk shows. Her essay here deals with how we rationalize our dishonest behavior and its harmful effects by saying, "Everybody does it."

The Thin Grey Line
Marya Mannes

1. "Aw, they all do it," growled the cabdriver. He was talking about cops who took payoffs for winking at double parking, but his cynicism could as well have been directed at any of a dozen other instances of corruption, big-time and small-time. Moreover, the disgust in his voice was overlaid by an unspoken "So what?": the implication that since this was the way things were, there was nothing anybody could do.

2. Like millions of his fellow Americans, the cabdriver was probably a decent human being who had never stolen anything, broken any law or willfully injured another; somewhere, a knowledge of what was probably right had kept him from committing what was clearly wrong. But that knowledge had not kept a thin grey line that separates the two conditions from being daily greyer and thinner—to the point that it was hardly noticeable.

3. On one side of this line are They: the bribers, the cheaters, the chiselers, the swindlers, the extortioners. On the other side are We—both partners and victims. They and We are now so perilously close that the only mark distinguishing us is that They get caught and We don't.

4. The same citizen who voices his outrage at police corruption will slip the traffic cop on his block a handsome Christmas present in the belief that his car, nestled under a "No Parking" sign, will not be ticketed. The son of that nice woman next door has a habit of stealing cash from her purse because his allowance is smaller than his buddies'. Your son's friend admitted cheating at exams because "everybody does it."

5. Bit by bit, the resistance to and immunity against wrong that a healthy social body builds up by law and ethics and the dictation of conscience have broken down. And instead of the fighting indignation of a people outraged by those who prey on them, we have the admission of impotence: "They all do it."

6. Now, failure to uphold the law is no less corrupt than violation of the law. And the continuing shame of this country now is the growing number of Americans who fail to uphold and assist enforcement of the law, simply—and ignominiously—out of fear. Fear of "involvement," fear of reprisal, fear of "trouble." A man is beaten by hoodlums in plain daylight and in view of bystanders. These people not only fail to help the victim, but, like the hoodlums, flee before the police can question them. A city official knows of a colleague's bribe but does not report it. A pedestrian watches a car hit a woman but leaves the scene, to avoid giving testimony. It happens every day. And if the police get cynical at this irresponsibility, they are hardly to blame. Morale is a matter of giving support and having faith in one another; where both are lacking, "law" has become a worthless word.

7. How did we get this way? What started this blurring of what was once a thick black line between the lawful and the lawless? What makes a "regular guy," a decent fellow, accept a bribe? What makes a nice kid from a middle-class family take money for doing something he must know is not only illegal but wrong?

8. When you look into the background of an erring "kid" you will often find a comfortable home and a mother who will tell you, with tears in her eyes, that she "gave him everything." She probably did, to his everlasting damage. Fearing her son's disapproval, the indulgent mother denies him nothing except responsibility. Instead of growing up, he grows to believe that the world owes him everything.

9. The nice kid's father crosses the thin grey line himself in a dozen ways, day in and day out. He pads his expenses on his income-tax returns as a matter of course. As a landlord, he pays the local inspectors of the city housing authority to overlook violations in the houses he rents. When his son flunked his driving test, he gave him ten dollars to slip the inspector on his second test. "They all do it," he said.

10. The nice kid is brought up with boys and girls who have no heroes except people not much older than themselves who have made the Big Time, usually in show business or in sports. Publicity and money are the halos of their stars, who range from pop singers who can't sing to ballplayers who can't read: from teen-age starlets who can't act to television performers who can't think. They may be excited by the exploits of spacemen, but the work's too tough and dangerous.

11. The nice kids have no heroes because they don't believe in heroes. Heroes are suckers and squares. To be a hero you have to stand out, to excel, to take risks, and above all, not only choose between right and wrong, but defend the right and fight the wrong. This means responsibility—and who needs it?

12. Today, no one has to take any responsibility. The psychiatrists, the sociologists, the novelists, the playwrights have gone a long way to help promote irresponsibility. Nobody really is to blame for what he does. It's Society. It's Environment. It's a Broken Home. It's an Underprivileged Area. But it's hardly ever You.

13. Now we find a truckload of excuses to absolve the individual from responsibility for his actions. A fellow commits a crime because he's basically insecure, because he hated his stepmother at nine, or because his sister needs an operation. A policeman loots a store because his salary is too low. A city official accepts a payoff because it's offered to him. Members of minority groups, racial or otherwise, commit crimes because they can't get a job, or are unacceptable to the people living around them. The words "right" and "wrong" are foreign to these people.

14. But honesty is the best policy. Says who? Anyone willing to get laughed at. But the laugh is no laughing matter. It concerns the health and future of a nation. It involves the two-dollar illegal bettor as well as the corporation price-fixer, the college-examination cheater and the payroll-padding Congressman, the expense-account chiseler, the seller of pornography and his schoolboy reader, the bribed judge and the stealing delinquent. All these people may represent a minority. But when, as it appears now, the majority excuse themselves from responsibility by accepting corruption as natural to society ("They all do it"), this society is bordering on total confusion. If the line between right and wrong is finally erased, there is no defense against the power of evil.

15. Before this happens—and it is by no means far away—it might be well for the schools of the nation to substitute for the much-argued issue of prayer a daily lesson in ethics, law, and responsibility to society that would strengthen the conscience as exercise strengthens muscles. And it would be even better if parents were forced to attend it. For corruption is not something you read about in the papers and leave to courts. We are all involved.

React....

to the essay by answering the following questions.

1. What is the thesis of the essay?

_____

_____

2. In what paragraph or paragraphs is the thesis best stated?

_____

3. What is "the thin grey line" referred to in the title?

_____

_____

4. Mannes uses many examples of "They all do it." List at least four?

   a. _____

   b. _____

   c. _____

   d. _____
5. What kind of heroes does Mannes say the youth of today admire?

_____

_____

6. Do you agree with the author's thesis? _____

   Why? _____

_____

_____

_____

7. Check the words from the essay you don't know or could not use correctly.

_____ a. cynicism (1)

_____ b. willfully (2)

_____ c. extortioners (3)

_____ d. impotence (5)

_____ e. ignominiously (6)

_____ f. erring (8)

_____ g. indulgent (8)

_____ h. absolve (13)

_____ i. chiseler (14)

_____ j. ethics (15)

Reread the words in the paragraphs indicated to see how they are used. Then go to the Vocabulary Section in the Appendix for more information and exercises.

Plan....

an essay on some aspect of human behavior.

Let's hope you have some ideas for an essay that stem from the Marya Mannes essay you just read or the THINK and REACT questions. If not, here are some specific situations that call for some behavioral action. Read each one; think about the behavior patterns each situation requires.

1. You are walking down the street. You are about to pass a man sitting in a car when he tosses a candy wrapper onto the sidewalk. There is a city trash can six feet away. What should you do and why?

   Possible essay subject: litterbug behavior.

2. You are in a course at college that you hate. It's a required course for graduation, but it's boring to you, and you don't particularly like the professor. You're not doing well in the class, and it's final exam time. Someone offers you, for a price, a copy of what is supposed to be the final. What will you do and why?

   Possible essay subject: forms of cheating; student cheating.

3. The doctor has just told your father that your mother, who has been ill for months, has only three to four months to live. Your father tells you, but says not to tell your mother. Your mother asks you to tell her what the doctor said because your father won't. What should you do and why?

   Possible essay subjects: deceit, telling lies.

4. You see a fourteen-year-old girl shoplifting in the department store where you are shopping. So far she has stolen a scarf and a necklace, and now you see she is about to take a bottle of perfume. What should you do and why?

   Possible essay subjects: shoplifting; stealing.

5. Your family is discussing abortion. Most everyone seems to be against it rather than for it. Suddenly your sixteen-year-old sister starts crying and runs from the room. What should you do?

   Possible essay subjects: abortion; moral behavior.

6. You are at a party. The wife of a friend of yours becomes overly attentive. Soon she lets you know in no uncertain terms that she would like to have an affair with you. She's attractive, and you admit to yourself that you wouldn't mind. What should you do?

   Possible essay subjects: adultery; flirting; faithfulness.

If none of these dilemmas help you select a topic, consider some of these ideas.

1. Why people gamble.
2. Why people are interested in pornography.
3. Euthanasia (mercy killing): right or wrong?
4. Should prostitution be legalized?
5. Segregation (racial, religious, or sexual) is (good, bad; moral or immoral).
6. What is sin?
7. Cruelty to animals (children, spouses).
8. Spying: a necessary evil.
9. The difference between lust and love.
10. Suicide as a freedom of choice.
11. Behavioral modification: good or bad?
12. Why people smoke.
13. Why people use drugs.
14. Are the Ten Commandments outdated?
15. Write a short essay in response to the following quote:
    "Trust is a social good to be protected just as much as the air we breathe or the water we drink." So argues Sissela Bok, a lecturer on medical ethics at Harvard Medical School, in her book *Lying*. Most Americans would readily agree. Yet Americans are finding it ever more risky to trust the world about them. Duplicity crops up so often and so widely that there are moments when it seems that old-fashioned honesty is going out of style. (Frank Trippett, "The Busting of American Trust." *Time*, October 20, 1980.)
16. In March 1980 a parent picked up a copy of *Ms.* magazine brought home from school by her high-school daughter. Inside she discovered a story that the parent claimed was "extremely offensive, and, further, immoral, obscene, and disgusting." Showing the magazine and complaining to the principal of the school, the parent was successful in getting the high school's subscription canceled. This set off a battle between some parents and fundamentalist religious groups on one side and civil libertarians, women's groups, teachers, and librarians on the other. A committee appointed by the school board recommended the magazine be available for students to read on library shelves. However, after a crowded, emotional board meeting the trustees voted to cancel the subscription, a policy that affects about 11,700 students. The American Civil Liberties Union filed suit against the school district to keep the district from restricting students' access to the magazine, claiming that the rights of students to receive information, the right of teachers to provide it, and the free press rights of the magazine have been violated by the school district. Pick a point of view, either for or against the cancellation of the magazine subscription and defend your ideas.

Practice 1. In your journal notebook or on a separate page, spend 10 to 15 minutes freewriting or exploring possible essay topics.

Practice 2. Now plan an essay on some topic. In the space below, write the topic or subject you have picked.

Topic:

_____

_____

Practice 3. Now write a working thesis for your topic.

Tentative Thesis Statement:

_____

_____

_____

_____

Below, list all the ideas you can think of to support your thesis. Then rearrange or group them into a proper order.

_____

_____

_____

_____

_____

_____

_____

_____

_____

Write...

(A) an outline for the first draft of your essay, using the rearranged list of supporting details.

Do an outline on a separate sheet of paper. Then go on to (*B*).

(B) a first draft.

On still another sheet of paper, write the first draft of your essay based on the outline you did in (*A*). Feel free to alter or change your first draft from the outline if you feel the change is for the better. Your outline is only a guide for writing, not the final word. When finished, go on to (*C*).

(C) sentences with proper agreement.

You already have seen in previous units how to write better and more mature sentences. In those units mention was made that every sentence must have a subject and a verb. It is important that you (1) use the correct verb form for the subject of the sentence and that (2) you use the correct pronoun when referring back to the subject.

Agreement of Subject and Verb

1. The rule for proper agreement of subjects and verbs is easy. Singular subjects take singular verbs; plural subjects take plural verbs. However, it is not always easy when you are writing to know which is the singular or plural verb form. Look at the examples below.

   The <u>tree</u> in the yard <u>grows</u> very fast.
   The <u>trees</u> in the yard <u>grow</u> very fast.

   Notice that a singular subject (*tree*) takes a singular verb form (*grows*). The plural subject (*trees*) takes a plural verb form (*grow*). Notice, too, that usually an *s* ending on a subject means it is a plural subject. Sometimes, however, this is not always the case, as the following examples show.

The <u>women</u> on our block <u>want</u> to organize a bridge club.
The <u>men</u> <u>went</u> to Las Vegas.
The <u>dog</u> and the <u>cat</u> <u>get</u> along well.

In all the preceding cases, the subjects are plural, but do not end with the letter *s.*

Check Your Understanding

For each of the following sentences, underline the subject with one line and the verb with two lines.

a. That music is one of my favorites.
b. In some colleges, boys and girls live in the same dormitories.
c. They forgot to meet us there.
d. My mother fixes television sets.
e. That television program makes me ill.

2. Sometimes, when writing, we use the wrong verb for the subject because of plural phrases or expressions that come between the subject and the verb. Look at the following examples.

Our <u>television,</u> as well as many other televisions, <u>is</u> not <u>built</u> to last beyond the warranty.
<u>Dr. Gibbons,</u> along with his three nurses, <u>appears</u> regularly on the program.
His <u>sisters,</u> who look very much like his brother, <u>are</u> not here today.

As you can see, the need to match the correct verb form with the subject can become difficult if the subject is not sorted out from the other nouns in the sentence.

Check Your Understanding

In the following sentences, underline the correct verb form.

a. Robert, as well as Jim and Paul, (were, was) late.
b. The hammer, along with my other tools, (were, was) left in the rain.
c. The boys, who don't care too much for their sister, (were, was) about to leave without her.
d. Television repairmen, along with auto mechanics, (has, have) poor reputations on the whole.
e. The crowd, paying no attention to the speaker, (is, are) starting to get restless.

3. The following words, when used as subjects, take singular verbs because they are considered singular subjects:

each	everybody	anyone	someone	neither	no one
every	everything	anybody	somebody	nobody	another
everyone	either	anything	something	nothing	

Notice the following examples:

> Each of us is concerned with the problem.
> Everybody wants him to win.
> Nothing is the way it was.
> Neither of them wants that to happen.

On the other hand, the following words may be used in either a singular or plural sense, depending upon the context of the sentence:

> any   all   more   most   none   some

Notice the following examples.

> Some of the stockings are too large.
> Some of the wood is wet.
> None of us are correct.
> None is correct.

Check Your Understanding

Underline the correct verb form in the following sentences.

a. Each of the three (has, have) a way to get there.
b. Either of them (is going, are going) to get it!
c. Some of the pants (are, is) damaged.
d. None of the answers (is, are) correct.
e. Anyone sensible (is, are) in agreement with me.

4. Two or more subjects linked by *and* usually take a plural verb even if the individual subject is a singular subject. However, when the words *each* or *every* are used before singular subjects linked by *and,* a singular verb is used.

   The principal and the teacher walk home for lunch.
   (The principal and teacher together make the plural, they. They walk home for lunch.)
   My mother, father, and sisters want to come to the play.
   (Taken together "they" want to come to the play.)
   Each novel and play has to be read by Friday.
   Every dog and cat likes to drag garbage from the trash cans.

Also, when two or more subjects are joined by the words *either . . . or, neither . . . nor,* the verb agrees with the subject closest to it.

> Either you or Sam buys tickets.
> Neither my girlfriend nor my best friends want to go.

Check Your Understanding

Underline the correct verb form in the following sentences.

a. The television and the radio always (break, breaks) down at the wrong times.
b. Dustin Hoffman and Robert Redford (are, is) my favorite actors.
c. Either the maps or the tablet (has, have) to be moved.
d. Each record and each album cover (have, has) to be marked.
e. Neither your parents nor mine (wants, want) to go.

5. Subjects that are plural in form, such as *pants, clothes, scissors,* and *glasses,* usually take a plural verb. However, subjects that are plural in form but singular in meaning, such as *mathematics, physics, economics, news, athletics, family, group,* and *class,* require singular verb forms. Notice the following examples.

My pants are torn.
Physics is a difficult subject for me.
Athletics is not required at this school.
The group is traveling by bus.

In addition, subjects that are stating an amount of something, such as money, weight, or time, require singular verbs.

Twenty-five dollars is too much to pay.
The doctor said four ounces of codeine is far too much.
Five weeks of vacation is ideal for the trip.

Check Your Understanding

Underline the correct verb form in the following sentences.

a. The entire family (want, wants) to watch the TV special.
b. Six dollars (is, are) a bargain.
c. Economics (is, are) my favorite subject this semester.
d. The scissors (is, are) not working correctly.
e. His trousers (is, are) frayed at the cuffs.

6. The singular verb form is used with the title of any written work, even if the title is plural. It is also always used when a sentence begins with *it.*

Arizona Highways is full of colorful illustrations.
The Los Angeles Times is a morning newspaper.
Indians of the Plains tells us a great deal about the history of the Cheyenne.
It is my favorite dish.
It is time for us to do something for her.

Check Your Understanding

Underline the correct verb in the following sentences.

a. *The Seven Minutes* (deal, deals) with obscenity.
b. It (is, are) the parents who demanded action.
c. *Plutarch's Lives* (tell, tells) us about famous Greeks and Romans.
d. Each one (tell, tells) it in his own way.
e. Neither that book nor these movies (show, shows) the truth.

Agreement of Pronoun and Subject

1. In order to keep from repeating your subject, you should use pronouns as a substitute. For instance,

   Awkward: The housewives said the housewives' demands on the stores were met.
   Better: The housewives said <u>their</u> demands on the stores were met.

Here is a list of pronouns that are used to replace subjects. There are more, but this list will stir your memory.

   me, my, mine, myself
   you, he, him, her, she
   they, them, these, this, that, their, its
   we, us, who, which, what

2. A pronoun has to agree in number with the subject or word it is replacing. Notice the following examples.

   The <u>students</u> left <u>their</u> books in the room.

   The <u>professor</u> told us about <u>his</u> personal problems.

   I know that <u>my</u> essay was well written.

   <u>They</u> wanted us to go in <u>their</u> car with <u>them.</u>

3. When the subject of a sentence is one of the words in the following list, a singular pronoun should be used.

someone	everyone	no one	person
somebody	everybody	nobody	man
something	everything	nothing	woman

Here are some examples:

   <u>Someone</u> should tell us about <u>his</u> or <u>her</u> own food.

   <u>Everyone</u> is responsible for <u>his</u> or <u>her</u> own food.

   <u>No one</u> can know what lies in <u>his</u> or <u>her</u> future.

4. When a collective noun such as *family, group,* or *class* is used as a singular subject, it requires a singular pronoun. When a collective noun is used as a plural subject, it requires a plural pronoun. Notice the examples below.

The family is having its third picnic this year.

The class will do their own projects rather than a group project.

Check Your Understanding

Supply the correct pronouns in the following blanks.

a. Someone left _____ bag here.

b. Everybody should do _____ own "thing."

c. Each person must give _____ report on Tuesday.

d. Anyone can join if _____ wants to do so.

e. The professors decided to take _____ problems to a lawyer.

Practices in Agreement

Practice 1. Change the verbs in the following sentences to agree with the subject of the sentence. Some sentences may be correct.

1. Our new car, like many new cars, don't seem to be as well built as older models.
2. My brothers, who look much like my dad, seems to have taken their physical characteristics from dad's side of the family.
3. John, as well as Mary and Ted, were late for class.
4. The students, bored with the speaker's topic, was getting restless and noisy.
5. Each of us are in need of the money.
6. My teacher, mother, and father want me to try for the scholarship.
7. Some of the pieces of wood is wet.
8. Anyone who wishes to go with us are welcome.
9. Each book and its cover have to be returned next week.
10. "Guadalajara" and "Sin ti" is on my favorite record of Mexican music.

Practice 2. Change the subjects of the following sentences to plural subjects, and change the verbs to fit the plural subjects. Some pronouns may also need to be changed to plural form.

1. The principal wants all parents to attend the meeting.

2. The letter took a long time to reach us.

3. The book is overdue at the library.

_____

4. The diamond ring fell through the grate.

_____

5. After eating his fill, the pony rubbed his neck on the fence.

_____

6. Only one of the boys wants to go with us.

_____

7. Their philosophy professor expects them to write good essay exams.

_____

8. The astronaut takes proper precautions before turning the dials.

_____

9. *The New York Times* is larger on Sunday than weekdays.

_____

10. The tree in the backyard is losing its leaves.

_____

Practice 3.   In the space provided, write the plural form of the verb listed.

1. to run _____

2. to cross _____

3. to see _____

4. to cause _____

5. to enjoy _____

6. to want _____

7. to restore _____

8. to remember _____

9. to think _____

10. to do _____

Practice 4. Change any of the pronouns used in the following sentences that do not agree with the subject.

1. Each person must tell the story in their own way.
2. Neither that car nor mine works as they should.
3. The doctors wanted to be certain he was understood.
4. Everybody wants to see an *A* on their paper.
5. Someone left their keys on the table.
6. Anyone can get some type of job if they really want to.
7. One of us must give our report on Tuesday.
8. The store has a reputation for not giving refunds for their faulty goods.
9. Every man and woman should vote according to their own conscience and judgment.
10. The group of laborers announced their decisions regarding the proposed labor law.

Practice 5. Write a sentence, using the following subjects and making certain there is a pronoun reference that agrees with the subject.

1. Each one of the members _____

_____

2. Neither you nor I _____

_____

3. The group of doctors _____

_____

4. Everyone must _____

_____

5. Either one _____

_____

6. None of the parents _____

_____

7. The class _____

_____

8. All of the members _____

_____

9. Nobody _____

_____

10. The pants _____

_____

Practice 6. Combine each set of sentences into one sentence. Use correct punctuation. The first one has been done for you.

1. a. Sammy ran quickly from the room.
   b. His face was wet with tears.
   Change *was wet:*

   His face wet with tears, Sammy ran quickly from the room.

   _____

   Or: Sammy ran quickly from the room, his face wet with tears.

   _____

2. a. The car slowed to a stop.
   b. The headlights were pointing right at us.
   Change *were pointing:*

   _____

   _____

3. a. When I saw him, Joe was sitting in front of the TV set.
   b. The dog was lying at his feet.
   Change *was lying:*

   _____

   _____

4. a. The men up and down the hills fought against the fire.
   b. They were sweating profusely.
   c. They were worried they might lose the battle against the flames.
   Change *were sweating* and *were worried:*

   _____

   _____

5. a. The coach sat on the bench alone.
   b. His head was hanging low.
   c. His hands were clutched together.
   Change *was hanging* and *were clutched:*

   _____

   _____

6. a. When the teacher returned, she could not believe the mess.
   b. Books were scattered on the floor.
   c. Graffiti were scribbled on the blackboards.
   d. Students were dancing on their desk tops.
   Use a dash after independent clause:

   _____

   _____

   _____

7. a. Janet hung up the phone.
   b. Janet was obviously pleased with the conversation.
   c. She had a huge smile on her face.
   Experiment with different possibilities:

   _____

   _____

   _____

8. a. "Shogun" cost over $25 million to produce.
   b. It was a television miniseries.
   c. "Shogun" almost reached as wide an audience as "Roots."
   Experiment with different possibilities:

   _____

   _____

   _____

Rewrite...
your first draft.

Before you begin to rewrite your essay, notice the short excerpt from a student's first and second draft for an essay dealing with the rise of alcoholism.

Student's First Draft	Instructor's Comments
The under-twenty-ones are not the only ones who are drinking more. In the past, middle-aged men was the most prone to alcoholism. Recently there been a big increase in alcoholism among people in their twenties and thirties and especially among women. In the '50s, the National Institute of Mental Health estimates that one of every six alcoholics was a woman the ratio now is one woman for every four men. These figures may be misleading. A nonworking woman find it easy to hide her habit. In some places the ratio between men and women problem drinkers are already equal, for example, in Floridas Dade County, authorities estimate that out of a population of 1,385,000 there probably is 78,000 alcoholics. Half women.	*This draft seems hurriedly written.* *Subj/verb agreement* *Word left out.* *Run-on (r.o.)* *Subj/verb agree* *New paragraph?* *"In some . . ." Agreement/* *Comma splice (c.s.) Need apostrophe* *subj/verb agreement/fragment* *Clean up your agreement problems, faulty sentence structures. Where possible combine sentences.*

Did you see all the errors in the first draft? Notice the changes made in the second draft below.

Student's Revised Draft	Instructor's Comments
The under-twenty-ones are not the only ones who are drinking more. In the past, middle-aged men were the most prone to alcoholism, but recently there has been a big increase in alcoholism among people in their twenties and thirties, especially among women. In the '50s, the National Institute of Mental Health estimates that one of every six alcoholics was a woman. Now, the	*A much tighter paragraph.* *Good job of sentence combining.* *Good transition from past to present.*

ratio is one woman for every four men; however, it may be higher since nonworking women find it easy to hide their habit at home.

Good sentence; concludes the paragraph nicely.

Good idea to start new paragraph here.

In some places, the ratio between men and women problem drinkers is already equal. For example, in Florida's Dade County, authorities estimate that out of a population of 1,385,000 there are probably 78,000 alcoholics, half of them women. Figures from other areas support this trend, which is growing at an alarming rate.

Good; the c.s. is eliminated, and the additional sentences here make this a much better paragraph.

Return now to the first draft you wrote on a separate sheet of paper at the beginning of this unit. Place a check mark in front of each of the following points as you reexamine your essay. Rewrite or make any corrections you feel would strengthen your essay.

_____ 1. Does your introductory paragraph contain your thesis or main idea regarding your topic?

_____ 2. Does your introductory paragraph attempt to draw your reader's interest?

_____ 3. Can you identify your topic sentences in each of your paragraphs?

_____ 4. Does your concluding paragraph summarize or clarify your point of view about your topic?

_____ 5. Have you used transitional words or expressions within sentences or paragraphs?

_____ 6. Have you corrected any sentence fragments, run-ons, or comma splices?

_____ 7. Have you used sentence variety, using the patterns discussed in the last Unit and sentence-combining techniques?

_____ 8. Have you checked each sentence for subject, verb, and pronoun agreement?

_____ 9. Have you shared your essay with someone for their comments and criticism?

When you are certain you have corrected your essay as needed, rewrite it, and give both your first draft and the final draft to your instructor.

UNIT

Think...

about self-control and self-discipline

Read...

about a case of lack of self-discipline
"On Being a Mess" by Elizabeth Ames

React...

to the essay

Plan...

an essay
Topics for an essay

Write...

(A) an outline for your essay
(B) a first draft
(C) with parallelism
Practices in parallelism

Rewrite...

your first draft

Think...

about self-control by answering the following questions.

1. Define what you think is meant by self-control. _____

_____

_____

2. Do you believe you have good self-control? _____

   Why? _____

3. Over what things, such as temper, emotions, weight, and so on, do you have

   good self-control? _____

_____

_____

4. Over what things do you *not* have good self-control? _____

_____

_____

5. When or under what circumstances do you think self-control of your desires

   is not desirable? _____

   Why? _____

_____

_____

6. What is the difference between self-control and discipline?

_____

_____

Read...

the following essay about the lack of self-control.

The following essay is a type of self-confessional. Many of us probably have difficulty disciplining ourselves in regard to something—studying, overeating, smoking, wasting time, and so forth. The author, Elizabeth Ames, confesses to us an area where she lacks self-control. Ms. Ames plans "to climb Mount Kilimanjaro as soon as she finishes cleaning her New York apartment."

On Being a Mess
Elizabeth Ames

1. I am one of those people who simply cannot clean up. To me, the prospect of an orderly living space is as remote—and problematic—as trying to climb Mount Kilimanjaro.

2. There's a definite syndrome of sloppiness. Many people, I've noticed, go about being sloppy in much the same way. I'm not sure what to call us. Mess-aholics? Mess-addicts? Whatever we are, the one thing we are *not* is slobs. Slobs wallow in their mess. Messy people (for want of a better label) groan over it. We're continually apologizing to the tune of, "My apartment is such a pigsty. My house is such a mess." We are always embarrassed.

3. When my place is at its worst, I frequently invite another Messy Person over. We'll engage in an odd one-upmanship that is both competition and consolation. "I'm sorry, the place is terrible." "You should see *mine*. It's ten times worse." "Oh, no, it isn't." "Yes, it is." Etc.

4. Messy People want to clean up, but we can't. Not that we don't try. We do, and probably more strenuously than most Neat People. I have scoured and dusted my tiny apartment on more sunny Saturdays than I can count. I have slogged through three-day marathons (attacking the kitchen, the living room, the bedroom and bathroom in turn). Yet somehow the apartment will not come to order. Soon after I've thrown in the sponge, I'm again tripping on the same sneakers and piles of underwear.

5. Omnivorous: We can never quite conquer the Mess. Rout it from the living room, and it withdraws to the bedroom. From there it may retreat under the bed or into dresser drawers. A protean monster, it forever changes form to evade us.

Reprinted by permission of Elizabeth Ames. Text originally appeared in *Newsweek*, July 7, 1980.

6. To complicate matters, it is also omnivorous. It eats my keys (usually before I go out). It eats my shoes. And worst of all, it eats my bills. That can have sticky consequences because who, after all, misses bills? Occasionally, it takes the threat of legal action for me to discover that the Mess devoured my bills before I had a chance to pay them.

7. Often the Mess seems to rule our lives. I have declined dozens of casual engagements because "I have to get rid of that Mess." Then there are the potential visitors I've had to meet in restaurants "because there is a giant Mess in my apartment."

8. Other times, the only way to subdue the Mess is to invite people to dinner. But even when I've labored over my apartment all afternoon—even when I think I have it licked—the Mess rears its ugly head.

9. "What about the newspapers on the floor?" a well-meaning friend will chide. "What about those files and legal pads on the dining-room table?"

10. "But I haven't *finished* those newspapers and I *work* on the dining-room table." My friends shake their heads sadly. I am surely a lost cause.

11. And that's on a good day. On bad days, the Mess takes over completely. There is no space at all on that dining-room table, or anywhere else for that matter. Everything I own is lost under the rubble. On tiptoe, I pick my way around the books and assorted papers, trying not to step on anything important.

12. On bad days I frequently cannot decide what to wear, partly because half my wardrobe—the clothes I wore last week—is heaped on the bedroom desk.

13. As for the kitchen, it can be downright scary. I dread opening the dark refrigerator, certain that some forgotten tomatoes have metamorphosed into new forms of life. Who knows what lurks in the sink? The dishes there form towers that lean precariously. They usually manage to fall over between 2 and 3 A.M.

14. I'm convinced that on one bad day I will enter my apartment and suddenly panic—thinking I've been robbed when I haven't. After all, how could a normal person wreak such havoc? I must be living with some invisible maniac, or a crazed gorilla.

15. Perhaps that is why so many Messy People feel "exposed" when a stranger glimpses their Mess. Beneath our attempts at denial, we have seen the enemy and he is certainly no crazed gorilla . . .

16. Reality, however, is not always easy to face. Thus we have devised several ingenious myths to justify our Mess—and ourselves. They are:

17. The Clean Mess. This myth is our primary protection against the gruesome label, "slob." Slobs, of course, live in filth. Messy People live amid a profusion of sterile objects. "What's wrong," we ask, "with some basically clean clothes lying around? At least they're not fungus."

18. The Intellectual Mess. According to this one, we are too busy pondering the state of the universe to bother with such earthly realities as unmade beds. We are creative nonconformists whose order is disorder. People with Intellectual Messes look down their noses at unimaginative organized souls. There's no challenge, they insist, in finding a dictionary *right away*. How routine. How dull.

19. It's My Mother's Fault. Behind nearly every Messy Person is a Meticulous Mother. We love to recount our childhood torments at her hands and bemoan its effects: "She ordered me to do the bathroom so many times! I now have convulsions at the sight of window cleaner . . . So much talk about eating off her floors warped my subconscious. I'm acting out delusions of being an animal." And so on.

20. It's My Apartment's Fault. People who rely on this complain, "There's no place left to put anything. My closets are full. What would I do with those things I'm saving for the Salvation Army? What would I do with my stuffed giraffe, Snookie? And those old broiler pans belonged to my grandfather!"

21. Such are the myths of Mess. Myths, because there are plenty of neat folks with brains, badgering mothers and small apartments. Being a mess is no blessing. The only way out is to probe your true motives, discard the excuses and accept responsibility. For me, that was a gut-wrenching process. It was so powerful, in fact, that I didn't wash dishes for two weeks.

React....

to the essay by answering the following questions.

1. What is the thesis of the essay?

_____

_____

2. What distinction is made between slobs and messy people?

_____

_____

3. Who is "the enemy" of messy people mentioned in paragraph 15?

_____

4. List the four myths messy people create to excuse themselves and briefly explain each:

   a. _____

   _____

   _____

   b. _____

   _____

   _____

   c. _____

   _____

   _____

   d. _____

   _____

   _____

5. Discuss why the last paragraph is or is not effective.

_____

_____

_____

6. Ames shows us very clearly one of her behavior patterns she is not proud to
   have. What are some behavioral patterns that show lack of self-discipline or
   responsibility that you have?

_____

_____

7. Check the following words you do not know or could not use correctly.

_____ a. remote (1)

_____ b. syndrome (2)

_____ c. one-upmanship (3)

_____ d. protean (5)

_____ e. omnivorous (6)

_____ f. subdue (8)

_____ g. metamorphosed (13)

_____ h. precariously (13)

_____ i. meticulous (19)

_____ j. badgering (21)

   Reread the words as they are used in the essay. Then go to the Vocabulary
Section in the Appendix for more information and exercises.

Plan...

an essay on self-control or self-discipline.

If the essay and the questions you answered did not stimulate your thinking about self-control, here is a list of ideas that might help you decide on a topic for an essay.

1. The trouble I get into when I don't control my emotions.
2. Self-control is not a general human characteristic; a person can have good self-control in some aspects of life and poor self-control in others. For instance . . .
3. People are losing control over themselves and their environment.
4. Can everyone learn to control his or her behavior?
5. Reasons I lose self-control.
6. How I try to control my habit of _____.
7. Ways to control overeating (or drinking or smoking, and so on)
8. How drugs can damage self-control.
9. The need for self-control against those idiots on the road.
10. The habits I need to control.
11. How one's environment hampers or helps self-control.
12. Adult temper tantrums I have seen.
13. Methods used by Schick Centers.
14. Pretend you are "Dear Abby" and a teenage girl writes, "I know this boy I'm seeing is just using me sexually, but I can't stop seeing him. What can I do?" Answer her question.
15. You are a college counselor, and a student explains his poor grades by stating that the surf has been up lately, and he's been cutting classes to get some surf in before it subsides. He knows he shouldn't be doing it, but he keeps hoping the surf will drop. What do you suggest and advise?
16. Your fourteen-year-old is caught shoplifting, not once, not twice, but three times. He explains he doesn't want to but can't help himself. "I just go out of control in the store," he tells you as his excuse. What do you say and do for him?
17. Read and think about the following quotes from Richard Bach's *Illusions: The Adventures of a Reluctant Messiah.* Write an essay based on your reaction to one of them:
    a. "Your only obligation in any lifetime is to be true to yourself. Being true to anyone else or anything else is not only impossible but the mark of a fake messiah."
    b. "Learning is finding out what you already know. Doing is demonstrating that you know it."
    c. "You are always free to change your mind and choose a different future, or a different past."
    d. "There is no such thing as a problem without a gift for you in its hands. You seek problems because you need their gifts."
18. Why I can't write an essay on self-control.

Practice 1. In your journal notebook or on a separate page, spend 10 to 15 minutes freewriting or exploring possible essay topics.

Practice 2. Now plan an essay on some topic. In the space below, write the topic or subject you have picked.

Topic:

_____

_____

Practice 3. Now write a working thesis for your topic.

Tentative Thesis Statement:

_____

_____

_____

_____

Below, list all the ideas you can think of to support your thesis. Then rearrange or group them into a proper order.

_____

_____

_____

_____

_____

_____

_____

_____

_____

Write...

(A) an outline for your essay.

On a separate sheet of paper write an outline for your essay, using the rearranged list of supporting ideas. When finished, turn it in to your instructor. When he or she has returned it, do (*B*).

(B) a first draft of your essay, using the outline you completed for your topic.

Do a first draft on a separate sheet of paper. When finished, go on to (*C*).

(C) with parallelism.

Parallelism in writing means that words and ideas used in sentences and paragraphs should express equal or matched words and ideas. Three types of parallelism will be explained to help make the definition clearer.

1. *Parallelism with words and phrases* is necessary for clarity of ideas and smoothness in reading. Notice how the verbs in the following sentence are not balanced or parallel in tense.

    Sharon files, types, and sometimes will run errands.

    The sentence should read:

    Sharon *files,*
        types, and sometimes
        runs errands.

Notice that the verb elements are all now the same tense. This is one type of parallelism. Here is another, more complicated example of faulty parallelism:

    Sharon learned how to type reports, to file correspondence, and smiles pleasantly.

The corrected sentence should read:

    Sharon learned how *to type reports,*
        to file correspondence, and
        to smile pleasantly.

For proper parallelism each series of verbs, adjectives, or phrases must be equal or matched in tense and word of phrase elements.

Check Your Understanding

Make each of the following sentences parallel by changing the incorrect elements.

a. He watched her sing, dance, and her acting.

b. I enjoy going to the movies, listening to music, and cards.

c. It is better to run than walking slowly.

d. We couldn't decide whether to go to the library or try going home.

2. Another type of parallelism is keeping a consistent *point of view* throughout your essay. In other words, if your point of view is "he" or "you" or "one," be consistent all the way through. Notice in the following example the *shift in point of view:*

> If one wishes to travel, he should save his money.

The correct parallelism would be:

> If <u>one</u> wishes to travel, <u>one</u> should save <u>one's</u> money.
>> *or:*
> If <u>he</u> wishes to travel, <u>he</u> should save <u>his</u> money.

Another example of poor parallelism is in the following sentence:

> Wrong:
> <u>John</u> <u>worked</u> on his car in the mornings, and his <u>afternoons</u> <u>were spent</u> surfing.

The correct structure would be:

> Right:
> <u>John</u> <u>worked</u> on his car in the mornings and <u>spent</u> his afternoons surfing.

Notice that in the wrong sentence *John* is the subject, but there is a needless change to *afternoons* as a subject of the second independent clause. In the corrected version *John* stays the subject for both clauses.

Check Your Understanding

Make each of the sentences parallel in point of view.

a. As we know where we are going camping, one should make plans for campsites.

b. Alan signed up for summer courses, but his summer was spent traveling.

_____

c. One never knows when he might be attacked on the streets.

_____

d. A person should make preparations for one's future.

_____

3. When a phrase in a sentence does not clearly or logically relate to another word or modify another word in the sentence, it is called a *dangling modifier*, another form of faulty parallelism. Notice in the examples that follow how the introductory clause does not modify or relate to any word in the sentence.

> Wrong:
> While eating my breakfast, a gun shot attracted my attention.
> (A gun shot can't eat breakfast.)
> Right:
> While eating my breakfast, I was attracted by a gun shot.
> (The introductory clause relates to the "I.")
> Wrong:
> Being intelligent and handsome, I hoped he would ask me for a date.
> (Is the "I" intelligent and handsome or the person who may ask for a date?)
> Right:
> I hoped he would ask me for a date because he's so intelligent and handsome.

Check Your Understanding

Change the dangling modifiers so that they are parallel to the proper elements in the sentence.

a. Looking out the door, an unusual bird caught my attention.

_____

b. Being bad grammar, the writer will not use dangling modifiers.

_____

c. When sitting, my shoulders tend to slump.

_____

d. Going home, it started to snow.

_____

Faulty or illogical parallelism is easier to recognize in drills such as these than in your own writing. It is suggested that you don't worry too much about parallelism as you write first drafts; but when you begin to write your final draft, examine each sentence for parallelism before you use it.

Practices in Parallelism

Practice 1. Supply the blank with words that are parallel to the ones already in the sentence.

1. Alice plans to be a typist, _____ or file clerk.

2. My dad likes hunting, _____, and sailing.

3. We will dance, _____, and sing all night.

4. After the movie, we _____,

   _____, and _____.

5. The teacher said that we were _____,

   _____, and _____.

Practice 2. Explain why *each* of the following sentences is not parallel.

1. The car slid to the left while daydreaming.

   _____

2. Because he was late, the boss fired him.

   _____

   _____

3. Sally helped her sister to put icing on the cake.

   _____

   _____

4. While watching the movie, my purse was stolen.

   _____

   _____

5. One should always try to do his best in whatever one undertakes.

   _____

   _____

Practice 3. Change *each* of the sentences in Practice 2 so that it is parallel.

1. _____

_____

2. _____

_____

3. _____

_____

4. _____

_____

5. _____

_____

Practice 4. Change the faulty parallelism in the following sentences.

1. She put on her bathing cap, walked to the diving board, changing her mind at the last minute.

_____

_____

2. After standing too long, my head begins to ache.

_____

_____

3. The actress spent months traveling to locations by jet, train, car, and once even rode a burro.

_____

_____

4. He always plays the piano with ease, with confidence, and takes pleasure in it.

_____

_____

5. Stunned by the end of the story, the television program left me very upset.

_____

_____

6. Man is really an animal and one should not expect so much from us.

_____

_____

7. Shaking his fist, he yelled and was making faces at the old man.

_____

_____

8. The instructor pretended to be stupid, but he is really very sharp.

_____

_____

9. Because it would not run, he sold the car.

_____

_____

10. She would rather watch TV with glasses on.

_____

_____

Practice 5. Combine each of the following sets of sentences into one effective sentence. Use any way that works. There is usually more than one way, but some sound or read better than others. Use correct punctuation.

1. a. A gift was promised to me.
   b. It was promised by my father.
   c. The gift was a Jeep.

_____

_____

_____

2. a. When Hank Aaron snapped his wrists, the bat hit the ball sending it over a 385-foot sign.
   b. It brought him his 715th home run.
   c. It broke the Babe's long-standing record.

_____

_____

_____

3. a. Some soldiers were across the gulch.
   b. They began shooting at me.
   c. But I got back to the others.
   d. I was not hurt at all.

_____

_____

_____

4. a. The horse was made of spirit.
   b. He himself was made of spirit.
   c. The trees were made of spirit.
   d. The grass was made of spirit.
   e. The stones were made of spirit.
   f. Everything was made of spirit in Crazy Horse's dream.

_____

_____

_____

5. a. In just three seconds, a cigarette makes your heart beat faster.
   b. It makes your blood pressure go up.
   c. Smoke takes the place of oxygen in your blood.
   d. It leaves cancer-causing chemicals in your body.

_____

_____

_____

_____

6. a. Next to parents, TV has become the most powerful influence on the beliefs of young people.
   b. TV influences young people's attitudes and values.
   c. TV affects the way humans learn to become human beings.

_____

_____

_____

_____

7. a. J. Allen Hynek is director of the Center for UFO Studies.
   b. He is a professor of astronomy at Northwestern University.
   c. He testified before the House Committee on Science and Astronauts.
   d. Hynek stated that the UFO problem may be far more complex than we
imagine.

_____

_____

_____

_____

8. a. Even though the government reports have linked smoking with cancer,
the U.S. Congress, in 1970, spent $84 million to help the tobacco indus-
try.
   b. Congress spent $2.7 million in research to find a new way to grow to-
bacco more cheaply.
   c. They spent $250,000 in advertising overseas to get foreign nations to buy
American tobacco.
   d. Congress guarantees a minimum price per acre for tobacco crops.

_____

_____

_____

_____

_____

Rewrite...

your first draft.

Here is another excerpt from a student's first and second drafts dealing with the topic "how to lose weight." Notice the difference in the two drafts.

Student's First Draft	Instructor's Comments
The successful method used by many weight-loss centers is called "self-administered aversion therapy. A person who wants to control the temptation for rich foods. The sight, smell, or thinking of such foods may cause an uncontrollable desire to eat. Here's how it works the person imagines himself in the kitchen. He looks up at a choclate cake on the top of the refrigerator. He wants a piece. He was really tempted. So he imagined eating a piece and getting sick. Each bite makes him sicker and sicker until he imagines he is vomiting all over his pants and shoes, this is what the overweight person continues to practice in his mind over and over again. Until the desire for the cake is gone.	*Is this the only method?* *Punctuation—define "aversion therapy"* *Frag.* *Parallelism problem* *Better to have two paragraphs: one defining, one explaining.* *r.o.* *sp.* *Shift in verb tenses.* *Try to sentence combine.* *Are the graphics of vomiting necessary?* *c.s.* *Frag.*

Compare the excerpt from the first draft with the second draft below.

Student's Revised Essay	Instructor's Comments
One successful method used by many weight-loss centers is called "self-administered aversion therapy." The object is to get the person to learn to hate or feel disgust toward rich foods normally craved. A person who can't control the desire to eat fattening foods usually is tempted through the sight, smell, or thought of such foods. Aversion therapy	*Better paragraph.* *You show it as "one" of other methods. Better defined than before.*

attempts to change the person's
feelings toward foods the person
loves.

Here is how aversion therapy
works. An obese man wants a piece of
chocolate cake. To get rid of his
desire, he imagines himself in the
kitchen, looking up at a chocolate
cake on the top of the refrigerator. He
reaches for a piece but feels himself
getting ill. He takes an imaginary bite
and feels really sick. As he tries to
swallow, he begins to vomit on his
pants and shoes. Over and over, the
man continues to practice in his mind
his aversion to foods he loves until the
desire is replaced by the dread of
being sick.

Good job of sentence combining

*The graphics are probably
necessary, especially since it's the
point of the therapy.*

You did a good job of revising.

Return now to the first draft you wrote on a separate sheet of paper at the
beginning of this unit. Read your essay aloud, and make any corrections you notice
need to be made. Then rewrite or make any corrections you feel would strengthen
your essay. Place a check mark in front of each of the following points as you
reexamine your essay.

_____ 1. Does your introductory paragraph contain your thesis or main idea
regarding your topic?

_____ 2. Does your introductory paragraph attempt to draw your reader's interest?

_____ 3. Can you identify your topic sentences in all your paragraphs?

_____ 4. Does your concluding paragraph summarize or clarify your point of
view about your topic?

_____ 5. Have you used transitional words or expressions within sentences
or paragraphs?

_____ 6. Have you corrected any sentence fragments, run-ons, or comma
splices?

_____ 7. Have you used variety in sentence structure, using the patterns discussed in Unit 9 and sentence-combining techniques?

_____ 8. Have you checked each sentence for subject, verb, and pronoun
agreement?

_____ 9. Have you checked for proper parallelism in your sentences?

When you are satisfied you have corrected your essay as needed, rewrite it,
and give both your first draft and the final draft to your instructor.

UNIT 12

Think...
about language

Read...

about obscene language
"Four-Letter Words Can Hurt You" by Barbara Lawrence

React...
to the essay

Plan...

an essay
Topics for an essay

Write...

(A) an outline for your essay
(B) a first draft
(C) using the correct words
Practices in correct word choice

Rewrite...

your first draft

about language.

1. How important to you is your language?

_____

_____

_____

2. Is it important to know more than your native language? _____

Why? _____

_____

3. Would the world be better off if all peoples spoke one language?

_____ Why? _____

_____

4. What language should be the universal language? _____

Why? _____

_____

5. Is speaking and writing correctly important? _____

Why? _____

_____

6. Many authorities feel that todays students are limited in their use and knowl-

edge of language because of TV. Do you agree? _____

Why? _____

_____

_____

7. S. I. Hayakawa, a well-known language expert, claims that "you just don't know anything unless you can write it." Agree or disagree.

_____

_____

_____

8. Is a composition class more of a headache to you than, say, a course in

   math, science, or psychology? _____

   Why? _____

   _____

9. Can language be "obscene"? _____

   Explain. _____

   _____

   _____

10. What words, if any, offend you? _____
11. What is the difference between the denotative and connotative meaning of a word?

   _____

   _____

about obscene language.

The next essay is written by a woman who deals with language as a part of her life. A poet, essayist, and teacher, Barbara Lawrence has a B.A. in French literature, an M.A. in philosophy and was an associate professor of humanities at the State University of New York's College at Old Westbury. She has been an editor at *McCall's*, *Redbook*, and *Harper's Bazaar*. Her essay here is actually an extended definition of obscenity as well as an explanation of what her title suggests.

Four-Letter Words Can Hurt You
Barbara Lawrence

1. Why should any words be called obscene? Don't they all describe natural human functions? Am I trying to tell them, my students demand, that the "strong, earthy, gut-honest"—or, if they are fans of Norman Mailer, the "rich, liberating, existential"—language they use to describe sexual activity isn't preferable to "phony-sounding, middle-class words like 'intercourse' and 'copulate'?" "Cop You Late!" they say with fancy inflections and gagging grimaces. "Now, what is *that* supposed to mean?"

2. Well, what is it supposed to mean? And why indeed should one group of words describing human functions and human organs be acceptable in ordinary conversation and another, describing presumably the same organs and functions, be tabooed—so much so, in fact, that some of these words still cannot appear in print in many parts of the English-speaking world?

3. The argument that these taboos exist only because of "sexual hangups" (middle-class, middle-age, feminist), or even that they are a result of class oppression (the contempt of the Norman conquerors for the language of their Anglo-Saxon serfs), ignores a much more likely explanation, it seems to me, and that is the sources and functions of the words themselves.

4. The best known of the tabooed sexual verbs, for example, comes from the German *ficken*, meaning "to strike"; combined, according to Partridge's etymological dictionary *Origins*, with the Latin sexual verb *futuere*; associated in turn with the latin *fustis*, "a staff or cudgel"; the Celtic *buc*, "a point, hence to pierce"; the Irish *bot*, "the male member"; the Latin *battuere*, "to beat"; the Gaelic *batair*, "a cudgeller"; the Early Irish *bualaim*, "I strike"; and so forth. It is one of what etymologists sometimes call "the sadistic group of words for the man's part in copulation."

5. The brutality of this word, then, and its equivalents ("screw," "bang," etc.), is not an illusion of the middle class or a crotchet of Women's Liberation. In their origins and imagery these words carry undeniably painful, if not sadistic, implications, the object of which is almost always female. Consider, for example, what a "screw" actually does to the wood it penetrates: what a painful, even mutilating, activity this kind of analogy suggests. "Screw" is particularly interesting in this context, since the noun, according to Partridge, comes from words meaning "groove," "nut," "ditch," "breeding sow," "scrofula" and "swelling," while the verb, besides its explicit imagery, has antecedent associations to "write on," "scratch," "scarify," and so forth—a revealing fusion of a mechanical or painful action with an obviously denigrated object.

6. Not all obscene words, of course, are as implicitly sadistic or denigrating to women as these, but all that I know seem to serve a similar purpose: to reduce the human organism (especially the female organism) and human functions (especially sexual and procreative) to their least organic, most mechanical dimension; to substitute a trivializing or deforming resemblance for the complex human reality of what is being described.

7. Tabooed male descriptives, when they are not openly denigrating to women, often serve to divorce a male organ or function from any significant interaction with the female. Take the word "testes," for example, suggesting "witnesses" (from the Latin *testis*) to the sexual and procreative strengths of the male organ; and the obscene counterpart of this word, which suggests little more than a mechanical shape. Or compare almost any of the "rich," "liberating" sexual verbs, so fashionable today among male writers, with that much-derided Latin word "copulate" ("to bind or join together") or even that Anglo-Saxon phrase (which seems to have had no trouble surviving the Norman Conquest) "make love."

8. How arrogantly self-involved the tabooed words seem in comparison to either of the other terms, and how contemptuous of the female partner. Understandably so, of course, if she is only a "skirt," a "broad," a "chick," a "pussycat" or a "piece." If she is, in other words, no more than her skirt, or what her skirt conceals; no more than a breeder, or the broadest part of her; no more than a piece of a human being or a "piece of tail."

9. The most severely tabooed of all the female descriptives, incidentally, are those like a "piece of tail," which suggest (either explicitly or through antecedents) that there is no significant difference between the female channel through which we are all conceived and born and the anal outlet common to both sexes—a distinction that pornographers have always enjoyed obscuring.

10. This effort to deny women their biological identity, their individuality, their humanness, is such an important aspect of obscene language that one can only marvel at how seldom, in an era preoccupied with definitions of obscenity, this fact is brought to our attention. One problem, of course, is that many of the people in the best position to do this (critics, teachers, writers) are so reluctant today to admit that they are angered or shocked by obscenity. Bored, maybe, unimpressed, aesthetically displeased, but—no matter how brutal or denigrating the material— never angered, never shocked.

11. And yet how eloquently angered, how piously shocked many of these same people become if denigrating language is used about any minority group other than women; if the obscenities are racial or ethnic, that is, rather than sexual. Words like "coon," "kike," "spic," "wop," after all, deform identity, deny individuality and humanness in almost exactly the same way that sexual vulgarisms and obscenities do.

12. No one that I know, least of all my students, would fail to question the values of a society whose literature and entertainment rested heavily on racial or ethnic pejoratives. Are the values of a society whose literature and entertainment rest as heavily as ours on sexual pejoratives any less questionable?

React....

to the essay by answering the following questions.

1. What is the thesis of the essay?

_____

_____

2. Do you agree or disagree with the author's thesis? _____

   Why? _____

   _____

3. By tracing the history of two synonyms for sexual intercourse, both of which she considers obscene, Lawrence shows the words suggest a violent action toward women (paragraphs 4 and 5). Are these words used today with violence and denigration in mind?

   _____ Explain. _____

   _____

4. Do you feel resentment or anger when you hear obscene words? _____

   What words do you consider obscene? _____

5. Lawrence's essay seems to aim primarily at the obscenity in language toward the female. What words does she leave out that women use to "denigrate" men? _____

   _____

6. Since Lawrence uses many words she calls obscene, can her own essay be considered such? _____

   Why? _____

   _____

7. Lawrence goes beyond the sexually obscene words into a broader definition of obscenity (paragraphs 11 and 12). What is her conclusion? _____

_____

8. Check the following words you don't know or could not use correctly.

_____ a. existential (1)

_____ b. inflections (1)

_____ c. etymological (4)

_____ d. sadistic (4 and 6)

_____ e. procreative (7)

_____ f. antecedent (5 and 9)

_____ g. aesthetically (10)

_____ h. piously (11)

_____ i. scrofula (5)

_____ j. pejorative (12)

Reread each word as it is used in the essay. Then turn to the Vocabulary Section in the Appendix for more information and exercises with the words.

Plan....

an essay dealing with some aspect of language.

If the Lawrence essay and the questions you have already answered have not given you any ideas for an essay, here are some dilemmas and suggestions to consider.

Dilemma A

Your five-year-old comes home from playing with a neighbor child. His hands are very dirty and he announces, "I have to wash this shit off my hands," and heads for the bathroom. You and your spouse never use the word *shit*, and you are shocked to hear your child say it. How do you react? What do you do about the neighbor child? What do you say, if anything, to your child and why?

Dilemma B

You are talking with one of your college students in your office. You mention you like her watch. She says she got a good deal on it and is proud that she "jewed the guy down" on the price. You are Jewish, and the phrase offends you. How do you react? What action, if any, do you take and why?

Dilemma C

You are working in an office at the Veteran's Administration. Your job is to open letters of request for help and channel them to the right person. You receive this letter:

Dear Sir:

Please help me. My husband had his project cut off 2 weeks ago and I haven't had any relief since then. Both sides of my parents are poor and I can't expect nothing from them, as my mother has been in bed for one year, with the same doctor, and won't change. Please send me my husband's form to fill out. I can't get any pay. I have 6 children, can you tell me why this is?

How do you help this person? How important is language in this case or others you can think of?

Here are some other topics to consider.

1. The place for four-letter words.
2. Should children be allowed to cuss?
3. Why four-letter words *shouldn't* hurt you.
4. The relationship between obscene words and pornography.
5. Language taboos.
6. What is obscenity in language?

7. Why people use obscene words.
8. The need for a universal language.
9. The importance of language.
10. We take language too much for granted.
11. Why we should know our native language better than we do.
12. Why aren't language classes more interesting?
13. Write the history of an English word and its changes over the centuries, such as the word *run.*
14. What I need to do about my own language skills.
15. The misuse of language in advertising.
16. Language of animals.
17. Read the following quotations. Pick one and react to it in an essay:
    a. "If there be any female chauvinists who have an insuperable tolerance of the word *man* (ignoring its basic meaning) they might logically start by taking the 'man' out of the woman." (Louis Foley, "You Can Overdo Being 'A Real Person,'" CEA *Forum,* 6, No. 1, October 1975, p. 9)
    b. "We have any number of compounds [compound words] which show *man* in its basic meaning of 'human being' without differentiation to sex: work*man*ship, sports*man*ship, craft*man*ship, pen*man*ship, and the like. Girls who learn to sail expertly—as many do—may be proud of their sea*man*ship. Would anyone suggest that the celebrated crack-shot Annie Oakley displayed wonderful *markspersonship?*" (Louis Foley, op. cit.)
    c. "Just as our thoughts can corrupt our language, so too can our language corrupt our thoughts, and in effect corrupt our behavior. When the Nazis repeated again and again in their propaganda directed to the German masses that the Jews were 'bacilli,' 'parasites,' and 'diseased,' the 'Final Solution' was made to appear less objectionable. This corrupted use of language made the Nazi oppression of the Jews more palatable to German audiences. Similarly, much of the language used by the Indians' oppressors was used not to define accurately who the Indian was, but to justify the suppression. As Peter Farb has indicated, 'cannibalism, torture, scalping, mutilation, adultery, incest, sodomy, rape, filth, drunkenness—such a catalogue of accusations against a people is an indication not so much of the depravity as that their land is up for grabs.' The language used to subjugate the Indians for almost five centuries has led to the defense of the indefensible, just as the oppressor intended." (Haig A. Bosmajian, "Defining the 'American Indian': A Case Study in the Language of Suppression," *The Speech Teacher,* March 1973)
18. Write an essay about your own language, commenting on how it differs in use with family friends, teachers, work, and the like.
19. The language of sports writers and announcers.
20. The language of politics.
21. The language of science.
22. The language of religion and prayer.

Practice 1. In your journal notebook or on a separate page, spend 10 to 15 minutes freewriting or exploring possible essay topics.

Practice 2. Now plan an essay on some topic. In the space below, write the topic or subject.

Topic:

_____

_____

Practice 3. Now write a working thesis for your topic.

Tentative Thesis Statement:

_____

_____

_____

_____

Below, list all the ideas you can think of to support your thesis. Then rearrange or group them into a proper order.

_____

_____

_____

_____

_____

_____

_____

_____

_____

Write...

(A) an outline for your essay.

On a separate sheet of paper write an outline for your essay, using the rearranged list of supporting ideas. When finished, turn it in to your instructor. When he or she has returned it, do *(B)*.

(B) a first draft of your essay, using the outline you completed for your topic.

Do a first draft on a separate sheet of paper. When finished, go on to *(C)*.

(C) using the correct words.

Using the correct word choice at the proper time in your essay is as important as proper sentence and paragraph control. If your word choice and usage are not appropriate for the type of essay you are writing, your essay will seem elementary or unsophisticated and thereby cause your reader to lose respect for your ideas. Although good writing often breaks rules of composition, it is a good idea to know what some instructors expect before making your own rules. This unit presents "traditional" concepts, but be aware that traditions and English instructors change.

Some formal writing does not permit the use of slang, jargon, and other informal vocabulary terms that we use in everyday speech or less formal writing. Because we speak more than we write, we sometimes use informal or incorrect language in our writing because of our speaking habits. This chapter will cover three areas of word usage: informal, formal, and commonly confused words. Keep in mind, however, that changes occur even in language and that much of contemporary writing uses both formal and informal language. You'll have to learn to conform temporarily to your instructor's whims. Later, you can be as creative as you want. For now, you need to learn differences in "acceptable" style.

1. Informal word usage

Here is an example of informal writing. The ideas are not difficult to understand, and the words used are not incorrect.

> I really dig that chick. She's a bright kid and grooves on a lot of stuff I dig, like rock, flicks, and Mex food. She's not one of those broads that goes around with her nose in the air or who tries to come on strong with her brain,

ya' know? She's got her head together. Besides that, she's really worth lookin' at, too. Man, I'd love to date her, but she's totally turned off by me.

The example is a "colorful" description, and it's doubtful that you had trouble understanding the ideas in the paragraph. The problem is that many of the words would not be acceptable in formal writing any more than making a "jack rabbit" stop during a driver's test would be acceptable.

Some day many of the words used in the sample paragraph may become standard or acceptable in formal English. For now, however, they are considered *slang,* and some grammarians do not even consider such speech as even informal English. Still, many instructors will not accept informal usage, whereas other instructors encourage it because it permits expression.

Here is an example of another informally written paragraph. See if you can spot the informal terms that might not be accepted by some instructors.

There's this here ad on TV where this kid and his old man are having a heart-to-heart talk about the kid's having lost a game of some kind. Well, the 2 of them are sitting in a car, and the kid's pop gives him a pitch about how it's OK to lose and all. Then a voice comes on and says something about remembering how your dad always had the right answers and stuff. It's real nostalgic, and then it turns out to be a phone ad trying to sell you on making more long distance calls to your family.

Some of the informal word choices are more obvious than others in the sample paragraph. Here is a list of the informal usage, what the formal usage would be, and the formal rule.

Informal	Formal	Rule or Reason
there's	there is	avoid contractions (exceptions are made when some contractions sound better)
it's	it is	same as preceding rule
ad	advertisement	use full word
TV	television	use full word
phone	telephone	use full word
old man	father	more polite
2	two	spell out numbers under one hundred
kid	boy	more polite
pop	father	more polite
OK	all right	avoid the use of slang
real	very	misuse of the word *real*
Well, . .		useless word; not needed

When you write formal essays, attempt to avoid the informal usages similar to those in the preceding list, but never at the expense of sounding "stiff."

Check Your Understanding

Change the following terms into more formal, standard English.

a. dig that chick: _____

b. photo: _____

c. got her head together: _____

d. they're: _____

e. nose in the air: _____

f. 24 members: _____

g. really mad: _____

2. Formal word usage

It has already been stated that in formal writing, at least for many grammarians, it is improper to use contractions unless they sound less awkward or stiff; and it is proper to use the full word, not abbreviations of words, to spell out numbers under one hundred, and to avoid using slang. This does not mean, however, that formal writing should be stiff or awkward sounding. For instance, it sounds too formal to write, "One should always hold one's cup with one's small finger extended." This is going overboard with formality. On the other hand, some grammarians feel that it is too informal to say, "You should always hold your cup with your small finger extended." They prefer, "A person should always hold his or her cup with his or her small finger extended." (Notice that the point of view in all three examples is parallel or consistent as was discussed in Unit 11.)

Here are some examples of formal and informal word choices.

Formal	Informal
alcoholic, dipsomaniac	drunkard, sot
unintelligent, backward	dumb, dunce, dope
police officer	cop, fuzz, pig
female	chick, broad, bird
small community	whistlestop, small town
youngster	kid, little guy
a great deal	lots, lots of, plenty
inferior, terrible	lousy, cruddy
outstanding, excellent	super, great, swell
very pretty	real pretty
certainly, truly	sure
extremely, very	awfully

 **Check Your Understanding**

Change any of the following words or terms to more formal words.

a. It's sure a lot of money.

b. That guy has lots of books.

_____

c. It's a super movie!

_____

d. She's real pretty.

_____

e. If you're not careful, you'll become a drunken sot.

_____

3. Commonly confused words

There seem to be many words that cause confusion in correct usage. Here is a list of most of the troublesome words. Carefully look them over.

accept and *except*
Accept means to receive or to say yes to an invitation.
Except means to exclude or with the exclusion of something.

>   She will *accept* the award at the banquet.
>   All the words *except* this one are on the list.

advice and *advise*
Advice is a noun and can be remembered as such because it has another noun in it—*vice.*
Advise is a verb meaning to give or offer solutions.

>   The counselor gave me poor *advice.*
>   The counselor *advised* me to take the class.

affect and *effect*
Affect means to influence.
Effect means to achieve or cause something if used as a verb and means the result of something if used as a noun.

>   The new law will *affect* many of us.
>   The doctors *effected* the new changes in the law.
>   The *effect* of the medicine is still not known.

all right and *alright*
All right is the correct spelling for a term meaning everything is correct or all is well.
Alright is not accepted as correct spelling for all right.

>   My answers were *all right.*
>   He's not *all right* in the head. (informal)

a lot
Usually, these two words are incorrectly spelled *alot.* Avoid using *a lot.*

already and all ready
Already refers to time and means before or by the time being discussed.
All ready means prepared.

>They had *already* arrived before we got there.
>They were *all ready* to leave by noon.

among and between
Among is used only when referring to three or more.
Between is used only when referring to two.

>We had no more than five dollars *among* us. (three or more)
>We had no more than five dollars *between* us. (two persons)

anyways and *anywheres*
Both words are incorrect; the correct forms are *anyway* and *anywhere.*

bad and *badly*
Bad is used with nouns and with verbs that refer to the five senses—*feel, smell, look, taste,* and *hear.*
Badly is used after most other verbs.

>It was a *bad* mistake. (used to modify a noun)
>He feels *bad.* (used after a verb referring to a sense)
>He spells *badly.* (used after most verbs *not* referring to senses)

bad, worse, and *worst*
Each of the three refers to different degrees of "badness."

>It was a *bad* accident. (positive)
>It was *worse* than your accident. (comparative)
>It was the *worst* accident of all. (superlative)

can and *may*
Can is a verb referring to the ability or ableness to perform.
May is used to request permission. Often, *can* is used incorrectly.

>I *can* go with you. (ability to go)
>*May* I go with you? (requesting permission)

can't hardly
An improper use of the term *can hardly.*

>She *can hardly* see through the windshield.

could of, should of, and *would of*

These are improper phrases meaning *could have, should have,* and *would have.* Often, the improper *could of* comes from the sound of the contraction *could've,* meaning *could have.*

> Mark *could have* won if he had tried harder.
> Mark *should have* won, but the referee was unfair.
> Mark *would have* won if the referee had seen the foul.

different from

Do not say, "Different than."

> His country's politics are *different from* ours.

etc.

This is a Latin abbreviation meaning "other things." It is best to avoid using the term. Think of other things to list rather than using *etc.,* which often means, "I can't think of anything more to list."

fast, faster, and *fastest*

Each of the three refers to different degrees of speed.

> His car is very *fast.* (positive)
> His car is *faster* than mine. (comparative)
> His car is the *fastest* of all. (superlative)

Check Your Understanding

Underline the correct word in the parentheses in the following sentences.

a. How did the new medicine (affect, effect) him?
b. Don't worry, it will be (alright, all right).
c. They are (all ready, already) to leave.
d. Just (among, between) us three, who is the winner?
e. The man's wife feels (bad, badly).
f. (Can, May) your daughter go with us?

Here are some more commonly confused words you should carefully look over.

here and *hear*

Here is an adverb.
Hear is a verb. (It has the word *ear* in it; ear = hear)

> *Here* is the car I want to buy.
> Do you *hear* that beautiful music?

infer and *imply*

To *imply* means that an author or speaker is suggesting some idea or meaning he or she is not stating outwardly.

Infer is what the reader or listener does when he or she reaches a conclusion based on supplied evidence or information.

> The author *implies* that the Mafia controls the market.
> On the basis of what the author says, I *infer* that the Mafia controls the market.

irregardless

This is incorrect for *regardless.*

> He will resign *regardless* of what you do.

is when and *is where*

These are both awkward phrases and should not be used.

> Incorrect: Spring *is when* the leaves and buds begin to appear on the plants.
> Better: Spring is the season when leaves and buds begin to appear on the plants.

its and it's

Its is possessive, just as *his, hers, yours,* and *ours* are.
No apostrophe for forming the possessive case in a pronoun is needed.
It's is the contraction for *it is* and nothing else.

> *Its* cage is near the window. (possessive)
> *It's* a nice cage. (contraction)

kind of and *sort of*

Both these phrases are informal and should not be used in formal writing.

> Informal: Her hair was kind of messy.
> Formal: Her hair was rather messy.
> Informal: He was sort of late.
> Formal: He was somewhat late.

lose and *loose*

Lose means no longer to have or know where something is.
Loose mean to set free or free from restraint.

> Did you *lose* your scarf?
> He let the dog *loose* from its leash.

shone and *shown*

Shone is the past tense of the verb *to shine.*
Shown is the past participle of the verb *to show.*

The sun *shone* brilliantly on the water.
We were *shown* through the house.

stationary and *stationery*
Stationary means not movable or not moving.
Stationery means writing paper and envelopes. (Keep in mind that paper ends in *er*
and so does *stationery*.)

The cash register is *stationary*.
The clerk used blue *stationery*.

their, there, and *they're*
Their is the possessive pronoun.
There is an adverb.
They're is the contraction of *they are*.

I went to *their* house.
I went *there* last night.
They're good friends of mine.

to, too, and *two*
To is a preposition.
Too is an adverb meaning also or implying more than what is needed, as in "too
much food."
Two is the spelling for the number.

They danced *to* the music.
We danced to the music, *too*. We danced *too* much.
We danced to the music until *two* in the morning.

who's and *whose*
Who's refers to the contraction *who is*.
Whose is the possessive case of *who*.

Who's going with me?
Whose coat is this?

Check Your Understanding

Underline the correct word in the parentheses in the following sentences.

a. The writer (infers, implies) that the truth will never be known.
b. I am going (irregardless, regardless) of what you say.
c. (Its, it's) impossible to tell from this information.
d. He likes his collars to be (lose, loose).
e. The (stationary, stationery) had a faint touch of perfume.
f. Let's all go (there, they're, their) with them.
g. I can't go because (there, they're, their) is (to, too, two) much to do.

Practices in Correct Word Choice

Directions: Check with your instructor to see whether or not you need to do all of these practices.

Practice 1. Identify the following words as either formal, informal, or slang words. Their use may determine your answer.

1. belly _____

2. stomach _____

3. gut _____

4. fib _____

5. misrepresentation _____

6. friend _____

7. sidekick _____

8. movie _____

9. flick _____

10. show _____

11. old lady _____

12. mother _____

13. dad _____

14. automobile _____

15. wheels _____

16. money _____

17. dough _____

18. bread _____

19. pot _____

20. bright _____

Practice 2. On a separate sheet of paper, write a sentence for each of the words you listed as informal or slang, and change the word to a more formal or acceptable word.

Practice 3. Choose the correct words for the blanks in the following sentences.

1. _____ unfortunate for him. (It's, Its)

2. _____ turn is it? (Whose, Who's)

3. Was _____ no mail today? (there, their, they're)

4. Mother, how late _____ I stay? (can, may)

5. _____ are your papers. (Hear, Here)

6. We were _____ (to, too, two) late to _____ (hear, here) the opening number.

7. I need more _____ to complete my letters. (stationary, stationery)

8. _____ going with you? (Who's, Whose)

9. Have you _____ Tom your new car? (shone, shown)

10. _____ go my good friends. (There, Their, They're)

11. _____ entering the building over _____. (their, there, they're)

12. Have you finished, _____? (to, too, two)

13. The kitten lost _____ ball. (its, it's)

14. We were _____ through the museum. (shown, shone)

15. Did you _____ your jacket? (loose, lose)

Practice 4. Write a *formal* sentence, using each of the following words. Make certain your sentences are expressed in formal terms.

1. *their:* _____

_____

2. *whose:* _____

_____

3. *loose:* _____

_____

4. *its:* _____

_____

5. *infer* _____

_____

6. *imply:* _____

_____

7. *fastest:* _____

_____

8. *different from:* _____

_____

9. *can:* _____

_____

10. *may:* _____

_____

11. *badly:* _____

_____

12. *between:* _____

_____

13. *all ready:* _____

_____

14. *already:* _____

_____

15. *affect:* _____

_____

16. *effect:* _____

_____

17. *advice:* _____

_____

18. *advise:* _____

_____

19. *accept:* _____

_____

20. *except:* _____

_____

Practice 5. Select the correct word for the blanks in the following sentences. Some of the word choices were not discussed in this chapter. If you are in doubt about any word, look it up in your dictionary.

1. She does not want to _____ the fact that she needs psychological help.
   a. accept   b. except

2. He _____ the older part so that it fit the new one.
   a. adopted   b. adapted

3. Let's hope the medicine will not have an _____ effect on her.
   a. adverse   b. averse

4. My _____ is not to _____ him on the matter.
   a. advise   b. advice

5. The story completely _____ him.
   a. alluded   b. eluded

6. I'm _____ to go.
     a. all ready   b. already

7. For years, he has _____ the guilt alone.
     a. born   b. borne

8. The new _____ building cost a fortune.
     a. capital   b. capitol

9. Upon this _____ , I'll build my home.
     a. cite   b. sight   c. site

10. The material felt very _____ to the touch.
     a. course   b. coarse

11. Why is _____ always served last?
     a. dessert   b. desert

12. She was _____ a waitress.
     a. formerly   b. formally

13. If you want to go, _____ fine with me.
     a. it's   b. its

14. Use the _____ one mentioned in the list above.
     a. latter   b. later

15. The tie was _____ about his neck.
     a. loose   b. lose

16. Wow, I _____ my history test!
     a. past   b. passed

17. He has been the _____ at this school for four years.
     a. principal   b. principle

18. He was _____ right, you know.
     a. quiet   b. quit   c. quite

19. The sun _____ brightly on the water.
     a. shown   b. shone

20. I am older _____ you are.
     a. than   b. then

Practice 6. Rewrite the following sentences so that they say what was really intended to be said. They are all taken from actual letters from wives, husbands, mothers, and fathers written to government agencies.

1. Please send me my elopment, as I have a four month old baby and his is my only support, and I need all I can get every day, to buy food and keep his close.

_____

_____

_____

2. I have already wrote to the President and if I don't hear from you, I will write to Uncle Sam, and tell him about both of you.

_____

_____

_____

3. Please send me a letter and tell me if my husband has made application for a wife and baby.

_____

_____

4. I am forwarding you my marriage certificate and my 2 children, one is a mistake as you can plainly see.

_____

_____

5. Please find out for certain if my husband is dead, as the man I am living with won't eat or do nothing until he knows for sure.

_____

_____

_____

6. I am annoyed to find out that you branded my child as illiterate, it is a dirty lie as I married his father 2 weeks before he was born.

_____

_____

_____

7. In accordance with your instructions, I have given birth to twins in the enclosed envelope.

_____

_____

8. I have no children as my husband was a truck driver and worked day and night when he wasn't sleeping.

_____

_____

_____

Rewrite...

your first draft.

Before you rewrite your essay, carefully read the following passages from a student's first and second drafts on an essay about how four-letter words are used in advertising to hurt us. Notice the changes, major and minor in the two drafts.

Student's First Draft	Instructor's Comments
All *help* really means is to aid or assist, but hear are some ways advertisers misuse the word *help*. A certain product can help prevent cavities. This doesn't mean it will stop or prevent cavities but we don't usually play attention to that part. Another example. A product claims it can help you feel young, it doesn't say it will or can make you feel young, just that it can *help* you feel young. But again, we don't usually pay attention to the four-letter word *help*.	*Poor topic sentence. Use transitional device to go from last paragraph to this one.* *Do you mean* hear? *"Certain product"—vague* *Wordy—rewrite* *Play* attention? *Frag.* *Rewrite; eliminate comma splice.* *Use more examples.* *Needs stronger concluding point for this paragraph.*

Here now is the student's revised portion of the essay. Notice how some parts are completely rewritten, something often necessary during revisions.

Student's Revised Draft	Instructor's Comments
Still another example of four-letter words advertisers use but distort is *help*. All *help* really means is to aid or assist in something. But here are some examples of the word *help* being used to mislead us about products:	*Much tighter topic sentence.* *Good transitional usage.*
. . . can help prevent cavities (not *will* stop or *will* prevent) . . . can help you feel young (not *will make you* young) . . . can help you look healthy (not *makes* you healthy) . . . can help overcome insomnia (not *overcome*)	*Good idea to list. The examples and their interpretation are clearer to see.*
In all cases, the four-letter word *help* allows the advertiser to use	*Good point and the idea connects with your thesis as well as your topic*

strong language after it, with most of
us remembering the strong word
rather than the qualifying word *help*
that gets the product manufacturers
off the hook.

sentence for this paragraph.

Return now to the first draft you wrote on a separate sheet of paper at the beginning of this unit. Read your essay aloud, and make any corrections you notice need to be made. Then rewrite or make any corrections you feel would strengthen your essay. Place a check mark in front of each of the following points as you reexamine your essay.

_____ 1. Does your introductory paragraph contain your thesis or main idea regarding your topic? If not, where does it appear?

_____ 2. Does your introductory paragraph attempt to draw your reader's interest?

_____ 3. Can you identify your topic sentences in all your paragraphs?

_____ 4. Does your concluding paragraph summarize or clarify your point of view about your topic?

_____ 5. Have you used transitional words or expressions within sentences and paragraphs?

_____ 6. Have you corrected any sentence fragments, run-ons, or comma splices?

_____ 7. Have you used sentence variety, using the patterns discussed in Unit 9 and sentence-combining techniques?

_____ 8. Have you checked each sentence for subject, verb, and pronoun agreement?

_____ 9. Have you checked for proper parallelism in your sentences?

_____ 10. Have you checked your word choices to make certain they are appropriate for the tone of your paper?

When you are satisfied you have corrected your essay as needed, rewrite it, and give both your first draft and the final draft to your instructor.

UNIT 13

Think . . .
about advertising and its effect on you

Read . . .
about advertising claims
"The Critical Evaluation of Advertising Claims"
by Jeffrey Schrank

React . . .
to the essay

Plan . . .
an essay
Topics for an essay

Write . . .
(A) an outline for your essay
(B) a first draft
(C) with clear-cut reasoning
Practices in recognizing fallacious reasoning

Rewrite . . .
your first draft

Think...

about advertising and its effect on you by answering the following questions.

1. Do you think the word *advertising* has a more negative or a more positive

   connotation for most people? _____

   Why? _____

   _____

   _____

   _____

2. Do you pay much attention to advertisements? _____

   Why? _____

   _____

   _____

   _____

3. When do you find advertisements most useful? _____

   _____

   _____

   _____

   _____

4. Do you think that you are sometimes fooled or "conned" by advertising gimmicks? _____ Why? _____

_____

_____

_____

_____

5. Advertisements pay for TV, radio, magazines, and newspapers. How different do you think the media would be without advertisements? _____

_____

_____

_____

6. Do you think advertising raises or lowers the cost of merchandise?

_____ Why? _____

_____

_____

_____

_____

about advertising claims.

The author of the following article, Jeffrey Schrank, is the editor of *Media Mix Newsletter* and at least three books, *Teaching Human Beings, Deception Detection* and *Snap, Crackle and Pop: The Illusion of Free Choice in America.* An ex-teacher, Schrank believes that education should help us develop insights into the ordinary. He is very concerned with consumer education and the need for us to be more aware of the effects of advertising, a constant part of our contemporary environment. See if you agree with the author's opinions about advertising claims.

The Critical Evaluation of Advertising Claims
Jeffrey Schrank

1. High school students, and many teachers, are notorious believers in their own immunity to advertising. These naive inhabitants of consumerland believe that advertising is childish, dumb, a bunch of lies, and influences only the vast hordes of the less sophisticated. Their own purchases, they think, are made purely on the basis of value and desire, with advertising playing only a minor supporting role. They know about Vance Packard and his "hidden persuaders" and the adman's psychosell and bag of persuasive magic. They are not impressed.

2. Advertisers know better. Although few people admit to being greatly influenced by ads, surveys and sales figures show that a well-designed advertising campaign has dramatic effects. A logical conclusion is that advertising works below the level of conscious awareness and it works even on those who claim immunity to its message. Ads are designed to have an effect while being laughed at, belittled, and all but ignored.

3. A person unaware of advertising's claim on him is precisely the one most vulnerable to the adman's attack. Advertisers delight in an audience that believes ads to be harmless nonsense, for such an audience is rendered defenseless by its belief that there is no attack taking place. The purpose of classroom study of advertising is to raise the level of awareness about the persuasive techniques used in ads. One way to do this is to analyze ads in microscopic detail. Ads can be studied to detect their psychological hooks, how they are used to gauge values and hidden desires of the common man. They can be studied for their use of symbols, color, and imagery. But perhaps the simplest and most direct way to study ads is through an analysis of the language of the advertising claim.

4. The "claim" is the verbal or print part of an ad that makes some claim of superiority for the product being advertised. After studying claims, students should be able to recognize those that are misleading and accept as useful information those that are true. A few of these claims are downright lies, some are honest statments about a truly superior product, but most fit into the category of neither bold lies nor helpful consumer information. They balanace on the narrow line between truth and falsehood by a careful choice of words.

5. The reason so many ad claims fall into this category of pseudoinformation is that they are applied to parity products, those in which all or most of the brands available are nearly identical. Since no one superior product exists, advertising is used to create the illusion of superiority. The largest advertising budgets are devoted to parity products such as gasoline, cigarettes, beer and soft drinks, soaps, and various headache and cold rememdies.

6. The first rule of parity claims involves the Alice-in-Wonderland use of the words "better" and "best." In parity claims, "better-" means "best" but "best" only means "equal to." If all the brands are identical, they must all be equally good, the legal minds have decided. So "best" means that the product is as good as the other superior products in its category. When Bing Crosby declares Minute Maid Orange Juice "the best there is," he means it is as good as the other orange juices you can buy.

7. The word "better," however, as grammarians will be pleased to hear, is legally as well as logically comparative and therefore becomes a clear claim to superiority. Bing could not have said that Minute Maid is "better than any other orange juice." "Better" is a claim to superiority. The only time "better" can be used is when a product does indeed have superiority over other products in its category or when the "better" is used to compare the product with something other than competing brands. An orange juice could therefore claim to be "better than a vitamin pill," or even that it was "the better breakfast drink."

8. The second rule of advertising-claim analysis is simply that if any product is truly superior, the ad will say so very clearly and will offer some kind of convincing evidence of the superiority. If an ad hedges the least about a product's advantage over the competition, you can strongly suspect it is not superior—maybe equal to but not better. You will never hear a gasoline company say, "We will give you four miles per gallon more in your car than any other brand." They would love to make such a claim, but it would not be true. Gasoline is a parity product, and, in spite of some very clever and deceptive ads of a few years ago, no one has yet claimed one brand of gasoline better than—and therefore superior to—any other brand.

9. To create the necessary illusion of superiority, advertisers usually resort to one or more of the following ten basic techniques. Each is common and easy to identify.

1. The Weasel Claim

10. A weasel word is a modifier that practically negates the claim that follows. The expression "weasel word" is aptly named after the egg-eating habits of weasels. A weasel will suck out the inside of an egg, leaving it to appear intact to the casual

observer. Upon closer examination, the egg is discovered to be hollow. Words or claims that appear substantial upon first glance but disintegrate into hollow meaninglessness on analysis are weasels. Commonly used weasel words include "helps" (the champion weasel), "like" (used in a comparative sense), "virtual" or "virtually," "acts" or "works," "can be," "up to," "as much as," "refreshes," "comforts," "tackles," "fights," "comes on," "the feel of," "the look of," "looks like," "fortified," "enriched," and "strengthened."

Samples of Weasel Claims

"*Helps Control* dandruff *symptoms* with *regular use.*"

The weasels include "helps control," and possibly even "symptoms," and "regular use." The claim is not "stops dandruff."

"Leaves dishes *virtually* spotless"

We have seen so many ad claims that we have learned to tune out weasels. You are supposed to think "spotless," rather than "virtually" spotless.

"Only half the price of *many* color sets"

"Many" is the weasel. The claim is supposed to give the impression that the set is inexpensive.

"Tests confirm one mouthwash *best* against mouth odor."

"Hot Nestles' cocoa is the very *best.*"

Remember the "best" and "better" routine.

"Listerine *fights* bad breath."

"Fights," not "stops."

"Lots of things have changed, but Hershey's *goodness* hasn't."

The claim does not say that Hershey's chocolate hasn't changed.

"Bacos, the crispy garnish that *tastes* just *like* its name."

2. The Unfinished Claim

11. The unfinished claim is one in which the ad claims the product is better, or has more of something but does not finish the comparison.

Samples of Unfinished Claims

"Magnavox gives you more."

More what?

"Anacin: Twice as much of the pain reliever doctors recommend most."

This claim fits in a number of categories; as an unfinished claim it does not say twice as much of what pain reliever.

"Supergloss does it with more color, more shine, more sizzle, more!"

"Coffee-mate gives coffee more body, more flavor."

Also note that "body" and "flavor" are weasels.

"You can be sure if it's Westinghouse."

Sure of what?

"Scott makes it better for you."

Makes what better? How is it better?

"Ford LTD—700% quieter."

When the Federal Trade Commission asked Ford to substantiate this claim, Ford revealed that they meant the inside of the Ford was seven hundred percent quieter than the outside.

3. The "We're Different and Unique" Claim

12. This kind of claim states simply that there is nothing else quite like the product advertised. For example, if Schlitz were to add pink food coloring to their beer, they could say, "There's nothing like new pink Schlitz." The uniqueness claim is supposed to be interpreted by readers as a claim to superiority.

Samples of "We're Different and Unique" Claims

"There's no other mascara like it."
"Only Doral has this unique filter system."
"Cougar is like nobody else's car."
"Either way, liquid or spray, there's nothing else like it."
"If it doesn't say Goodyear, it can't be Polyglas."
"Polyglas" is a trade name copyrighted by Goodyear. Goodrich or Firestone could make a tire exactly identical to the Goodyear one and yet couldn't call it "Polyglas"—a name for fiberglass belts.
"Only Zenith has Chromacolor."
Same as the "Polyglas" gambit. Admiral has Solarcolor and RCA has Accu-color.

4. The "Water Is Wet" Claim

13. "Water is wet" claims say something about the product that is true for any brand in that product category (e.g., "Schrank's water is really wet"). The claim is usually a statement of fact, but not a real advantage over the competition.

Samples of "Water Is Wet" Claims

"Mobil: the Detergent Gasoline"
Any gasoline acts as a cleaning agent.
"Great Lash greatly increases the diameter of every lash."
"Rheingold: the natural beer"
Made from grains and water as are other beers.
"SKIN smells differently on everyone."
As do many perfumes.

5. The "So What" Claim

14. This is the kind of claim to which the careful reader will react by saying, "So what?" A claim is made that is true but gives no real advantage to the product. This is similar to the "water is wet" claim except that it claims an advantage that is not shared by most of the other brands in the product category.

"Geritol has more than twice the iron of ordinary supplements."
But is it twice as beneficial to the body?
"Campbell's gives you tasty pieces of chicken and not one but two chicken stocks."
Does the presence of two stocks improve the taste?
"Strong enough for a man but made for a woman"
This deodorant claim says only that the product is aimed at the female market.

6. The Vague Claim

15. The vague claim is simply not clear. This category often overlaps with others. The key to the vague claim is the use of words that are colorful but meaningless, as well as the use of subjective and emotional opinions that defy verification. Most contain weasels.

Samples of Vague Claims

"Lips have never looked so luscious."
Can you imagine trying to either prove or disprove such a claim?
"Lipsavers are fun—they taste good, smell good and feel good."
"Its deep rich lather makes hair feel new again."
"For skin like peaches and cream"
"The end of meatloaf boredom"
"Take a bite and you'll think you're eating on the Champs Elysées."
"Winston tastes good like a cigarette should."
"The perfect little portable for all-around viewing with all the features of higher-priced sets"
"Fleischmann's makes sensible eating delicious."

7. The Endorsement or Testimonial

16. A celebrity or authority appears in an ad to lend his or her stellar qualities to the product. Sometimes the people will actually claim to use the product, but very often they don't. There are agencies surviving on providing products with testimonials.

Samples of Endorsements or Testimonials

"Joan Fontaine throws a shot-in-the-dark party and her friends learn a thing or two."
"Darling, have you discovered Masterpiece? The most exciting men I know are smoking it." (Eva Gabor)
"Vega is the best handling car ever made in the U.S."
This claim was challenged by the FTC, but GM answered that the claim is only a direct quote from *Road and Track* magazine.

8. The Scientific or Statistical Claim

17. This kind of ad uses some sort of scientific proof or experiment, very specific numbers, or an impressive-sounding mystery ingredient.

Samples of Scientific or Statistical Claims

"Wonder Bread helps build strong bodies 12 ways."

Even the weasel "helps" did not prevent the FTC from demanding this ad be withdrawn. But note that the use of the number "12" makes the claim far more believable than if it were taken out.

"Easy-Off has 33% more cleaning power than another popular brand."

"Another popular brand" often translates as some other kind of oven cleaner sold somewhere. Also, the claim does not say Easy-Off works thirty-three percent better.

"Special Morning—33% more nutrition"

Also an unfinished claim.

"Certs contains a sparkling drop of Retsyn."

"ESSO with HTA"

"Sinarest. Created by a research scientist who actually gets sinus headaches."

9. The "Compliment the Consumer" Claim

18. This kind of claim butters up the consumer by some form of flattery.

Samples of "Compliment the Consumer Claims"

"If you do what is right for you, no matter what others do, then RC Cola is right for you."

"We think a cigar smoker is someone special."

"You pride yourself on your good home cooking. . . ."

"The lady has taste."

"You've come a long way baby."

10. The Rhetorical Question

19. This technique demands a response from the audience. A question is asked and the viewer or listener is supposed to answer in such a way as to affirm the product's goodness.

Samples of Rhetorical Questions

"Plymouth—isn't that the kind of car America wants?"

"Shouldn't your family be drinking Hawaiian Punch?"

"What do you want most from coffee? That's what you get most from Hills."

"Touch of Sweden: could your hands use a small miracle?"

20. Teaching someone how to build a log cabin or how to make yogurt is more exciting (or at least "different") than teaching the complexities of processed food deceptions, or the ins and outs of misleading ads from banks and savings and loan associations. But for 205 million Americans learning to stalk wild asparagus is far less important than learning to stalk honest value for hard-earned money in the neon neatness of the grocery store.

React...

to the essay by answering the following questions.

1. What is the thesis of the article? _____

_____

_____

2. Who or what type of person does the author claim to be most vulnerable to

advertising claims? _____

_____

_____

3. How does the author claim advertisers use the words *best* and *better* to their

advantage? _____

_____

_____

4. In your own words, define each of these basic advertising techniques:

a. the weasel claim _____

_____

b. the unfinished claim _____

_____

c. the "We're Different and Unique" claim _____

_____

d. the "Water Is Wet" claim _____

_____

e. the "So What" claim _____

_____

f. the vogue claim _____

_____

g. the endorsement or testimonial _____

_____

h. the scientific claim _____

_____

i. the "Compliment the Consumer" claim _____

_____

j. the rhetorical question _____

_____

5. Do you basically agree or disagree with the author's thesis? _____

Why? _____

_____

_____

_____

6. Check the following words from the essay that you do not know or could not use correctly.

_____ a. notorious (1)

_____ b. hordes (1)

_____ c. belittled (2)

_____ d. rendered (3)

_____ e. gauge (3)

_____ f. parity (5)

_____ g. hedges (8)

_____ h. deceptive (8)

_____ i. aptly (10)

_____ j. substantial (10)

Take the time now to reread the words in the paragraphs indicated by parentheses. Then go to the Vocabulary Section in the Appendix for more information and exercises using these words.

Plan...

an essay on some aspect of advertising.

If you do not have an idea for an essay of your own, look over these suggestions and topics to see if there is one you can use or modify.

1. Respond to this quotation: "Advertising: what is it? Education. Modern education, nothing more or less. School teachers and college professors arrogantly believe they are educators. We advertisers teach more and better."

2. Children aged five and under, watch an average of 23.5 hours of TV a week. (Adults watch 44 hours per week.) This means that by the time the child graduates from high school, he or she will have watched about 15,000 hours of TV. He or she will have seen 350,000 commercials and watched 18,000 murders. Next to parents, TV has become the most powerful influence on the beliefs, attitudes and values of young people. TV is affecting the way humans learn to become human beings. Discuss what the future of our society will be based on this information.

3. An advertisement in *Playboy* or *Playgirl* for the Chevrolet Division of General Motors is apt to be for a Corvette or other sporty model, whereas the ad in *McCall's* or *Ladies Home Journal* tends to be for a station wagon. Explain the reason behind such advertising.

4. Using the following lines from advertisements (or pick your own ads) write an essay showing the falseness of such claims:
   a. Our cars have the lowest sticker prices in America.
   b. Coca-Cola: It's the real thing!
   c. Three out of four doctors recommend the major ingredient in Anacin for the relief of headache pain.
   d. New Salem Ultra: the first ultra low tar that stands for refreshment.
   e. Camel: Where a man belongs.
   f. From $14.95

5. Read the following quotes. Pick one and write an essay in reaction to it:

   a. The consumer of mouthwash pays about $9 per gallon for a solution whose main ingredient is alcohol (5 to 25 percent). In 1971, the Federal Trade Commission challenged all medicinal claims for mouthwashes and complained that the claim of Listerine to "kill germs by the millions on contact" is of no medical significance. The ad-educated consumer is willing to pay four times more for mouthwash than for milk in spite of a study by the National Academy of Sciences which found that "There is no convincing evidence that any medicated mouthwash, used as part of a daily hygiene regimen, has therapeutic advantage over saline solution [salt water] or even water.

   b. Growing up, especially in the second decade of life, is mined with explosive changes, physical and emotional. It's the time when young people are supposed to gain competence, to learn who they are in the world and how they'll survive. It's an even tougher business today when kids are unemployed and kept in age ghettos of schools. The teen-agers I know are often acutely aware that they are regarded as useless, if not downright dangerous. There is no way for them to test living skills. The rites of passage have been reduced to drinking, driving and sex. The only value they seem to have is as consumers. So they are being sold sex along with their deodorants and shampoo and eyeliner and movie stubs. (Ellen Goodman, "The Marketing of Kidsex," *Los Angeles Times,* October 5, 1980.)

c. In a year-long study at a Chicago food chain, twice as many people bought a certain brand of margarine under a well-known brand name as the identical margarine sold under the store label even though the store brand was less expensive.

If you don't like any of those ideas, kick these topics around.

1. Evaluate an advertisement from a popular magazine, and identify what claim or claims are being used in the ad.
2. The effects of advertising on children.
3. Advertising: Yesterday and today (1900—today). Look through some old magazines in the library.
4. Fraudulent advertising: What to do about it.
5. What advertising says about our social values.
6. How to conduct a successful advertising campaign.
7. Does advertising insult the intelligence of the American people?
8. Life without advertising.
9. Compare the advertising claims of two similar products (Colgate vs. Crest toothpaste, Tide vs. All, and so on).
10. Products or businesses that should not be advertised.
11. Should doctors/lawyers be allowed to advertise?
12. A rebuttal to Schrank's thesis.
13. Why we buy or want to buy what we see advertised.
14. Does hard-sell advertising work?
15. Who really responds to advertising?
16. The language of advertising: symbols and truth.

Practice 1. In your journal notebook or on a separate page, spend 10 to 15 minutes freewriting or exploring possible essay topics.

Practice 2. Now plan an essay on some topic. In the space below, write the topic or subject.

Topic:

_____

_____

Practice 3. Now write a working thesis for your topic.

Tentative Thesis Statement:

_____

_____

_____

_____

Below, list all the ideas you can think of to support your thesis. Then rearrange or group them into a proper order.

_____

_____

_____

_____

_____

_____

_____

_____

Write...

(A) an outline for your essay.

On a separate sheet of paper, write an outline for your essay, basing it on your rearranged list of support. When finished, turn it in to your instructor for a final check before you actually begin writing your essay. When it has been approved by your instructor, start on (B).

(B) a first draft of your essay, using the outline you completed.

Do a first draft on a separate sheet of paper. When finished go on to (C).

(C) with clear-cut reasoning.

Showing good, clear-cut reasoning in your essays is just as important as showing good structure and grammar. In fact, it may be even more important because the reason for writing is to communicate your ideas to a reader. Your ideas need to be grounded on reason and logic rather than on fallacies in your argument or thinking.

Fallacies in logical reasoning occur when an argument or belief is based on an incorrect belief or judgment. There are many different types of fallacious reasoning. The most common ones are described in the following sections so that you can attempt to avoid them in your writing.

1. The bandwagon fallacy

The bandwagon fallacy is reasoning based on the premise that "because everyone else is doing it, why shouldn't I?" Here are some examples of bandwagon fallacies in logic:

> Councilman A: We'd better pass a law banning nudity on the beach.
> Councilman B: Why?
> Councilman A: Because all the other cities along the coast are doing so.

Notice that there is no logic given as to the need to pass a law against nudity on the beach, only the fact that other cities are doing it.

2. The circular reasoning fallacy

Sometimes circular reasoning is referred to as "begging the question." It means that the argument or point being proved just goes in a circle rather than offering any logic proof. Here is an example to help clarify the definition.

> Councilman A: We'd better pass a law banning nudity on the beach.
> Councilman B: Why?
> Councilman A: Because nudity is immoral.
> Councilman B: How do you know?
> Councilman A: The best ministers say so.
> Councilman B: How do you know who the best ministers are?
> Councilman A: They're the ones who feel nudity is immoral.

Notice the fallacious reasoning just goes in a circle. Councilman A wishes to prove that nudity is immoral because the best ministers say so and then claims that the best ministers are the ones who feel nudity is immoral.

3. The contradiction

A contradiction is a statement or argument that is opposite or contrary to a previous position held by the same writer. Notice the following example.

> Councilman A: We'd better pass a law banning nudity on the beach.
> Councilman B: Why?
> Councilman A: Because all nudists are weirdos, and they'll give our beaches a bad name.
> Councilman B: But the mayor is a nudist.
> Councilman A: Well, that's different. He's not in the same category.

Councilman A says that all nudists are weirdos but contradicts himself when he discovers the mayor is a nudist. Such reasoning is fallacious.

4. False analogy or association

A false analogy is the comparing of two items, ideas, or situations that cannot logically be compared. For example,

> Councilman A: We'd better pass a law banning nudity on the beach.
> Councilman B: Why?
> Councilman A: Nudity will attract the criminal elements to our town.

Councilman A equates nudity with crime and criminals, which does not logically follow any more than saying that because Jim Smith has a wonderful father that Jim will also make a wonderful father.

✔ Check Your Understanding

Identify the type of fallacious reasoning made in each of the following examples.

a. Harold Pinter's play *The Homecoming* is his greatest play. All the best critics say so, and the best critics are the ones who know the best plays.

   Type of reasoning: _____

b. We should start an Ethnic Studies Division on our campus. All the best colleges are doing it.

   Type of reasoning: _____

c. I'm not going to see Loretta Limp's new movie because she associates with immoral people.

   Type of reasoning: _____

d. All teachers like to give heavy homework assignments. Ms. Green doesn't give too many assignments, though.

   Type of reasoning: _____

5. The hasty generalization

Fallacious reasoning also occurs when an overall statement or conclusion is based on only one or two examples. Notice Councilman A's hasty generalization in the following example.

> Councilman A: We'd better pass a law banning nudity on the beach. Most people are in favor of it.
> Councilman B: How do you know?
> Councilman A: I've received four letters about the problem, and three of them are in favor of passing the law.

Although Councilman A's mail may primarily be in favor of the law, a survey of four letters is much too limited to offer accurate public feelings. More information is needed.

6. Oversimplification

Oversimplification makes a problem or position seem more or less important than it really is. Again, notice the councilman's reasoning.

> Councilman A: We must pass a law banning nudity on the beach!
> Councilman B: Why?
> Councilman A: If we don't we'll have every nudist in the country coming here and cluttering up our beaches.

7. Rationalization

When we find a false reason for doing something in an attempt to cover all real reasons, we are *rationalizing*. The councilman is rationalizing in the following example.

Councilman A: What is the public's feeling about the proposed ban on nudity at the beaches?

Councilman B: Four to one against it.

Councilman A: Oh? Well, I'm against it, too.

Councilman B: I thought you were for the law.

Councilman A: That was before I studied all the facts.

Councilman A is rationalizing that he changed his mind because he "studied all the facts." Actually, he realizes that the voting public is four to one *against* the law; so he feels it safe to change his view.

8. Transfer reasoning (guilt by association and testimonial)

There are two types of transfer reasoning. One of the fallacious reasoning types is the *guilt-by-association* thinking. This occurs when something known as bad or evil or disliked by a large majority of people is linked to someone or something being attacked.

Councilman A: Nudists are a bunch of long-haired hippie-types who have no respect for God or their great country.

The other type of fallacious transfer reasoning is the *testimonial reasoning,* which uses a well-known personality's endorsement of an idea or product even though that person lacks authority on the subject.

Councilman A: We'd better pass a law banning nudity on the beach.

Councilman B: Why?

Councilman A: Reverend Holcombe, the great evangelist minister, says that nudity will corrupt the minds of our youth.

With all due respects to the evangelistic minister, it is doubtful that he is an authority on nudism and what causes the corruption of our youth's minds. Yet because Councilman A respects him, he transfers the minister's ideas as his own. No logical reasoning takes place in his decision.

Check Your Understanding

Identify the type of fallacious reasoning used in each of the following examples.

1. I don't see why everyone is so worried about ecology. Everything will work itself out.

   Type of reasoning: _____

2. I know I've quit smoking, but if I don't smoke this carton of cigarettes my girl gave me, I'll hurt her feelings.

   Type of reasoning: _____

3. Don't vote for him. His father used to be active in the Communist movement back in 1930.

Type of reasoning: _____

4. "Everybody needs milk; even Vicki Carr."

Type of reasoning: _____

5. All kids love hot dogs; so buy Johnny one, too.

Type of reasoning: _____

Practices in Recognizing Fallacious Reasoning

Practice 1. In your own words, define the following terms.

1. bandwagon argument: _____

_____

2. circular reasoning: _____

_____

3. contradictory reasoning: _____

_____

4. false analogy: _____

_____

5. hasty generalization: _____

_____

6. oversimplification: _____

_____

7. rationalization: _____

_____

8. guilt by association: _____

_____

9. testimonial: _____

_____

10. fallacious: _____

_____

Practice 2. Analyze the type of fallacious reasoning being used in the following examples and write your comments in the spaces provided.

1. All Catholics are opposed to abortion.

_____

_____

2. Sam Slick will make an excellent governor. His father is one of the wealthiest men in the state and has given Sam the best education possible.

_____

_____

3. Smoking marijuana is not detrimental to anyone. I know. I've smoked it for several years.

_____

_____

4. I would never vote for him. All the long-haired hippies want to see him in office.

_____

_____

5. If I am elected, I will end social inequality and rid this country of poverty.

_____

_____

6. The tax money spent on space exploration is a waste. The money would be better spent on ending poverty in this country.

_____

_____

7. The Russians now have a larger submarine fleet than we have; so we had better build more subs.

_____

_____

8. I should never have walked under that ladder this morning. That's why I had this accident.

_____

_____

9. Because the medicine the doctor prescribed for my father worked so well for him, he gave it to my brother when he got sick.

_____

_____

10. I am a Methodist because what was good for my parents is good enough for me.

_____

_____

Practice 3.   Follow the directions given for each of the following items.

1. Name a person or a group you could cite as an authority for an essay on

   a. alcoholism: _____

   b. dangers of pro-boxing: _____

   c. benefits of milk: _____

   d. acupuncture: _____

   e. natural foods: _____

   f. grammar: _____

   g. babies: _____

2. Change the following generalization to a logical statement: Because eighteen-year-olds can vote, they should be allowed to drink.

_____

_____

3. Change the following statement so that it is more logical: Teenagers love rock music.

_____

_____

4. Identify what is wrong with this statement; then change it, using a better comparison: Learning to drive is as easy as falling off a log.

_____

_____

5. List reasonable evidence you could use for an essay on: Christmas has/has not lost its true meaning.

_____

_____

_____

6. Rewrite the following fallacy so that it is logical: Doberman pinschers are mean dogs; they even attack their owners.

_____

_____

7. Using guilt by association, make a fallacious statement about a police officer.

_____

_____

8. What types of reasoning could you use to prove to a friend that black cats do not cause bad luck?

_____

_____

9. Discuss what is wrong with the following logic:
Husband: Boy, you sure make lousy coffee.
Wife: Well, you're not perfect either, you know!

_____

_____

10. Change the following statement so that it is more logical: If we don't build bigger bombs than the Russians, they will take over the world.

_____

_____

Practice 4. Select an advertisement from a magazine, and analyze it for (1) the type of advertising claim and (2) any fallacies in reasoning suggested by the words and pictures. Do this analysis on a separate sheet of paper, and attach the ad to it.

Rewrite...

your first draft.

Return now to the first draft you wrote on a separate sheet of paper at the beginning of this unit. Place a check mark in front of each of the following points as you reexamine your essay for those items. Rewrite or make any corrections you feel would strengthen your essay.

_____ 1. Does your introductory paragraph contain your thesis or main idea regarding your topic?

_____ 2. Does your introductory paragraph attempt to draw your reader's interest?

_____ 3. Can you identify your topic sentences in all your paragraphs?

_____ 4. Does your concluding paragraph summarize or clarify your point of view about your topic?

_____ 5. Have you used transitional words or expressions within sentences or paragraphs?

_____ 6. Have you corrected any sentence fragments, run-ons, or comma splices?

_____ 7. Have you used sentence variety, using the patterns discussed in Unit 9 and sentence-combining techniques?

_____ 8. Have you checked each sentence for subject, verb, and pronoun agreement?

_____ 9. Have you checked for correct punctuation on the basis of what you learned in Unit 8?

_____ 10. Have you checked for parallelism in point of view, verb usage, and sentence sense?

_____ 11. Have you checked for the correct word choice?

_____ 12. Have you checked for fallacious reasoning or faulty logic in your essay?

When you are certain you have corrected your essay as needed, rewrite it and turn in the final draft to your instructor.

Appendixes

Appendix 1

Part One: Vocabulary Development
Part Two: Useful Affixes

Appendix 2

Some Spelling Hints

Appendix 3

Part One: Some Principal Verb Parts
Part Two: Supplemental Drills

Appendix 1

Part One: Vocabulary Development

Here is a pronunciation guide to help you sound out words you don't know:

ă	as in pat	ā	as in pay	ə, the schwa, is short as in
ĕ	as in pet	ē	as in be	ə = about
ĭ	as in it	ī	as in pie	ə = item
ŏ	as in pot	ō	as in toe	ə = edible
ŭ	as in cut	ū	as in usurp	ə = gallop
o͝o	as in took	o͞o	as in boot	ə = circus

Note: Words are defined according to their use in the essays.

Unit 1: Words Defined

1. **tedious** (tē′dē əs)—boring; tiresome; monotonous.
2. **trivial** (triv′ē əl)—of little importance; commonplace.
3. **trite** (trīt)—worn out with overuse; lacking interest or originality.
4. **vacuity** (vă kyo͞o′ə tē)—an empty space; emptiness of mind.
5. **abstract** (ăb străkt′)—not easily understood; theoretical rather than having concrete existence.
6. **hedge** (hĕj)—to avoid committing oneself; to be cautious.
7. **linguistics** (lĭng gwis′tics)—the science of language.
8. **euphemism** (yo͞o′ fo mĭz əm)—use of an unoffensive term instead of one that might offend; for example, "to pass away" instead of "to die."
9. **jargon** (jar′gən)—the specialized language of a trade, profession, or particular group.
10. **induce** (in do͞os′)—to stimulate or cause something to happen.

 ## Check Your Understanding

I. Fill in the blanks with the correct word from the preceding list.

1. After having second thoughts, Jerry might _____ on his promise to loan me his car.

2. You can tell my instructor knows something about _____ because she is always making reference to the connection of certain words with speech patterns.

3. When my mother scolded my brother, his eyes showed a _____ of mind.

4. Some of the work Jackie does is very _____ , but most of it she finds interesting.

5. Most discussions at cocktail parties are _____ and lack depth of thought.

6. The doctor's use of _____ had me thoroughly confused.

7. Our essays are not supposed to be about such things as our personnal experiences; rather, they are to deal with _____ thought.

8. Colorful words often _____ an emotional response or mental picture.

9. Calling someone "not right upstairs" instead of saying "mad" is an example of _____ .

10. What he contributed to the play was _____ in comparison to her efforts.

II. On a separate sheet of paper write a sentence for each of the words for this unit. Feel free to add or drop suffixes such as *ly*, *ful*, *ness*, *able*, *tion*, and so forth (see page 330) to fit your sentences. Suffixes change words to different parts of speech. For example, in place of using the word *tedious*, you might want to change it from an adjective (The tedious exercise bored me.) to *tediously*, an adverb (He tediously talked on and on, boring me.).

Unit 2: Words Defined

1. **relevance** (rĕl′ə vănce)—the state of being immediately useful; applicable to what is happening at the time.
2. **pedantry** (pĕd′n trē)—over or undue attention to detail or rules without having a true understanding; learning for learning's sake, not for practical application.
3. **counter to** (koun′ tər)—against; opposite to; not with or together.
4. **ecological** (ĕk ə lŏj′ĭ kəl)—of or pertaining to the relationship between organisms and their environment; in this case, the schools should attempt to "balance" students' education with what they *don't* get from the media.
5. **yin and yang** (yĭn/yăng)—from the Chinese dualistic philosophy of opposites meaning that if there is good, there is also bad, happy and sad, strong and weak, and so forth; *yin* is the female, passive symbol, and *yang* is the masculine, active symbol.
6. **dominant** (dŏm′ə nənt)—superior; predominant; main; leading; strongest.
7. **devoid** (dĭ void′)—empty; without; lacking.
8. **semantics** (sə măn′ tĭks)—the study or science of meaning in language.
9. **ambience** (ăm′ bē əns)—environment; atmosphere; surroundings; setting.
10. **alternative** (ôl tŭr′ nə tĭv)—choice; substitute.

Check Your Understanding

I. Fill in the blanks with the correct word from the preceding list.

1. Postman believes that schools should take an _____ approach to what should be taught by supplying the education society does not.

2. Jan's mother is the _____ one in her family.

3. Paul does not see the _____ of being required to take biology as an English major.

4. The present abortion laws are _____ the church's beliefs.

5. The union leader presented an _____ to the company's proposal.

6. Sitting in the emergency ward, Sara felt the _____ of a nurse's life.

7. The idea that opposites are a reality of life can be expressed through

   _____ .

8. Working on his degree, Wally got so hung up in _____ that he failed to see the usefulness of what he was learning in everyday life.

9. The movie was _____ of any true meaning.

10. His study of _____ turned John into a word detective, tracing the history of many words he thought he knew.

II. On a separate sheet of paper write a sentence for each word from this unit. Feel free to change the words by adding necessary suffixes, such as *ly, ness, ful, able, tion,* and so on.

Unit 3: Words Defined

1. **idyllic** (ī dĭl′ ĭk)—simple; natural; the way one wants things to be.
2. **hedonistic** (hēd′ n ĭs tĭc)—pursuing pleasure above all else; pleasure-oriented.
3. **exquisite** (ĕks′ kwĭ zĭt)—beautifully made or designed.
4. **suited** (sōōt′ ed)—having met the requirements; fitted for a task or position.
5. **formidable** (fŏr′ mə də bəl)—admirable; awe-inspiring; it can also mean arousing fear or dread.
6. **level** (lĕv′ əl)—informal usage here means to tell the truth; be honest.

7. **potential** (pə tĕn′ shəl)—possible; likely; probable; in this case, women who could be mothers.
8. **justify** (jŭs′ tə fī)—to prove; to defend; to explain reasons.
9. **fair game** (idiom)—free to be taken; free to use or attack; free to question or take issue with.
10. **succumbing** (sə kŭm′ ing)—giving in to.

Check Your Understanding

I. Fill in the blanks with the correct word from the preceding list.

1. José is well _____ for the job because of his previous experiences.

2. Movies and television often make the era of the fifties seem _____, but, as I remember it, things weren't all that wonderful.

3. The instructor tried to _____ why he gave so many *D's.*

4. _____ with me; I want the truth.

5. Living a _____ life-style often appears to be selfish to many people.

6. Do you think their team will make a _____ opponent for our team?

7. Unfortunately for Tom, he thought all the girls in bikinis were _____ for him, but they soon showed him otherwise.

8. Her _____ dress was the envy of the other models.

9. It appeared Pete was _____ to his wife's dominating ways.

10. Shirley has the _____ to be a good journalist, but refuses to develop her talents.

II. On a separate sheet of paper write a sentence for each word from this unit. Feel free to change the words by adding or dropping suffixes, such as *ly, ness, ful, able, tion,* and so on, to fit your sentences.

Unit 4: Words Defined

1. **precise** (prĭ sīs′)—clearly expressed; exact.
2. **exhortation** (ĕg zor tā′ shən)—strong argument or advice.

3. **persecuting** (pur′ sə kyōōt ing)—annoying; harassing; bothering unpleasantly.
4. **literally** (lĭt′ ər əlē)—actually; really; exactly that.
5. **passively** (pas′ iv lē)—yielding without effort; inactive; uncaring; detached.
6. **mainliners** (mān′ līn ərs)—people who inject narcotics straight into the vien (slang)
7. **perennially** (pə rĕn′ ē al lē)—appearing continually; everlasting; lasting through the years.
8. **contempt** (kən tĕmpt)—disrespect; open disobedience.
9. **permissive** (pər mĭs′ ĭv)—allowing; tolerant; in this case, the reference is to Dr. Spock, whose famous baby-raising book taught parents to be permissive toward their children.
10. **vested interest** (vĕs′ tĭd)—a strong concern for something from which one will benefit; in this case, the Bureau of Narcotics has vested interests in keeping certain drugs illegal so that they can keep their jobs and positions.

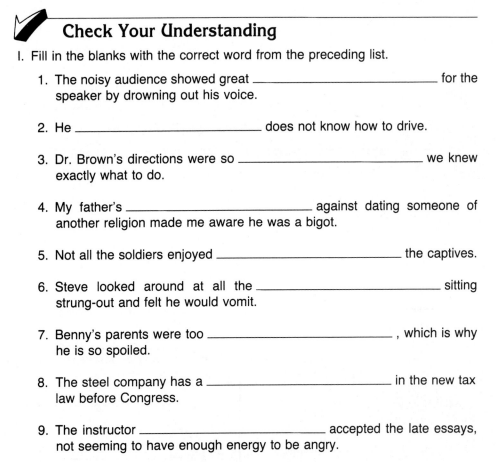

Check Your Understanding

I. Fill in the blanks with the correct word from the preceding list.

1. The noisy audience showed great _____ for the speaker by drowning out his voice.

2. He _____ does not know how to drive.

3. Dr. Brown's directions were so _____ we knew exactly what to do.

4. My father's _____ against dating someone of another religion made me aware he was a bigot.

5. Not all the soldiers enjoyed _____ the captives.

6. Steve looked around at all the _____ sitting strung-out and felt he would vomit.

7. Benny's parents were too _____ , which is why he is so spoiled.

8. The steel company has a _____ in the new tax law before Congress.

9. The instructor _____ accepted the late essays, not seeming to have enough energy to be angry.

10. Speeding on the highways seems to go on _____.

II. On a separate sheet of paper write a sentence for each word from this unit.

Feel free to change the words by adding or dropping suffixes, such as *ly, ness, ful, able, ible, tion,* and so on.

Unit 5: Words Defined

1. **intercollegiate** (ĭn tər kə lē′ jĭt)—involving two or more colleges.
2. **hypocritical** (hĭp ə krĭt′ĭ kl)—insincere; pretending to believe or feel things not really believed or felt.
3. **fiscal** (fĭs′ kəl)—pertaining to finances.
4. **lamentable** (lam′ən tə bəl)—sorrowful; mournful or exhibiting sorrow over.
5. **psychic** (sī kik)—pertaining to the human mind; extraordinary mental processes.
6. **adulation** (ăj ŏŏ lā shun)—excessive praise or flattery.
7. **zealous** (zĕl′us)—overly enthusiastic.
8. **myriad** (mir′ ē əd)—an indefinitely great number.
9. **intramural** (ĭn trə myŏŏr′ əl)—within a school or college.
10. **intrusion** (ĭn trŏŏ′ shun)—unwelcome entry; an unwanted interruption.

Check Your Understanding

I. Fill in the blanks with the correct word from the preceding list.

1. The president of the college prefers intramural sports programs rather

   than _____ programs.

2. In the last _____ years, the company grossed $200,000 worth of business.

3. The wind's _____ on our picnic forced us to go home.

4. The _____ recruiting sergeant almost talked Frank into joining the marines.

5. The _____ given to sports heroes by young people reflects part of their sense of values.

6. Sharon claims to have _____ powers and believes in ESP.

7. The destruction of his house during the fire is _____ .

8. There is a _____ of television sets in the world.

9. Some of the students want to organize some _____ games to be played every week.

10. I find it _____ for him to give a speech on ecological needs and then drive away in his Cadillac.

II. On a separate sheet of paper write a sentence for each of the words for this unit. Feel free to change the words by adding or dropping suffixes to fit your sentences.

Unit 6: Words Defined

1. **hypothetical** (hī pə thet′ ĭ kəl)—an assumption used as the basis for action; in this case, refers to the so-called average person.
2. **semantically** (sə măn′ tik əl lē)—pertaining to the meaning in language.
3. **patriarchal** (pā′ trē ark′ əl)—led or ruled by male members of a family or tribe.
4. **inherent** (ĭn hĕr′ ənt)—forming an essential part; intrinsic.
5. **unabridged** (ŭn ə brĭjd′)—not changed or condensed.
6. **pejorative** (pĭ jor′ ə tiv)—downgrading; tending to make worse.
7. **surreptitiously** (sur əp tĭsh′ əs lē)—secretly or stealthily.
8. **ludicrous** (lo͞o′ dĭ krəs)—foolish; absurdly laughable.
9. **discretion** (dĭs kresh′ ən)—freedom to act or to judge on one's own.
10. **condescension** (kon′ dĭ sen′ shun)—disdain shown by making it seem that you are coming down to the level of inferiors.

Check Your Understanding

I. Fill in the blanks with the correct word from the preceding list.

1. She used a _____ word when discussing the Equal Rights Amendment and offended the women's delegation.

2. An _____ part of any essay is the conclusion.

3. Use an _____ dictionary.

4. His argument was so _____ that no one could believe he meant it.

5. At night the children crept down the stairs _____.

6. Because she was raised in a strong _____ family, she was less interested in getting involved in women's lib activities.

7. _____ speaking, woman is not one with the species of man, but a distinct subspecies.

8. Given a _____ situation, you may be right, but in reality I'm not too sure.

9. You may pay me back at your _____ .

10. Harry's _____ to the group's wishes offended many.

II. On a separate sheet of paper write a sentence for each of the words for this unit, and turn it in to your instructor. Feel free to change words by adding or subtracting suffixes to fit your sentences.

Unit 7: Words Defined

1. **beneficiary** (bĕn ə fish′ ē ĕr ē)—one who receives a benefit or gains something from another.
2. **gaudy** (gah′ dē)—glaring; showy; overdone; pretentious.
3. **oppression** (a prĕsh′ ən)—the act of holding back or down or limiting freedom.
4. **complied** (kəm plīd′)—obeyed; went along with; did what was asked.
5. **evaded** (i vād′ əd)—escaped; avoided; eluded.
6. **dossier** (dŏs′ē ā)—a collection of papers or information on a subject; a file.
7. **ploy** (ploi)—a trick; to obtain an advantage by some strategy.
8. **diversity** (dī vur′ sə tē)—variety; distinction.
9. **plaintiffs** (plān′ tifs)—the ones who bring a lawsuit against someone; opposite of defendants.
10. **drones on** (drōns)—boringly goes on; dully continues.

Check Your Understanding

I. Fill in the blanks with the correct word from the preceding list.

1. Sammy Davis is often criticized for the _____ jewelry he wears.

2. During lectures, my accounting instructor just _____ as though he were a machine.

3. When I asked if I was adopted, my mother _____ my question, which shook me.

4. Later, I discovered it was a _____ because she thought it was a stupid question.

5. The FBI had a _____ an inch thick on the kidnapper.

6. Paula _____ when her boss asked her to dinner because she feared she might lose her job if she didn't.

7. Social _____ is not new to many minorities.

8. To Jerry's surprise, the old man he helped get to the bus everyday made

   Jerry a _____ of an insurance policy.

9. The _____ lied during the trial, but there was no way the defendants could prove it.

10. The _____ of musical ability makes Oregon an exciting group.

II. On a separate sheet, write a sentence for each of the words for this unit. Feel free to add or drop suffixes if need be.

Unit 8: Words Defined

1. **staminal** (stăm′ ə nəl)—having stamina or strength; pertaining to the stamen (pollen-bearing organ of the flower).
2. **occult** (ŏ kŭlt′)—having to do with magic or witchcraft; mysterious and beyond human understanding.
3. **debunked** (dĭ bŭngkt′)—past tense of the verb *to debunk,* meaning to disprove or show as false.
4. **flaunt** (flont)—to show or display in a crude or brazen manner.
5. **renascent** (rĭ năs′ ənt)—born anew, rising again into being.
6. **statute** (stach′ o͞ot)—a law; an authoritarian rule.
7. **mystique** (mĭ stēk′)—a collection of attitudes or opinions associated with someone or something that gives special or almost superhuman status to the person or thing.
8. **esoteric** (ĕs ə ter′ ĭk)—beyond normal understanding or ability; understood by only a select few.
9. **emanation** (em ə nā′ shun)—anything that flows out from a source; a flowing out.
10. **stargazer** (star′ gā zər)—someone who studies the stars; a daydreamer.

Check Your Understanding

I. Fill in the blanks with the correct word from the preceding list.

1. Astrologers are sometimes called _____.

2. _____ that we receive from others are sometimes call vibrations.

3. The boy's story was _____ by the police investigation.

4. The book was so _____ and beyond my experiences that I could not understand it.

5. After reading a book on the _____, he became
interested in witchcraft.

6. The _____ clearly states that wearing con-
cealed weapons is a punishable offense.

7. A _____ has developed regarding Martin Luther
King, Jr.

8. The movie served as a _____ source for his
desire to learn *karate*.

9. Watch her _____ her new diamond ring.

10. Astrology is _____ among many teen-agers.

II. On a separate sheet of paper write a sentence for each of the words for this
unit, and turn it in to your instructor. Feel free to add or drop suffixes to fit
your sentences.

Unit 9: Words Defined

1. **eminently** (ĕm′ ə nənt lē)—outstandingly in performance or character; promi-
nently.
2. **humanoid** (hyōo′ mə noid)—a synthetic person; resembling a human being.
3. **iridescent** (ir ə dĕs′ ənt)—producing a display of rainbowlike colors.
4. **continuity** (kŏn tə nōo′ə tē)—unbroken; state of being continuous.
5. **transience** (trăn′ shəns)—state of moving from place to place often.
6. **inextricably** (ĭn ek′ stri kə blē)—in a way too tangled to get free; inescapably.
7. **sumptuous** (sŭmp′ chōo əs)—lavish; suggesting great expense or size.
8. **boutiques** (bōo tēk′)—small shops dealing in fashionable clothes.
9. **radically altered** (răd′ ĭ kəl lē)—changed greatly or drastically.
10. **supplant** (sə plant′)—replace.

Check Your Understanding

I. Fill in the blanks with the correct word from the preceding list.

1. The _____ reflection of lights on the water attracted our eyes.

2. Recently, science fiction movies seem to contain the use of a _____ somewhere in the story.

3. Helen opened two _____, one on Fifth Avenue and the other on Main Street.

4. Her boutique on Main Street is very _____.
5. Because his parents were migrant farm workers, his life was based on

_____.

6. Harold's story has great _____.

7. The characters in the story are _____ bound together.

8. The new model aircraft will _____ the X-R model.

9. The design for the new aircraft has been _____ from the first one.

10. The lead actress is _____ qualified for the part.

II. On a separate sheet of paper write a sentence for each of the words for this unit, and turn it in to your instructor.

Unit 10: Words Defined

1. **cynicism** (sĭn′ ə sĭz em)—belief in the worst of everyone and everything.
2. **willfully** (wĭl′ ful lē)—on purpose; deliberate.
3. **extortioners** (ĕk stor′ shin ers)—those who obtain money or favors from others by threatening or pressuring them.
4. **impotence** (ĭm′ pə təns)—lacking strength or power; weak.
5. **ignominiously** (ĭg′ nō mĭn′ ē əs lē)—shamefully; disgracefully.
6. **erring** (ĕr′ ing)—going astray; making a mistake.
7. **indulgent** (ĭn dŭl′ jənt)—permissive; lenient; giving in easily to other's desires.

8. **absolve** (ăb zŏlv′)—to clear of blame; forgive.
9. **chiseler** (chĭz′ lər)—one who cheats or deceives.
10. **ethics** (ĕth′ ĭks)—the moral rules and standards seen fit by a society.

 ## Check Your Understanding

I. Fill in the blanks with the correct word from the preceding list.

1. Mac's _____ was caused by a long illness from which he never really regained his strength.

2. The _____ were not as clever as they thought and were apprehended quickly by the police.

3. On his deathbed, he asked the priest to _____ him of his sins.

4. If he had practiced better _____, he might not have so many sins from which to be absolved.

5. _____ can be catching and before you know it, everyone is on a negative kick.

6. Charles Manson acted so _____ in court, the judge had him removed.

7. Why would anyone want to follow his _____ ways when trouble is the obvious outcome?

8. How _____ a parent should be is a controversial subject among psychologists and doctors.

9. The sniper _____ shot down innocent people for the fun of it.

10. How can you trust that _____, Tom, when he's been caught cheating so often?

II. On a separate sheet, write a sentence for each of the words for this unit. Add or drop suffixes as needed for your sentences to read correctly.

Unit 11: Words Defined

1. **remote** (rĭ mōt′)—far away; distant.
2. **syndrome** (sĭn′ drōm)—symptoms or signs that indicate a condition or quality, such as syndromes of sloppiness.

3. **one-upmanship** (wŭn ŭp′ mən shĭp)—the art of going one step better.
4. **protean** (prō′ tē ən)—able to take on different shapes or forms.
5. **omnivorous** (ŏm nĭv′ ər us)—taking in or consuming everything.
6. **subdue** (sŭb dōō′)—conquer; overcome; defeat.
7. **metamorphosed** (mĕt ə mor′ fōzd)—transformed; changed from one form to another.
8. **precariously** (prĭ kăr′ ē əs lē)—dangerously; unstable.
9. **meticulous** (mə tĭk′ yə ləs)—extremely careful; precise; fastidious.
10. **badgering** (băj′ ər ing)—pestering; bothering; annoying.

✔ Check Your Understanding

I. Fill in the blanks with the correct word from the preceding list.

1. Dan has an _____ mind and seems to be interested in everything.

2. Plastic Man has a _____ body that can change into any shape he wants.

3. The truck hung _____ on the edge of the cliff, seeming as though it might fall at any time.

4. My little sister keeps _____ me to take her to the movies.

5. When Joe and I get together to talk over old times in the service, it becomes a real game of _____ to see who can lie the best.

6. There is a _____ possibility Henrietta will get an *A* in English, but don't count on it.

7. Sharon's appearance is always so _____ that it makes me want to mess up her hair or something.

8. There's definite _____ for mid-semester blahs.

9. Try to _____ your desire to drop the course.

10. After his years in the service, his whole personality was _____.

II. On a separate sheet, write a sentence for each of the words for this unit. Add or drop suffixes as needed for your sentences to read correctly.

Unit 12: Words Defined

1. **existential** (ĕg zĭ stĕn′ shəl)—based on experience; dealing with what exists.
2. **inflections** (ĭn flĕk′ shəns)—changes in pitch and tone when pronouncing words.
3. **etymological** (ĕt ə mə lŏj′ ĭ kəl)—pertaining to the origin and history of words and their development.
4. **sadistic** (sə dĭs′ tĭk)—cruel; extremely mean for enjoyment purposes.
5. **procreative** (prō′ krē ā tĭv)—capable of reproducing; child-producing powers.
6. **antecedent** (ăn tə sēd′ ənt)—prior; one that precedes or comes before.
7. **aesthetically** (ĕs thĕt′ ik əl lē)—artistically; tastefully; pertaining to a love of beauty.
8. **piously** (pī′ əs lē)—in this case, hypocritically shocked, although the word can mean very religious and devout.
9. **scrofula** (skrŏf′ yə lə)—swelling of the glands.
10. **pejorative** (pĭ jor′ ə tiv)—downgrading; making something worse; derogatory.

 ## Check Your Understanding

I. Fill in the blanks with the correct word from the preceding list.

1. Being a foreigner, his _____ made it difficult to understand his questions.

2. He _____ refused to throw rocks at the church windows.

3. Stan's _____ statements under oath made matters worse for his attorney to defend him.

4. Robert's philosophy of life is certainly not _____ but more spiritual in nature.

5. The soldier's _____ powers were ruined as a result of the wound he received.

6. I was Betty's _____ and held that position for two years before leaving.

7. The _____ background of the little word *run* is interesting.

8. The _____ killer wasn't satisfied that she murdered them; she committed brutal acts on their bodies.

9. The word _____ is archaic and seldom used anymore.

10. Mindy's apartment is _____ decorated and pleasant to visit.

II. On a separate sheet, write a sentence for each of the words for this unit. Add or drop suffixes as needed for your sentences to read correctly.

Unit 13: Words Defined

1. **notorious** (nō tor′ ē əs)—known widely for unfavorable things.
2. **horde** (hōrd)—a swarm or large group.
3. **belittle** (bĭ lĭt′ l)—to make someone seem small or unimportant.
4. **rendered** (rĕn′ dərd)—given or offered up.
5. **gauge** (gāj)—to measure or evaluate.
6. **parity** (păr′ ə tē)—equality in value.
7. **hedges** (hej′ əs)—holds back or avoids commitment.
8. **deceptive** (dĭ sĕp′ tiv)—misleading.
9. **aptly** (ăpt′ lē)—appropriately.
10. **substantial** (səb stăn′ shəl)—solid or real.

Check Your Understanding

I. Fill in the blanks with the correct word from the preceding list.

1. Some _____ products are advertised as superior to others when, in fact, they are not.

2. The comment from the instructor was intended to _____ the class for being so noisy.

3. The bill collector wanted to know when the next payment would be

_____.

4. That horse is _____ named Devil; it's thrown me twice and bitten me four times.

5. He earns a _____ income from selling real estate.

6. _____ of shoppers will be coming through that door at 9 o'clock.

7. Al Capone is _____ for his crimes.

8. If Patsy _____ paying her debt, she's in for trouble.

9. His speech was _____ and did not deal with the facts.

10. The foreman's job is to _____ our work and then compare it with the other departments' work.

II. On a separate sheet of paper write a sentence for each of the words for this unit, and turn it in to your instructor. Add or drop suffixes as needed.

Part Two: Useful Affixes

The term *affixes* refers to *prefixes* (syllables added to the beginning of a word that affect the word's meaning) and *suffixes* (syllables added to the end of a word that affect the word's meaning).

Useful Prefixes with Negative Meanings

dis—disappear
il—illogical
im—immature
in—inappropriate

ir—irrational
mis—misread
non—nonviolent
un—unheard

Check Your Understanding

Add one of the prefixes above to the following words, and then define its new meaning. When a prefix ends with the same letter as the beginning of the main word, include both letters (*mis + spelling = misspelling*).

Prefixed Word   Definition

1. _____ moral   _____

2. _____ literate   _____

3. _____ accurate   _____

4. _____ done   _____

5. _____ agree   _____

Useful Prefixes Concerning Position

Prefix	Meaning	Example
ante	before	antedate
inter	between	interstate

intra	inside	intravenous
pre	before	prepare
post	after	postdate
re	back	repay
retro	back	retroactive
sub	under	subtitle
trans	across	transport

Check Your Understanding

Add one of the prefixes above to the following words, and then define its new meaning.

Prefixed Word   **Definition**

1. _____ turn   _____

2. _____ view   _____

3. _____ spect   _____

4. _____ marine   _____

5. _____ atlantic   _____

Other Useful Prefixes

Prefix	Meaning	Example
a	without	apathy
anti	against	antiaircraft
auto	self	automatic
hyper	more, extra	hyperactive
mono	one	monopoly
poly	many	polytechnic
semi	half	semicircle
super	more, extra	supersensitive
ultra	more, extra	ultrarich
uni	one	uniform

Check Your Understanding

Add one of the prefixes above to the following words, and then define its new meaning.

Prefixed Word   **Definition**

1. _____ mobile   _____

2. _____ logue   _____

3. _____ finished   _____

4. _____ man   _____

5. _____ cycle   _____

6. _____ syllabic   _____

Useful Suffixes

Suffix	Meaning	Example
able	able to be or do	replaceable
ate	full of	legitimate
dom	state of	freedom
ful	full of	resentful
hood	state of	motherhood
ible	able to be	responsible
less	none	penniless
ment	state of	wonderment
ness	state of	wilderness
ship	state of	friendship
tion	action	separation

Note: When a suffix begins with the same letter as the end of the main word, include both letters (*soul* + *less* = *soulless*).

Check Your Understanding

Add one of the above suffixes to each of the words in the following list, and then define its new meaning.

Suffixed Word   **Definition**

1. truth _____   _____

2. widow _____   _____

3. segregate _____   _____

4. relation _____   _____

5. respect _____   _____

6. adult _____   _____

7. serf _____   _____

8. reason _____   _____

9. martyr _____   _____

10. agree _____   _____

Appendix 2

Some Spelling Hints

As you know, printed letters represent the sounds of spoken words. The letters we use are divided into two major categories: *vowels* and *consonants*. *Vowels* are *a, e, i, o, u,* and sometimes *y*. *Consonants* are all the other letters in the alphabet. These letters represent different sounds, and some letters have several sounds of their own. Here are some rules and examples to help you understand English spellings.

The Final, Silent *e*

With short, usually one-syllable words, a silent *e* on the end of a word changes the sound of the vowel that comes before it from a short vowel sound to a long one. Notice the following examples by sounding out the words.

at	ate (the final *e* is silent but changes the *a* sound)
can	cane
cap	cape
car	care
mop	mope
fat	fate
hat	hate
pan	pane
bit	bite
wag	wage

A final, silent *e* is generally dropped before a suffix beginning with a vowel, but is kept when a suffix begins with a consonant. Notice the following examples.

Example: care (silent finale *e*)	caring (*e* is dropped because the suffix begins with a vowel)
care (silent final *e*)	careful (*e* is *not* dropped because the suffix does not begin with a vowel)
Example: become (silent final *e*)	becoming (*e* is dropped because the suffix begins with a vowel)
Example: write (silent final *e*)	writing (*e* is dropped because the suffix begins with a vowel)
Example: require (silent final *e*)	requirements (*e* is *not* dropped because the suffix does not begin with a vowel)

Example: desire (silent final *e*)   desirable (*e* is dropped because the suffix begins with a vowel)

Check Your Understanding

Write the correct spelling for the following words:

1. write + ing _____

2. replace + able _____

3. notice + ing _____

4. chose + en _____

5. safe + ty _____

6. come + ing _____

7. arrange + ment _____

8. arrange + ing _____

9. imagine + ary _____

10. deceive + ing _____

Words With ie And ei

The best way to learn when to use *ie* or *ei* is to memorize the following verse and then use it.

> Write *i* before *e*
> Except after *c*
> Or when sounded like *a*
> As in *neighbor* and *weigh*.

Although the rule of the verse is not 100 percent true, it applies in enough cases to make it worth the time to learn. Notice the following examples.

"*i* before *e* except after *c*"

no c	c
believe	receive
brief	conceive
chief	receipt
achieve	ceiling

experience	deceive
belief	conceit
thief	perceive
piece	

"*e* before *i* when sounded like *a*"

neighbor	freight
weigh	sleigh
eight	rein

The rule does not apply to foreign words we now use in our language, such as *reveille,* nor does the rule apply to words when the *ie* or *ei* are part of two different syllables, such as *science* (sci-ence), *weird* (we-ird), or *ingredient* (in-gre-di-ent).

 Check Your Understanding

Fill in the blanks with *ie* or *ei.*

1. p_____ce

2. perc_____ve

3. bel_____f

4. rec_____pt

5. br_____f

6. bel_____ve

7. ch_____f

8. ach_____ve

9. w_____gh

10. conc_____ve

The Final Consonant

When a word ends with a consonant that has a vowel before it, you double the consonant when a suffix beginning with a vowel is being added. This rule applies to all one-syllable words.

Example: win (final consonant) win*ning* (double the consonant because the suffix begins with a vowel)

Example: thin (final consonant) thin*ner* (double the consonant because the suffix begins with a vowel)

Example: plan (final consonant) plann*ed* (double the consonant because the suffix begins with a vowel)

When a word of more than one syllable is accented on the last syllable and ends with a consonant with a vowel before it, you usually double this final consonant.

Example: control (con-TROL) —accent on last syllable
—last syllable ends in consonant ⎫
—vowel comes before consonant ⎬ controlled
⎭

Example: equip (e-QUIP) —accent on last syllable
—last syllable ends in consonant } equipped
—vowel comes before consonant

As in most spelling rules, there are always exceptions. Here are some of the most common exceptions. Even though the last syllable is not accented, you still add the double consonant:

transfer = transferred
exel = excellent

When a word of more than one syllable that ends with a consonant with a vowel before it is *not* accented on the last syllable, you usually do *not* double the final consonant.

Example: pocket (POCK-et) —accent *not* on last syllable
—last syllable ends in consonant } pocketing
—vowel comes before consonant

Example: marvel (MARV-el) —accent *not* on last syllable
—last syllable ends in consonant } marvelous
—vowel comes before consonant

Example: travel (TRAV-el) —accent *not* on last syllable
—last syllable ends in consonant } traveled
—vowel comes before consonant

Check Your Understanding

In the following blanks, correct the spelling of any misspelled word in the list. (*Hint:* Find the root word first.)

1. forgoten _____

2. winner _____

3. occurence _____

4. beginer _____

5. equipped _____

6. different _____

7. thiner _____

8. submitting _____

9. controled _____

10. slaming _____

Final *y:* Plural Spellings and Suffixes

When a word ending in *y* has a consonant before it, drop the *y* and add *ies* when you change the word to plural.

Example: baby (a consonant before the *y*) babies
Example: safety (a consonant before the *y*) safeties

When a suffix beginning with *i* is added to a word ending in *y*, keep the *y*.

> Example: baby—babying (suffix begins with *i; y* is kept)
> Example: carry—carrying (suffix begins with *i; y* is kept)

When a suffix beginning with any letter except *i* is added to a word ending in *y*, change the *y* to *i*.

> Example: luxury—luxurious (suffix begins with letter other than *i*)
> Example: study—studious (suffix begins with letter other than *i*)

Check Your Understanding

I. Change the following words to plurals.

1. turkey _____

2. cemetery _____

3. boundary _____

4. jealousy _____

5. story _____

II. Change the following words as indicated.

6. busy + ly _____

7. beauty + ful _____

8. angry + ly _____

9. study + ing _____

10. category + es _____

Commonly Confused Words

The following list contains words that are often misspelled or misused because they are similar in some respect. Look them over, and, if necessary, look up in the dictionary the ones you don't know.

accept, except	bare, bear	capital, capitol
advice, advise	berth, birth	choose, chose
altar, alter	born, borne	cite, site, sight

coarse, course
conscience, conscious
decent, descent, dissent
desert, dessert
device, devise
dyeing, dying
hear, here

its, it's
later, latter
loose, lose
passed, past
peace, piece
personal, personnel
principal, principle

quiet, quite, quit
right, rite, write
stationary, stationery
to, too, two
weak, week
who's, whose
your, you're

Appendix 3

Part One: Some Principal Verb Parts

Present	Past	Past Participle (used only with helping verbs, such as *have, has, had, am, is, was,* and so on)
arise	arose	arisen
awake	awoke	awakened
beat	beat	beaten
become	became	become
begin	began	begun
bend	bent	bent
bet	bet	bet
bite	bit	bitten or bit
blow	blew	blown
break	broke	broken
bring	brought	brought
build	built	built
burst	burst	burst
choose	chose	chosen
cling	clung	clung
creep	crept	crept
deal	dealt	dealt
dive	dived (dove)	dived
do	did	done
draw	drew	drawn
drink	drank	drunk
drive	drove	driven
drown	drowned	drowned
eat	ate	eaten
fall	fell	fallen
flee	fled	fled
fling	flung	flung
fly	flew	flown
forbid	forbade	forbidden
freeze	froze	frozen
go	went	gone
grow	grew	grown
hang (execute)	hanged	hanged
hang (suspend)	hung	hung
hide	hid	hidden
keep	kept	kept
know	knew	known

lay	laid	laid
lead	led	led
lend	lent	lent
lie	lay	lain
lose	lost	lost
raise	raised	raised
read	read	read
ring	rang	rung
rise	rose	risen
see	saw	seen
set	set	set
shake	shook	shaken
shine (glow)	shone	shone
shine (polish)	shined	shined
show	showed	shown
shrink	shrank	shrunk
sing	sang	sung
sink	sank	sunk
slay	slew	slain
speak	spoke	spoken
spin	spun	spun
spring	sprang	sprung
steal	stole	stolen
sting	stung	stung
strike	struck	struck
swear	swore	sworn
swim	swam	swum
swing	swung	swung
tear	tore	torn
throw	threw	thrown
wake	woke	wakened
wear	wore	worn
wring	wrung	wrung
write	wrote	written

Part Two: Supplemental Drills

Exercises in Subject-Verb Usage

Drill A. In the following sentences, underline the subjects with one line and the verbs and auxiliaries with two lines.

1. The reruns of "M.A.S.H." are more enjoyable than some of the newer programs.

2. The cat and the mouse scurried around the cabin.
3. In some colleges, men and women live in the same dormitories.
4. The flower blossoms are bright and colorful.
5. Mr. Petersen, along with his wife, left for England today.
6. Mr. Petersen's children, as well as their friends, did not want them to go.
7. Please go to the store for me before it closes.
8. Each of us is aware of her problems.
9. Some of the cars are a total wreck.
10. None of us want to do it.

Drill B.   In the following sentences, underline the correct verb form.

1. Sales of SCUBA equipment (has, have) dropped during the winter months.
2. Orchid corsages (is, are) very popular at proms.
3. An orchard, of all the different types of flowers, (are, is) the most popular.
4. Jane, as well as Alice and Paul, (were, was) late.
5. The girls, who don't care much for their brothers, (was, were) about to leave without them.
6. My mother, father and sisters (wants, want) to come, too.
7. Everybody (was, were) ready to help him.
8. Each book and short story (have, has) to be read by the end of the week.
9. Mathematics (is, are) my favorite subject.
10. Joey (don't, doesn't) want to go with us.

Drill C.   In the blanks, write in the correct form of the verb in parentheses.

1. Neither my girlfriend nor my best friends _____ to go. (to want)

2. The television and the stereo set always _____ down when I need them. (to break)

3. Either the divan or the chair _____ to be moved. (to have)

4. Our new dishwasher, like many new appliances, _____ not seem to be built too well. (do)

5. Julia _____ n't want to go with us. (do)

6. The coin _____ through the grate. (fall)

7. *Shogun* _____ with, among other things, the difficulty in learning humility. (to deal)

8. The diving teams _____ n't want to compete in the shark tagging tomorrow. (do)

9. After eating, the cat _____ its paws. (to clean)

10. Neither the book nor the movie version _____ the truth. (to show)

Exercises in Correct Usage

Drill D. Correct anything you see wrong in the following sentences—agreement, verb usage, correct words, punctuation, and so forth.

1. My sister Kate don't care what she say to no one.

_____

2. Moe will except the award at the meeting tonight.

_____

3. It don't matter to me, man!

_____

4. I didn't want to go anyways its a dumb way to spend money.

_____

5. That night in jail was the baddest night I ever spend.

_____

6. I can't hardly believe I got through it.

_____

7. Sammy could of won if he hadn't tripped.

_____

8. Its the best candy in the world.

_____

9. Jackie went to there house last night. For dinner.

_____

10. The man who came to dinner.

_____

Exercises in Sentence Combining

Drill E. On another sheet of paper, combine each set of sentences below into one sentence. You are free to use words such as *who, which, that, although before, because,* and so on, as well as changing verbs to *ing* endings. There is no one answer, but many options. Compare your versions to others'.

1. a. José was strong and quick.
   b. José was not particularly heavy.
   c. Being strong and quick aided José's running ability.
2. a. Shirley picked up a hitchhiker.
   b. He looked down and out.
   c. The hitchhiker had a little dog.
3. a. My aunt Polly arrived on Sunday.
   b. We were not ready for her arrival.
   c. Her room was not prepared.
4. a. The colonel moved among his troops.
   b. He briefed his staff before he moved among his troops.
   c. The colonel seemed to be looking for someone in particular.
5. a. Mac went home to await the election result.
   b. Mac voted early.
   c. He was a candidate for mayor.
6. a. Broward Community College is excellent in most respects.
   b. It has upgraded its vocational course offerings.
   c. It also prepares students who want to go on to a four-year college.
7. a. *The Reader's Digest* has a large circulation.
   b. It condenses everything from its original form.
   c. It rewrites everything to a fourth-to-sixth grade level.
   d. I prefer to read things in their original form.
8. a. I read James Michener's novel *Centennial.*
   b. It was made into a television miniseries.
   c. I preferred the book to the TV program.
   d. The book seemed more realistic.

Index